# Navigating the AI Job Market: A Survival Guide for the Age of Generative AI

***For Indian AI and Data Science Professionals: GCCs, Layoffs, and the Long Game***

**Joy Bose**

# Table of Contents

## Back Matter / Appendices

# Author's Note

The structural analysis in this book draws on publicly available research. First-person anecdotes, including the interview experiences and assignment questions described in Chapter 9 and Appendix G, are real. Employer and company names have been deliberately left out throughout, not because the events did not happen, but because the substance of what was asked and what it revealed matters more than who asked it. Illustrative figures used to describe patterns across the industry, references to "the senior data scientist" or "the GCC engineer," are composite, drawn from many conversations rather than any single person.

# Preface

### *Why I Wrote This, and Who It Is For*

I am writing this in Bengaluru in 2026, in the middle of my own job search.

I want to say that plainly, at the start, because it shapes everything that follows. I wrote this from inside the uncertainty that many of you reading this are navigating right now, not from the comfort of a tenured position or the vantage point of someone who has already figured it out.

I have spent over seventeen years working in machine learning and data science, in product companies and research settings across Bengaluru and abroad. I hold a PhD in computational neuroscience, an MSc in Psychology and Neuroscience of Mental Health, and a Master of Laws (LLM), three disciplines that between them say something about how I think about intelligence, organisations, and the structures that govern both. I have spent several years writing about what I have learned, in research papers, in books, and in articles that have reached a wide professional audience.

By most external measures, this is a substantial profile. And yet here I am, in the middle of a job search, feeling many of the things this book describes: the uncertainty about where the field is going, the anxiety about whether my skills are still current, the particular discomfort of being highly qualified in a market that is moving faster than any qualification can track.

I am telling you this not to perform vulnerability, but because I think the pretence that career guides are written by people who have transcended career difficulty is one of the things that makes them less useful than they could be. The person who has never felt behind has probably never been in a field moving fast enough to matter.

## What This Book Is

This book is a map of the generative AI job market as it actually exists in 2026, not as the press releases describe it, not as the LinkedIn posts perform it, but as the people working inside it experience it.

It is about the paradox at the centre of this market: that AI is simultaneously creating new roles and automating the tasks those roles were meant to perform. That the field is expanding rapidly while individual positions become harder to land. That the professionals most at risk from automation are often the experienced ones, not the junior ones, because automation targets the tasks that experience was previously required to perform.

It is about the Indian context specifically: the GCC ecosystem, the credentialing culture, the family pressures, the particular shape of the job market in Bengaluru and Hyderabad and Pune, while remaining relevant to anyone working in this field anywhere in the world. India is not a footnote to the global AI story. It employs nearly two million technology professionals, it is the back-end of a significant fraction of the world's AI infrastructure, and the questions it faces about the quality and nature of that work are questions the whole field needs to grapple with.

It is about the psychology of working in a field that never lets you rest: the imposter syndrome, the performative learning, the particular pain of watching peers get promoted, the family expectations that do not map onto non-linear career realities.

And it is about the long game: what a twenty-year career in AI might actually look like if you navigate it with deliberateness rather than just reacting to whatever the market demands next.

## What This Book Is Not

It is not a technical manual. There are no code samples, no framework tutorials, no step-by-step guides to implementing a RAG pipeline. Those resources exist in abundance, and they are not what most people are missing.

What most people are missing is a clear-eyed account of what the field actually looks like from the inside, the structural forces that shape it, the psychological pressures that accompany it, and the strategic thinking that allows someone to navigate it over decades rather than just surviving the next hiring cycle.

It is also not a book that tells you everything will be fine. Some of what is happening in the AI job market is genuinely difficult, and pretending otherwise would not serve you. Experienced professionals are being displaced by automation in ways that are not temporary. The GCC model that employs a significant fraction of India's technology workforce is under structural pressure that will not resolve simply by waiting. The skills that made someone hireable three years ago are not sufficient today, and the skills that are sufficient today will shift again.

What I can offer is not reassurance but orientation: a way of understanding what is happening clearly enough to make good decisions about how to respond to it.

## Where This Book Comes From

The chapters that follow draw on several years of writing about data science, machine learning, and the AI job market: several years of research, a working paper on the structural dynamics of India's Global Capability Centre sector, and the accumulated experience of working in, thinking about, and writing about this field for longer than I sometimes care to admit.

They also draw on conversations with colleagues who are navigating the same uncertainty, with junior professionals who are trying to enter a field that keeps shifting its entry requirements, with senior professionals who built careers on skills that are now being automated, with people who left stable GCC roles to pursue independent work and found it both harder and more rewarding than they expected.

The research on GCCs that underlies several chapters was undertaken not as an academic exercise but because of a genuine need to understand, in a rigorous way, why so many talented people working in prestigious organisations felt that their work was smaller than their capabilities. The answer turned out to be structural rather than personal, and it is one of the most important things in this book.

## How to Read This Book

The chapters are designed to be read in sequence, but they are also self-contained enough to be read in the order that your current situation demands.

If you are in the middle of a job search right now, Chapter 11 (on what to do if you have just been let go) and Chapter 9 (on the interview landscape in 2026) are where to start.

And if you want to read what the interview process itself reveals about the company on the other side of the table, Chapter 10 covers that directly.

If you are employed but uncertain about whether your current role is developing you or merely consuming you, Chapter 8 (on the GCC trap and how to identify whether a role has real context density) is the most immediately useful.

If you are early in your career and trying to understand the shape of what lies ahead, the four phases described in Chapter 4 (Tool User, Builder, Translator, Shaper) will give you a framework for understanding where you are and what comes next.

If you are asking the bigger questions, about sustainability, meaning, and what a long career in this field could actually look like, Chapter 12 is where those questions are addressed directly.

And if you are sitting with the particular kind of anxiety that comes from working in a field that never quite lets you feel ready, Chapter 6 was written specifically for that moment.

## A Note on the Indian Context

Throughout this book, I write about the Indian technology market specifically: the GCC ecosystem, the Naukri and LinkedIn job landscapes, the IIT credential culture, the family pressures that accompany career decisions in a society where professional success is not a private matter.

This is not parochialism so much as a recognition that general career advice, written mostly in and for the American technology context, often travels poorly. The structural dynamics of the Indian market, the social context within which Indian professionals make career decisions, and the specific opportunities and constraints of working in Bengaluru or Hyderabad rather than San Francisco or London are different enough to warrant their own treatment.

At the same time, the core of what this book addresses, namely the paradox of the GenAI job market, the psychological pressures of working in a fast-moving field, the structural dynamics of execution-oriented organisations, and the principles of long-term career navigation, applies wherever you are reading this. The Indian lens sharpens the analysis. It does not limit it.

## A Final Word Before We Begin

The AI career behaves like a loop more than a ladder, cyclical, sometimes disorienting, requiring periodic reinvention rather than steady upward progression. This is not a comforting thought if you were hoping for a cleaner path. But it is an accurate one, and accuracy is more useful than comfort when you are trying to navigate something real.

The professionals who thrive over a long career in this field are not the ones who found the right ladder and climbed it without interruption. They are the ones who learned to move through the loop consciously: to recognise when reinvention was required, to build the habits that made reinvention possible, and to hold their sense of self loosely enough that it did not shatter when a particular version of their career became obsolete.

This book is an attempt to help you do that, wherever you are in the loop, whatever the market looks like when you are reading this, and whatever version of yourself you are in the process of becoming.

Let us begin.

*Joy Bose*

*Bengaluru, May 2026*

# Chapter 1: The Landscape Has Changed

## *Jobs, Automation, and the Paradox at the Centre of the GenAI Market*

Something unusual is happening in the AI job market, and it is worth stating plainly before we try to navigate it.

The market is expanding rapidly. Between early 2023 and early 2025, the proportion of AI-related job postings in India doubled, from 2.9 percent to 6.5 percent of all vacancies. India now ranks third in the global AI vibrancy index, supported by a tech-savvy workforce and accelerating enterprise adoption. The generative AI market in India alone was valued at approximately USD 1.5 billion in 2025 and is projected to reach USD 6.2 billion by 2034. Eighty-seven percent of Indian enterprises report actively using AI in at least one business function. The demand is real, the investment behind it is real, and the urgency is real.

At the same time, getting hired has never felt harder. Professionals with strong technical backgrounds are submitting dozens of applications and hearing nothing. People who were comfortably employed two years ago find that their skills have been reclassified as baseline rather than differentiating. Experienced engineers at major technology companies are being laid off in numbers that would have seemed implausible five years ago.

Both of these things are true simultaneously. The market is abundant and the market is brutal. Understanding why requires looking at what is actually driving both sides of the paradox.

## A New Operating System

Generative AI is best understood as infrastructure rather than a product category or a set of tools, a new layer on which other things get built, in the way that the internet was infrastructure for the software industry of the 2000s, or cloud computing was infrastructure for the 2010s.

Each previous infrastructure shift created enormous demand for people who could build on the new layer, displaced people whose skills were optimised for the previous one, and eventually settled into a new normal where the infrastructure became invisible and the premium moved to whatever was built on top of it.

The GenAI shift is following a similar pattern, but faster. The time between a new capability appearing and that capability being commoditised has compressed dramatically. What required a specialised team in 2022 can be implemented by a competent developer with good prompting skills in 2025. What requires specialised skill in 2025 will be a framework call in 2027.

This compression is what makes the job market feel simultaneously full of opportunity and impossible to enter. The opportunity is real. But the window between a skill being valuable and that skill being assumed is shorter than any previous technology wave has produced. Current research suggests that technical skills in AI can become outdated within eighteen to twenty-four months, a rate of obsolescence with no precedent in earlier technology careers.

## The Job Title Explosion

A search on LinkedIn or Naukri in 2026 returns a taxonomy of roles that did not exist three years ago: Generative AI Engineer, GenAI Data Scientist, LLM Integration Architect, LLMOps Engineer, RAG Developer, Prompt Engineer, Context Engineer, Director of GenAI, Chief AI Officer. Sometimes GenAI skills appear as requirements inside existing titles, Machine Learning Engineer, Data Scientist, without a new title being created at all.

The postings span every sector: consulting, healthcare, finance, logistics, education, government. On the surface this looks like a moment of extraordinary opportunity.

Beneath the surface, the reality is more complicated. For nearly every posting, there are now hundreds of applicants, sometimes thousands. Recruiters receive resumes within minutes of a listing going live. Online forums are full of accounts of professionals submitting fifty or sixty applications without a single substantive response. In many cases, the initial screening is performed by AI systems whose criteria are opaque, the particular irony of AI professionals being filtered out by AI tools being one of the stranger features of this market.

The job titles are proliferating. The hiring is not keeping pace with the proliferation.

## Jobs Everywhere, Hires Nowhere

Why the dissonance? Three forces are driving it simultaneously.

Generative AI is doing more than create new jobs: it is automating the tasks those jobs were meant to perform. AI tools can now generate code, document APIs, debug errors, draft communications, design interfaces, and produce structured analysis in domains that previously required years of human expertise. What previously required a team of junior engineers can be prototyped in hours using the right combination of prompts and APIs.

Skill obsolescence has accelerated at the same time, to the point where yesterday's differentiator becomes today's baseline before the professional who developed that differentiator has had time to leverage it. The person who spent eighteen months becoming genuinely expert in prompt engineering finds that prompt engineering is now a listed prerequisite rather than a valued specialisation. The person who built RAG pipelines before RAG was a common term finds that RAG is now the expected foundation, not the headline.

And the volume of candidates has been amplified by the very tools that are displacing some of the work. AI-assisted resume writing, cover letter generation, and application processes mean that the signal-to-noise ratio in hiring has collapsed. A posting that might have received two hundred applications three years ago receives two thousand today, many of them polished to similar surface quality by similar tools. Hiring managers are overwhelmed, and the filters they apply to manage the volume are crude and sometimes counterproductive.

## The Productivity Paradox

The standard narrative about AI and productivity is that AI tools make everyone more effective. This is broadly true, with an important qualification that most career guides ignore.

Generative AI tools boost overall productivity by an average of 14 percent across the workforce, with particularly significant gains among novice workers, productivity increases of up to 34 percent have been documented for lower-skilled professionals performing well-defined tasks. AI effectively compresses the performance distribution, narrowing the gap between experienced and inexperienced workers on tasks where the AI can substitute for the experience premium.

This compression has a direct consequence for experienced professionals: it erodes the wage premium that years of experience previously commanded for tasks that AI can now replicate adequately. The senior data scientist who spent five years developing intuition for data cleaning, feature engineering, and model debugging finds that a junior analyst with good AI tool literacy can produce comparable outputs on routine work. The specific tasks in which the experience was accumulated are becoming substitutable, even if the judgment that comes from years of real problem-solving is not.

More striking is a finding that rarely appears in the productivity headlines. For complex, context-heavy tasks, the kind of work that senior engineers actually spend most of their time on, AI tool usage can *increase* completion times by as much as 19 percent, because of the cognitive overhead required to review, correct, and integrate AI-generated outputs that are plausible-looking but subtly wrong. The tools that accelerate junior work can slow down senior work when the task requires genuine expertise to evaluate the output correctly.

This is why the professionals most affected by the current wave of automation are often not the most junior. They are the experienced engineers whose value proposition was built around performing, efficiently and reliably, exactly the tasks that AI now handles adequately. The automation has not reached the top of the complexity curve. It has carved out the middle of it.

## Automation by Design

The capabilities of current large language models have expanded at a pace that has repeatedly surprised even the researchers building them. These models generate code, document APIs, debug errors, draft communications, design interfaces, and produce structured analysis in domains that previously required years of human expertise.

This is a present reality reshaping employment at scale, not a hypothetical concern for the future.

In 2025 and into 2026, Microsoft, Google, Amazon, Meta, and IBM all made significant workforce reductions, with a substantial proportion attributed explicitly or implicitly to efficiencies made possible by AI systems. The cuts were not concentrated in the roles that previous automation waves typically displaced, routine physical labour, basic data entry, simple customer service. They were concentrated in engineering, analysis, and knowledge work: the roles that the technology sector had previously treated as automation-proof.

In India, the picture is pointed. Analysis of industry data from early 2026 suggests that Indian IT firms reduced more positions in the first quarter of 2026 than in all of 2025, with cuts concentrated in execution-oriented teams. The sectors most affected were those where the work was most amenable to AI substitution: routine code generation, standard testing, templated reporting, basic data pipeline maintenance. These are precisely the tasks that a significant fraction of India's technology workforce has been hired to provide, a structural vulnerability that the sector's official narrative of innovation has largely obscured.

The AI transformation has revealed an unexpected pattern. Previous waves of automation primarily displaced low-skill, repetitive physical labour. This wave is disproportionately affecting experienced knowledge workers, senior backend engineers, established data scientists, mid-level analysts, whose years of experience were accumulated performing tasks that AI can now replicate adequately. The premium previously associated with that experience has eroded not because experience itself became less valuable, but because the specific tasks it was applied to became substitutable.

## The Geographic Reality

For Indian professionals, the job market is not uniform across cities. The concentration of AI hiring follows infrastructure and investment patterns that are worth understanding before deciding where to focus a search.

Bangalore accounts for 11 percent of AI-related job postings in India, reflecting its established software ecosystem and concentration of global R&D centres. Hyderabad follows at 9.57 percent, driven by investment in data infrastructure and public-private partnerships. Pune accounts for 6.95 percent, with a significant manufacturing and automotive AI presence. Chennai contributes 6.62 percent, concentrated in SaaS and logistics AI applications.

These four cities together account for roughly a third of all AI job postings in India. The remainder is distributed across Mumbai, Delhi-NCR, and a long tail of emerging technology hubs. The practical implication for job seekers is that geographic flexibility, or at minimum a willingness to target remote roles within distributed GCC environments, materially expands the available opportunity set.

The premium for AI skills is also geographically concentrated. The 28 percent wage premium that AI-focused roles command over general positions, significantly higher than the 12 percent premium for general digital skills, is most consistently available in these four cities. Roles in emerging hubs may carry the title but not always the compensation.

## What This Means Before You Read Further

The landscape described in this chapter is genuinely difficult. It would not serve you to pretend otherwise, and this book does not try to.

What it offers instead is orientation. The professionals who navigate this market well are not the ones who were unaffected by its difficulties. They are the ones who understood the structural forces clearly enough to position themselves on the right side of the shifts, toward work that is becoming more valuable rather than more substitutable, toward roles with genuine context density rather than execution mandates being automated, toward the habits of continuous repositioning that make each disruption faster to recover from than the last.

The next chapter maps what the market is actually hiring for in 2026, and what it takes to be genuinely competitive in it. The rest of the book addresses how to build and sustain a career in conditions that will continue to shift.

# Chapter 2: What the Market Is Actually Hiring For

***Roles, Skills, and How to Position Yourself in 2026***

The job descriptions tell you what companies say they want. The hiring patterns tell you what they are actually doing. In the GenAI market of 2026, there is a meaningful gap between the two, and navigating that gap is one of the more practically important skills available to a job seeker.

This chapter maps the roles that are genuinely in demand, the skills that differentiate competitive candidates from the mass of applicants, and the specific dynamics of the Indian market that shape how those roles are filled and what they actually involve once you are inside them.

## The Role Taxonomy: What JDs Actually Say

An analysis of current postings across LinkedIn, Naukri, and global hiring platforms reveals six categories of genuine demand, each with distinct skill requirements, experience targets, and career trajectories. The distinctions between them matter: the preparation required for each is different, and applying for the wrong category is one of the most common and correctable mistakes in a job search.

### Generative AI Developer / LLM Developer (2–5 Years Experience)

This is the largest category by volume and the entry point for most mid-career professionals transitioning into GenAI work. Core requirements from actual JDs include: RAG pipeline architecture using vector databases such as Pinecone, Weaviate, FAISS, or

ChromaDB; prompt engineering and chain-of-thought techniques; proficiency with LangChain and LlamaIndex; API integration with major LLM providers (OpenAI, Anthropic, Google); and Python fluency at production grade.

For LLM Developer roles specifically, expectations shift toward fine-tuning using LoRA and QLoRA, model optimisation and quantisation, and experience with Hugging Face Transformers. These roles require three to five or more years of experience and expect genuine hands-on depth rather than tutorial-level familiarity.

### MLOps Engineer (3–4 Years Experience)

MLOps has completed its transition from specialisation to baseline expectation. Current JDs for these roles require CI/CD pipeline implementation for ML workflows, containerisation with Docker and Kubernetes, model drift monitoring using tools like Evidently AI, experiment tracking with MLflow, and increasingly, familiarity with serving frameworks like vLLM and Triton for efficient inference.

The emphasis in 2026 JDs has shifted noticeably toward cost management and inference optimisation alongside reliability. A candidate who can demonstrate that they reduced inference costs by a meaningful margin, or kept a production system running reliably through a model update cycle, is more compelling than one who simply lists the tools.

### Agentic AI Engineer / Multi-Agent Architect (3–5 Years Experience)

This is the fastest-growing category and the one with the widest gap between supply and demand. JDs in this space require familiarity with agent orchestration frameworks including CrewAI, AutoGPT, Microsoft Semantic Kernel, and LangGraph. Specific technical expectations include implementing Chain-of-Thought and ReAct reasoning frameworks, building memory systems for context persistence across multi-step tasks, designing tool-calling schemas, and developing evaluation frameworks, often referred to as LLM-as-a-Judge, to score agent performance on reasoning quality and task completion.

The Model Context Protocol (MCP) is appearing in forward-looking JDs as an emerging standard for how AI agents securely access local data and tools. Familiarity with it is currently a differentiator; by 2027 it will likely be a baseline expectation.

### AI Research Scientist (PhD or Equivalent, 0–3 Years Post-Qualification)

The research tier remains the pinnacle of the technical hierarchy, focused on the invention of new algorithms and the expansion of the theoretical limits of machine intelligence. Major organisations, Meta, NVIDIA, Microsoft, Capital One, and others, are actively seeking PhD-level candidates with expertise in LLM pre-training, post-training, and reinforcement learning from human feedback. Publication records at venues like NeurIPS, ICML, and ICLR are weighted heavily. Proficiency in PyTorch and JAX is expected.

This category is relevant to a small fraction of job seekers but worth understanding for two reasons: it defines the frontier against which applied roles are judged, and it is the direction that some mid-career professionals with strong research instincts and academic connections can move toward.

### AI Governance, Ethics, and Security (Emerging, Variable Experience)

This category is newer and currently smaller by volume, but growing rapidly as regulation increases and organisational risk awareness around AI systems matures. AI Security Specialists protect LLMs and data pipelines against adversarial attacks including prompt injection and data exfiltration. Governance roles focus on compliance with frameworks including the EU AI Act, India's DPDP Act, the NIST AI Risk Management Framework, and ISO/IEC 42001.

In the Indian market, this category is underrepresented relative to its likely future importance. Professionals with technical depth combined with legal or regulatory background, your LLM, your domain expertise in a regulated sector, are positioned to occupy these roles before the market fully prices in the demand. This is a genuine first-mover opportunity for people with unusual cross-disciplinary profiles.

### LLM Systems / AI Platform Engineer (4–8 Years Experience)

This category barely existed as a separate posting before 2024 and is still often folded into MLOps or Senior ML Engineer titles, but the JDs are now distinct enough to treat it as its own archetype. The work is serving models rather than building applications on top of them: deploying open-weight models such as Llama, Qwen, and Mistral with inference engines like vLLM, Triton, or TensorRT-LLM, managing GPU clusters on Kubernetes, capacity planning and autoscaling, quantisation decisions, inference cost engineering, and observability for model serving. Requirements typically combine strong Python and Kubernetes with genuine understanding of GPU memory, batching, and the internals of at least one serving stack.

The cleanest way to understand where this role sits is a three-way distinction that also explains a great deal about how interviews are drifting. Applied AI engineers work at the application layer, RAG, agents, evaluation, prompts; their core question is how to improve answer quality. AI platform engineers run the models those applications call; their core question is how to serve five hundred concurrent users on as few GPUs as possible. Model and inference engineers work below both, on attention kernels, parallelism, and compiler-level optimisation; their question is how to squeeze out more tokens per second, and outside a handful of companies these roles are rare. The three profiles are genuinely different jobs, but as Chapter 9 discusses, interviewers increasingly move across the boundary between the first two inside a single conversation, so a candidate positioned in one category needs at least conversational depth in the next one down.

In the Indian market this category is growing for a structural reason: regulated clients. Banks, telecom operators, healthcare providers, and government bodies increasingly refuse to send confidential data to external model APIs, so they self-host open models, and the GCCs and consulting firms serving them need people who can make those deployments fit, scale, and stay affordable. The positions are fewer than application-layer roles and concentrated in central platform teams, but the candidate pool that can genuinely do the work is thinner still, which is what a premium looks like before the market fully prices it.

## The Skills Hierarchy

Across all six categories, a consistent hierarchy of competencies has emerged from JD analysis. Understanding where your skills sit in this hierarchy is more useful than simply listing everything you know.

### Baseline Expectations

These are the skills that get you past the first filter. Having them does not make you competitive. Not having them disqualifies you.

Python fluency and standard machine learning libraries. Working knowledge of major LLM APIs. Basic prompt engineering and chain-of-thought techniques. Understanding of vector databases and semantic search. Familiarity with at least one orchestration framework such as LangChain or LlamaIndex. These were differentiators in 2022. They are the floor in 2026.

### Differentiating Competencies

These are the skills that make you genuinely competitive once past the initial filter.

Experience with model fine-tuning using LoRA or QLoRA. Familiarity with AI agents and the Model Context Protocol.

Knowledge of deployment optimisation, scalability, and cost management, the ability to run a smaller quantised model efficiently is increasingly valued over the ability to call a frontier model API. Understanding of AI safety and alignment principles at a practical level. The ability to design evaluation metrics and benchmarks, one of the most consistently undervalued and underdemonstrated skills in the market. Cross-functional collaboration with non-technical stakeholders, which sounds soft and is genuinely rare.

### Skills That Command Premium

These are the skills that make you the candidate rather than a candidate.

Expertise in multimodal AI, the integration of vision, audio, and text. In 2026, live-interaction products are increasingly requiring multimodal capability as standard. Experience with constitutional AI, red-teaming, and adversarial evaluation. Track record of successful AI product launches, not models built but systems shipped, maintained, and demonstrated to have delivered business outcomes. Deep domain expertise in a regulated or data-rich sector combined with technical depth. Understanding of the regulatory landscape at a level that allows you to design for compliance from the first architecture decision.

The professionals commanding the highest salaries and most interesting opportunities in the Indian market typically possess skills from all three tiers, with deep expertise in at least one area from the third category. In concrete terms, agentic AI lead roles are currently reaching 45 to 55 LPA for candidates with that combination. The overall wage premium for AI-focused roles versus general technology roles stands at 28 percent, significantly higher than the 12 percent premium for general digital skills.

## The Mathematical Foundations Have Not Been Abstracted Away

A persistent belief in the market is that higher-level APIs and frameworks have reduced the need for mathematical depth. The 2026 JD landscape does not support this belief.

Across senior roles, there is a renewed emphasis on foundational theory, not as a box-checking exercise but because it is essential for diagnosing training instabilities, understanding model behaviours, and performing effective fine-tuning. Machine learning engineer interviews at technical companies routinely include questions about the bias-variance tradeoff, the mathematical basis of regularisation techniques, gradient descent and backpropagation, and the derivation of common loss functions.

The key mathematical disciplines remain linear algebra (foundational for neural network computations), calculus (essential for understanding optimisation), probability theory (critical for predictive modelling and uncertainty quantification), statistics (vital for evaluation metrics and A/B test design), and optimisation theory (which differentiates research-level talent from tool users). These are not new requirements. What is new is that the market is explicitly re-emphasising them after a period in which framework fluency was sufficient to get hired.

The practical implication is that candidates who have been relying on API calls without understanding what is happening beneath them are increasingly exposed in technical interviews. If your mathematical foundations have atrophied during years of applied work, rebuilding them is more valuable interview preparation than adding another framework to your resume.

## The Agentic Shift: A New Design Paradigm

The most significant structural change in what the market demands is the transition from building static AI features to designing autonomous agentic systems. Agentic AI refers to systems capable of independent planning, tool usage, memory management, and cross-agent delegation to achieve complex goals.

This transition requires a shift in mindset that goes beyond learning new frameworks. Prompt engineering, crafting effective instructions for a single model call, is a different cognitive task from designing a reasoning loop in which an agent plans, executes, evaluates its own output, and decides whether to retry or delegate. The latter requires thinking about failure modes, memory architecture, tool selection logic, and evaluation criteria in ways that single-call prompt work does not.

Current JDs for agentic roles specify capabilities that did not exist as hiring requirements two years ago: implementing ReAct frameworks to guide agent reasoning, building context persistence systems so agents can remember previous actions across multi-step tasks, designing multi-agent collaboration structures where specialised agents work together on decomposed subtasks, and developing LLM-as-a-Judge evaluation systems to score agent performance automatically.

For candidates in Phase 2 of the loop, the Builder phase, this is the most important new territory to enter. The market for people who can design and ship reliable agentic systems is significantly less saturated than the market for people who can implement RAG pipelines, which was the frontier eighteen months ago.

## The ATS Problem and What to Do About It

A growing proportion of initial candidate screening in 2026 is performed by automated systems, applicant tracking systems and increasingly AI-powered screening tools, before a human sees a resume.

These systems optimise for keyword matching and structural patterns, not for a nuanced reading of your actual experience. A resume that communicates your competence effectively to a thoughtful hiring manager may perform poorly in automated screening if it uses different terminology than the job description.

The adaptation required is translational, not dishonest. If you have been building retrieval-augmented generation systems under an internal project name no one outside your organisation would recognise, call it RAG. If you have been doing LLMOps work under a generic data engineering title, make that explicit. If your experience with agentic systems has been described internally as workflow automation, use the current market terminology alongside it.

Match the language of the job description where it accurately describes what you have done. Do not claim skills you do not have. But do not allow terminology gaps to filter you out of roles for which you are genuinely qualified.

In the Indian market specifically, Naukri's search and ranking algorithms reward keyword density differently than LinkedIn's. If you are using both, and you should be, the profile optimisation is not identical across the two platforms. Naukri skews toward title and skills section keywords; LinkedIn rewards connected narrative and endorsements alongside keywords.

Recruiters at senior levels are increasingly supplementing ATS screening with direct searches for public evidence of capability: GitHub repositories, arXiv preprints, participation records at NeurIPS and ICML, and Medium or Substack writing. The candidate with a well-documented public project is findable in ways that a strong private resume is not.

## The Organisational Context: Big Tech vs GCC vs Startup

The skills hierarchy above applies across all roles, but what those skills are used for varies significantly depending on the type of organisation. Understanding this before you apply shapes both your preparation and your evaluation of whether a role will develop you.

Big Tech organisations, Amazon, Microsoft, Google, and their equivalents, offer access to massive datasets, enormous compute resources, and highly specialised roles. A Software Development Engineer at Amazon might focus specifically on AI tools for third-party sellers; an Applied Scientist on the Alexa team focuses on voice interaction optimisation. These roles offer clear promotion tracks, significant compensation, and the credibility of a brand-name employer. They also tend toward specialisation and incremental innovation within established systems.

GCC environments, as discussed in Chapter 8, vary enormously in the degree to which they involve genuine strategic work versus execution against specifications set elsewhere. The skills hierarchy applies in all of them, but your opportunity to develop differentiating and premium skills depends heavily on where the role sits in the context density matrix. A GCC role with genuine product ownership develops you; a GCC role that processes well-defined specifications does not, regardless of what the job description says about innovation.

Startups require generalist capability and end-to-end ownership. A founding AI hire at a startup may be responsible for establishing ML best practices, making infrastructure decisions, building evaluation frameworks from scratch, and eventually hiring the team around them. These roles are higher risk, higher intensity, and, for the right person at the right stage, significantly more developmental than a comparable title at a larger organisation.

Mid-market and SaaS companies often represent the best balance: enough scale to have real production systems and real users, enough ambiguity to require genuine problem-solving, and enough flexibility to allow the kind of cross-functional work that develops the Translator skills described in Chapter 4.

## The Illusion of Readiness

Online learning platforms have made it easier than ever to acquire the vocabulary of new skills quickly. They have also created a persistent gap between feeling ready and being ready in the sense that interviewers are probing for.

The gap has little to do with intelligence or effort. It comes down to the difference between knowing how a technology works in a tutorial context and knowing how it fails in a production context. Courses teach the former. Experience in real systems teaches the latter.

The practical implication is that building something, a working project using current tools, applied to a real problem, documented and deployable, is more valuable interview preparation than completing additional courses. The project demonstrates applied competence. The course demonstrates that you were willing to pay for access to a video series.

If you are currently in a role that does not provide opportunities to build with current tools, build on the side. The project does not need to be elaborate. It needs to be finished, working, and yours to explain in depth. A RAG pipeline applied to a domain you know well, documented clearly on GitHub, with a brief Medium post explaining what you built and what you learned, covers more interview ground than three certifications.

The psychological dimension of the readiness gap, the particular anxiety of a field that perpetually moves the competence threshold, is addressed in Chapter 6. What is worth noting here is that the anxiety is real and almost universal, which means it is not useful information about your specific competence relative to other candidates. Almost everyone applying for these roles feels underprepared in some dimension. The ones who succeed are not the ones who feel most ready. They are the ones who can demonstrate most clearly what they have actually built.

What the market wants, in the end, is not the person who knows the most, but the one who can build reliably, learn continuously, and bring sound judgment to problems no tool can solve on its own. The chapters that follow address how to demonstrate each of these things.

# Chapter 3: The Indian IT Sector Specifically

### *What the Automation Wave Means If You Are Working in Bengaluru, Not San Francisco*

Most writing about AI and job displacement is written from an American vantage point, about American technology companies, for an American audience. The layoffs at Microsoft and Google and Amazon are real and they matter, but they are not the primary concern of the two million technology professionals working in India's GCC ecosystem, in its IT services firms, in its product startups, and in the research centres that have made Bengaluru and Hyderabad two of the most important technology cities in the world.

The Indian technology sector faces a version of the automation challenge that is structurally distinct from what is happening in Silicon Valley. The displacement falls mainly on the execution layer, the large, well-organised, highly competent workforce that India built over three decades to deliver technology services to the world, rather than on highly paid engineers at frontier AI companies. That workforce is now facing a set of pressures that its own success made possible, and the official narrative of the sector has been slow to acknowledge what is actually happening.

This chapter is about what is actually happening.

## The Workforce India Built

To understand what is at risk, you need to understand what was built. Between roughly 1990 and 2020, India constructed the world's largest technology services workforce, starting from cost arbitrage and progressively moving up the value chain through application development, systems integration, and increasingly sophisticated engineering. By 2024, the GCC sector alone employed approximately 1.9 million professionals and generated USD 64.6 billion in revenue. But this workforce was built on a particular kind of work: technically skilled, process-oriented execution of well-defined tasks. Writing code to specifications. Testing software against requirements. Managing data pipelines. These are not trivial tasks, but they are tasks defined by someone else, bounded by someone else's requirements, measured by someone else's criteria. They are, in the framework of Chapter 8, execution-oriented roles. The automation wave of 2025 and 2026 is targeting exactly this kind of work.

## What the Numbers Show

The gap between the official narrative and the on-the-ground reality became harder to ignore in early 2026.

The employment data told a story the official narrative was slow to acknowledge. Analysis of hiring and attrition data from early 2026 indicated that Indian IT firms reduced more positions in the first quarter of 2026 than in all of 2025, cuts concentrated in execution-oriented teams: software testing functions, routine code development, data processing and pipeline maintenance. These were not the cuts of companies in financial distress. They were the cuts of companies that had found a more efficient way to do the work those teams had been doing.

The EY GCC Pulse Report for 2025 found that 58 percent of GCCs were investing in agentic AI and 83 percent were scaling generative AI projects. Read optimistically, these numbers describe an industry embracing transformation. Read carefully, they describe an industry automating exactly the execution tasks that the majority of its workforce is employed to perform.

The Zinnov five-year GCC landscape report found that only 18 percent of GCCs had reached transformation hub status, the level at which genuine innovation work is being done, while 44 percent remained portfolio hubs and 25 percent were functioning as satellite units. These are execution-oriented configurations. The 82 percent of GCCs that are not transformation hubs are the organisations where the automation pressure is most acute, because their work is most substitutable.

## The Specific Tasks Being Automated

It is worth being concrete about what AI is actually replacing, because the popular narrative, "AI is coming for your job", is both true and misleading. AI is replacing specific tasks rather than Indian technology professionals wholesale, and those tasks happen to make up a large share of what a large share of the workforce spends most of its time doing.

**Routine code generation.** A significant proportion of the code written in production systems at service companies and execution-oriented GCCs is template code: CRUD operations, API endpoints, data transformation logic, boilerplate that follows established patterns. AI coding tools, GitHub Copilot, Cursor, Claude Code, generate this code faster and with fewer errors than most developers write it manually. The junior developer whose primary contribution was writing this code is not being replaced by AI; they are being made redundant by it.

**Software testing.** Test case generation, test script writing, regression testing, and basic QA processes are among the most automated tasks in the 2026 technology stack. Companies that previously employed large testing teams are discovering that AI-assisted testing tools can cover the same regression surface with a fraction of the headcount. This has hit Indian IT services firms particularly hard because testing was one of the first functions systematically offshored, and the teams built around it are large.

**Data pipeline maintenance.** Monitoring data pipelines, debugging data quality issues, writing transformation scripts, and maintaining ETL processes, these are tasks that a significant fraction of data engineering and data science roles in execution-oriented environments spend most of their time on. AI tools are not eliminating this work entirely, but they are dramatically reducing the human time required per unit of work done.

**Templated reporting and analysis.** Generating regular business reports, producing dashboards from defined data sources, writing analysis summaries for recurring business reviews, these are tasks that many data analyst roles are primarily defined by. LLM-based tools can produce these outputs from structured data with minimal human intervention.

**Technical support and documentation.** First and second-line technical support, internal documentation writing, knowledge base maintenance, these are functions where AI tools have achieved genuine substitution in many organisational contexts.

The pattern across all of these is the same: tasks that are well-defined, repetitive, bounded by clear requirements, and measurable against objective criteria are the tasks that AI is most effectively replacing. These are also, not coincidentally, the tasks that execution-oriented organisations, service companies, satellite GCCs, basic shared services centres, are primarily structured to perform.

## Who Is Most at Risk

The risk is not distributed evenly, and the distribution is counterintuitive in ways that the official narrative does not acknowledge.

**Junior professionals in execution roles** face the most immediate risk to their entry paths. The traditional model, join a service company or a GCC at entry level, spend two to three years learning the basics through relatively routine work, then progress, is under pressure because the routine work that constituted the learning curve is being automated. The path still exists but it is narrower, and the rate at which companies are hiring at entry level for execution roles has declined noticeably in the 2025–2026 period.

**Mid-level professionals with commodity skill sets** face a different risk: not immediate displacement but the gradual erosion of the premium their experience commanded. The data scientist with five years of experience who has been doing standard analysis work, maintaining existing pipelines, and producing regular reports is discovering that AI tools allow a junior analyst with good tool literacy to produce comparable outputs. The years of experience are not valueless, but the tasks in which they were accumulated are becoming substitutable, and the compensation premium that attached to those tasks is compressing.

**Senior professionals in management roles without technical depth** face a third kind of risk. The manager who rose through the ranks in an execution-oriented environment, whose value was in orchestrating large teams doing well-defined work, is discovering that AI tools reduce the optimal team size for that work. Fewer people doing equivalent work means fewer management layers are needed. This is the pattern behind the disproportionate impact of recent cuts on mid-level managers and senior delivery leads at Indian IT firms.

What the risk distribution reveals is that the automation wave is carving out the execution-oriented middle, not primarily the most junior or the most senior, hitting the large, well-compensated, professionally stable tier of professionals who built solid careers on competent delivery of well-defined work. This is the tier that the

Indian technology sector's three-decade growth story produced in the largest numbers, and it is the tier under the most acute pressure.

## What Is Not Being Automated

Equal clarity about what is not being automated is as important as clarity about what is.

**Judgment in ambiguous situations** is not being automated. The ability to look at a problem that has not been fully defined, to ask the right questions to clarify it, to propose an approach that accounts for constraints the requester did not know to articulate, and to adapt when the initial approach encounters unexpected obstacles, this is the work that AI tools consistently fail at in ways that are immediately visible to anyone who has tried to use them for genuinely novel problems.

**Trust-based relationships with clients and stakeholders** are not being automated. The human dimension of technology delivery, understanding what a client actually needs rather than what they asked for, navigating organisational politics, building the credibility that allows a technical recommendation to be heard by a non-technical decision-maker, these are capabilities that remain fundamentally human.

**Creative problem definition** is not being automated. Identifying the right problem to solve, framing it in a way that makes it tractable, and recognising when a proposed technical solution is solving the wrong problem, these are Phase 3 and Phase 4 skills that AI tools do not possess and are not close to possessing.

**Domain expertise combined with technical skill** is not being automated. The professional who understands Indian financial regulation and can build AI systems that comply with it, or who understands clinical workflows and can design AI tools that integrate into them, or who understands agricultural supply chains and can deploy prediction systems that account for the specific patterns of Indian agricultural data, these combinations of depth are not substitutable by general-purpose AI tools.

**Systems thinking at scale** is not being automated. Understanding how a technology system interacts with the human and organisational systems around it, anticipating second-order effects, designing for failure modes that are not obvious from the requirements, this is the work that the most valuable senior professionals are primarily doing, and it is work that AI tools assist with rather than replace.

The pattern is consistent: the work that is not being automated is the work that requires genuine understanding of context, consequence, and human complexity. The work that is being automated is the work that can be fully specified in advance, measured objectively, and repeated at scale. The division between these categories maps almost exactly onto the division between execution-oriented roles and high-context-density roles described in Chapter 8.

## The Narrative Gap

The official narrative of the Indian technology sector in 2026 describes a transition: from execution to innovation, from delivery to strategy, from cost arbitrage to cognitive arbitrage. This narrative is not false, the transition is real, and there are genuine examples of GCCs and service companies that have made it meaningfully. But the narrative gap between what is being described and what is being experienced by the majority of the workforce is significant and widening.

NASSCOM reports describe transformation hubs and innovation mandates. The Zinnov data shows that 18 percent of GCCs have reached this status. The remaining 82 percent employ the majority of the sector's workforce, and for the people working in them, the experience looks less like cognitive arbitrage and more like increasing efficiency pressure, shrinking team sizes, and the quiet awareness that the work they are most expert in is becoming less economically valuable.

The gap matters for individual professionals because it shapes the advice they receive. If you believe the official narrative, that your organisation is becoming a transformation hub, that the innovation mandate is real, that the work is moving up the value chain, you may be waiting for a transition that is not coming, in an organisation that is not positioned to make it. If you understand the actual distribution, that most GCCs are in the lower-right quadrant of the context-bandwidth matrix, that the governance reform required to move them is not happening at the pace the narrative implies, you can make better decisions about where to invest your development and when to move.

## The Sovereign AI Dimension

One dimension of the Indian automation story that is genuinely distinct from the global narrative is the emerging investment in sovereign AI infrastructure.

India's government and domestic technology companies are investing in the development of foundation models and AI infrastructure that does not depend on American providers. Initiatives like Krutrim (Ola's foundation model), the Bhashini platform for Indic language AI, and various government-backed efforts to build GPU infrastructure and training capability represent a genuine domestic AI industry in early formation.

For Indian technology professionals, this creates a set of opportunities that are not visible if you are only looking at the global market. The need for professionals who understand Indic language model fine-tuning, who can work with Indian regulatory requirements from the ground up, who have domain expertise in

Indian agriculture, healthcare, finance, or governance, and who can build AI systems that serve a linguistically diverse population of 1.4 billion people, these are not generic AI skills. They are specifically Indian AI skills, and the domestic market for them is growing.

The skills hierarchy from Chapter 2 still applies, you need the technical foundations regardless of which market you are targeting. But the domain layer on top of those foundations looks different if you are targeting domestic Indian AI opportunities rather than GCC execution roles or global tech firms. Understanding Indian regulatory frameworks (DPDP Act, RBI fintech guidelines, IRDAI insurance regulations), having linguistic competence in one or more Indian languages beyond English, and having domain knowledge of specifically Indian problems and contexts, these are assets in the domestic market that have no equivalent in the global AI skills conversation.

None of this is a reason to ignore the global market. It does mean recognising that the Indian technology workforce has assets specifically valuable in the domestic context, and that the domestic context is developing its own AI industry that will need them.

## What to Do With This Information

The structural analysis in this chapter points in a clear direction, even if it does not make the path comfortable.

The execution layer is under sustained pressure that will not reverse. The work that defined career stability for a large fraction of the Indian technology workforce over the last two decades is becoming less economically valuable at a rate that institutional communication is not honestly acknowledging. This is a structural shift, not a temporary disruption that patience will resolve.

The professionals who navigate it well are not the ones who deny it or wait for their organisation to manage the transition for them. They are the ones who understand clearly which side of the execution-versus-judgment divide their current work sits on, and who take deliberate action to move toward the judgment side before the execution side contracts further around them.

That action does not require leaving your current organisation immediately. It requires building, within your current role or alongside it, the capabilities that sit above the execution layer, the problem framing skills, the domain depth, the public portfolio of work, the relationships with people who are doing high-context-density work, the understanding of what it would actually take to move into a role that is not primarily defined by well-specified execution.

Chapter 4 describes what that progression looks like across the four phases of the career loop. Chapter 5 maps the specific skills that constitute the judgment layer in 2026. Chapter 8 gives you the framework for evaluating whether any specific role, including your current one, is positioned above or below the innovation threshold.

The automation wave is real. The Indian technology sector's reckoning with it is underway, even if the official account of that reckoning is several years behind the reality. The professionals who read the actual situation clearly, and act on what they read, are the ones for whom the loop continues productively rather than painfully.

The execution layer is contracting and the judgment layer is not, which leaves a fairly practical question for the next stretch of your career: which one are you actually building toward?

# Chapter 4: The Career Is a Loop, Not a Ladder

## *A Phase-by-Phase Map for AI Engineers and Data Scientists*

Most people entering AI think they are climbing a ladder. They are not.

They are stepping onto a loop that will quietly make their skills obsolete every few years and then ask them to begin again. The ladder model, entry level, mid level, senior, lead, principal, director, implies that progress is linear, cumulative, and upward. Master the current level and you advance to the next. Your experience compounds predictably. The destination is visible from the starting point.

The loop model is less comfortable and more accurate. Progress happens in cycles rather than increments. Each cycle requires learning something genuinely new, not just deepening what you already know. The skills that made you valuable in the previous cycle become the baseline in the next one, and the premium you earned for having them transfers only partially, if at all. The destination is not visible from the starting point because the field itself changes shape while you are moving through it.

In 2021, being an AI engineer meant knowing how to train a Transformer. In 2024, it meant knowing how to prompt one. By 2026, it means knowing how to fix the system when the model hallucinates and starts corrupting your production database at 2am. The technical centre of gravity has shifted three times in five years. It will shift again.

If you are still climbing the ladder you started on at graduation, you are probably climbing a ghost. What follows is a map of the loop, phase by phase, with the traps, the transitions, and the India-specific realities that most career guides do not bother to address.

## Phase 1: The Tool User (0 to 2 Years)

What you think you are doing: Learning AI.

What you are actually doing: Learning how AI fails.

At this stage, everything feels exciting. Python, pandas, scikit-learn, maybe some PyTorch. A Kaggle competition. A few online courses. You feel close to the frontier.

In reality, most early-career roles are about execution: running pipelines, cleaning data, debugging why the model that worked perfectly in development refuses to behave in production. The gap between the AI you learned about in the course and the AI you encounter in a real codebase is one of the most disorienting experiences of an early career. The course showed you a clean problem with a clean dataset and a satisfying accuracy metric. The job shows you six months of accumulated technical debt, upstream data that changes schema without warning, and a stakeholder who wants results by Friday.

The most valuable lesson in this phase is how models fail, not how they work. Messy data, broken assumptions, label leakage, silent drift, class imbalance that nobody noticed for six months. Pay attention to those failures. They are worth more than ten Kaggle gold medals.

### The India-specific reality of Phase 1

One trap specific to the Indian context: a strong college brand can delay the reckoning. The IIT or NIT credential opens doors in the first two years. Hiring managers give the benefit of the doubt. The interview process is slightly easier. The first role comes more readily.

After Year 2, interviewers look at GitHub, not your college name. What you built matters more than where you studied. The professionals who understood this early, who used the credential to get in the door and then immediately started building a record of actual work, come out of Phase 1 significantly ahead of those who continued to rely on the credential as the primary signal of their value.

The other India-specific reality is that many Phase 1 roles sit inside GCC environments where the work is execution-oriented almost by design. As discussed in Chapter 8, this is a structural feature of how those organisations are built, not a reflection of your potential. Use Phase 1 in a GCC to learn the fundamentals of production systems, how code actually gets deployed, how pipelines actually fail, how stakeholder communication actually works, and build your portfolio on the side with problems that are yours to define.

## What to build in Phase 1

Learn Python at production grade, not notebook grade. Write functions, modules, and unit tests. AI graduates who write clean, tested code are meaningfully more employable than those who only know the math.

Learn SQL properly: window functions, CTEs, query optimisation. Not just SELECT *.

Learn Git: version control everything, including notebooks, from day one.

Choose one deep learning framework and go deep on it rather than shallow on three. PyTorch is the current standard for research-adjacent work. TensorFlow remains widely used in production systems.

Deploy something. Not a notebook. An actual API endpoint that takes input and returns a prediction. Use FastAPI. Host it on a free cloud tier. This one step puts you ahead of most fresh graduates in a way that no certification replicates.

The trap at this stage

Becoming an API wrapper with confidence. Stringing together LLM calls and calling it building AI. The barrier to making something that looks impressive has never been lower. The barrier to making something that actually works reliably in production has not changed. Do the foundational work first. Abstract it later.

## Phase 2: The Builder (2 to 5 Years)

### The shift that has to happen here

You move from notebooks to systems. This is the most technically demanding transition in an AI career. You are now expected to deploy models, build pipelines that do not break when upstream data changes, work alongside software engineers, and handle latency, scale, and drift.

Welcome to MLOps. In 2026, it is no longer a specialisation. It is a baseline expectation for anyone working on production AI systems.

There is also a quieter shift in what building means. Most production teams have moved away from heavy fine-tuning toward in-context learning and RAG. Fine-tuning a model on proprietary data is expensive and brittle. A well-designed RAG pipeline over a good knowledge base frequently outperforms a fine-tuned model at a fraction of the cost and maintenance overhead. A good builder in 2026 knows this distinction and applies it correctly rather than reaching for fine-tuning because it sounds more sophisticated.

### The core toolkit, in learning order

Years 2 to 3: MLflow for experiment tracking, Docker for containerisation, one cloud ML service (SageMaker, Vertex AI, or Azure ML), Airflow or Prefect for pipeline orchestration.

Years 3 to 4: Kubernetes basics, model monitoring with Evidently AI or Prometheus and Grafana, CI/CD pipelines for ML workflows.

Years 4 to 5: RAG pipeline design, vector databases such as Pinecone or Weaviate, LLMOps tooling, agentic workflow frameworks like LangGraph.

Start with MLflow, Docker, and one cloud platform. Everything else builds on top of those foundations.

## Two skills most people skip

**Model optimisation**: A senior AI engineer in 2026 can do more than call a frontier model API. They can run a smaller, quantised model on a private cloud and save a company significant money every month. Small models like Llama 3 or Mistral, properly optimised, frequently outperform large frontier models for specific enterprise tasks. Learn quantisation, ONNX export, and efficient inference basics.

**Agentic system design**: The industry has moved from chatbots to agents. Understanding how to design multi-agent workflows, how tasks pass between agents, how failures get caught, how hallucinations get contained, is a real differentiator at this level.

## The India-specific reality of Phase 2

This is where the service company versus product company question becomes most consequential. Engineers who started in service companies often feel permanently behind peers who went directly into product companies. The anxiety is understandable but mostly wrong.

The skills gap is real at Year 2. By Year 5, what matters is what you built, not where you built it. A RAG pipeline deployed at a mid-sized service company solving a genuine problem is more compelling to a hiring manager than three years of supporting a legacy codebase at a brand-name firm. The transition from service to product company is possible at any point in Phase 2. It requires one solid proof-of-work project, not a pedigree correction.

## The 80 percent rule nobody warns you about

Once you are in production work, you will find that most of your time is data plumbing, not modelling. Broken pipelines, upstream schema changes, data quality fires, retraining triggers. Engineers who treat this as a distraction from the real work plateau. Engineers who embrace it become indispensable. The ability to keep a production system running reliably is rarer and more valued than the ability to train a slightly more accurate model.

### The trap at this stage

Becoming a model-plus-dashboard machine: train model, build dashboard, present results, repeat. Useful, yes. Replaceable, also yes. Stop thinking in terms of models. Start thinking in terms of systems. How does the data flow? What happens when the model fails? Where does it fit inside a larger product? These questions separate a builder from an executor.

## Phase 3: The Translator (5 to 10 Years)

### What changes

Less coding. More thinking.

At this stage, your role shifts whether you like it or not. You spend more time framing problems before they reach engineering, talking to product and leadership, and deciding what not to build. This last skill, knowing what not to build, is the most underrated one at this level.

You are no longer judged primarily by how accurate your model is. You are judged by whether the work mattered.

The signal that someone has stopped growing at this phase is rarely dramatic. It is a quiet shift from being needed to being optional. The person is still technically capable. They can still build things. But they are no longer the one shaping what gets built. That transition happens slowly, and then all at once.

## The skills that actually matter here

Problem framing: Taking a vague business question, why are users churning, why is this process taking so long, why is revenue declining in this segment, and converting it into a precise, solvable ML problem with the right success metric. This is rarer than it sounds and more valuable than almost any technical skill.

AI pruning: Many organisations in 2026 are dealing with AI fatigue. Too many tools, too many models, nothing talking to each other properly. The most valuable thing a senior person can often say is: we do not need a custom model here. We need a better database schema and a simple rule. Knowing when not to use AI is now a senior-level skill.

System design: Designing an end-to-end AI solution, data ingestion, preprocessing, model, serving, monitoring, retraining, coherently and at scale. This is a standard senior interview question and a daily requirement of the job.

Domain depth: An AI engineer who understands credit risk, clinical trial data, or telecom fraud is far harder to replace than a generalist. Pick a domain and go deep. The investment compounds in ways that technical skill investment alone does not.

## The plateau most people hit

This is where many careers stall, not from lack of skills, but from avoiding the discomfort of judgment work. People stay in execution mode because execution is familiar and judgment is exposed. You can be wrong about a model's accuracy metric and explain why technically. Being wrong about whether a project was worth doing at all is harder to defend.

The signal that you have made the transition: you are the person others come to when they cannot figure out what the problem actually is, not just when they need it solved.

A practical step: volunteer to own a project end to end. Not just the model. Requirements gathering, stakeholder alignment, deployment, post-launch monitoring, and business review. Do this once, even imperfectly, and you will learn more about career progression than any certification.

## Phase 4: The Shaper (10 or More Years)

### What the job actually looks like

At senior levels, the boundaries dissolve. Research, engineering, and product blur together. Your day looks less like doing AI and more like defining strategy, making build-versus-buy decisions on foundation models, evaluating whether a problem warrants an AI solution at all, and building institutional knowledge across teams.

The most senior AI professionals are not necessarily the best at any single technical skill. They have taste. They can see which technical bets are worth making, which shortcuts will cost dearly later, and which problems the organisation has not yet thought to ask. Taste is accumulated rather than learned. It comes from having been close to enough decisions, good and bad, to have developed a reliable intuition about which way they tend to go.

### The reinvention reality

Almost nobody reaches this phase without at least one uncomfortable reinvention. Computer vision specialists whose market contracted. Spark engineers whose ecosystem shifted. Research scientists who had to learn the product side from scratch. That is not failure. That is the loop working as designed.

The engineers who thrive long-term are the ones who move through disruption faster, not the ones who avoid it. The capacity to reinvent, to let go of a previous identity, to be a beginner again in a specific domain, to rebuild credibility in a new context, is the most durable skill available in a field that changes this quickly.

Ethics and governance at this level

In Phases 3 and 4, the build-versus-buy decision turns on compliance and risk as much as cost. A senior leader in 2026 must account for data sovereignty, where data lives and who has legal access to it. Algorithmic bias, moving beyond accuracy to audit for fairness and explainability, particularly in regulated industries. And the emerging regulatory landscape, the EU AI Act, India's DPDP Act, and the compliance frameworks that will shape what can be built and deployed in each jurisdiction.

These are not additions to the technical role. They are the technical role, at this level.

## The Salary Number Game

Here is a pattern that derails more AI careers than any technical gap.

People start tracking their career in salary multiples. They should be at three times their Year 1 package by Year 3. They should hit a certain number by thirty. They optimise entirely for the number.

The problem is that this lens is almost entirely backward-looking. It measures what the market paid for your skills last year, not what your skills will be worth in three years.

More useful questions: What is your work actually adding, stated clearly in one sentence? Is your work strategic or interchangeable, could a team elsewhere do exactly what you do, for less? What is the real cost of this role, does the increment come with hours and conditions that erode the capacity for learning that will determine your value in five years?

Optimise for learning rate and optionality, especially in the first ten years. The money follows the skills. It rarely works convincingly the other way around.

## On Watching People Get Promoted Ahead of You

This deserves its own section because almost nobody writes about it honestly.

At some point, someone you started alongside will be promoted ahead of you. Before you. And it will feel like something, not necessarily envy in its pure form, but a complicated mixture of self-doubt, comparison, and something close to grief about the version of the story you had been telling yourself.

A few things worth holding onto.

Titles are not synchronised. Careers are not races with a shared clock. Some people accelerate early and plateau. Some move slowly and then compound. The comparison is almost always between your internal experience, every doubt, every mistake, every moment of uncertainty, and someone else's external presentation.

Their path is not your data. If someone became VP at thirty-two by spending five years in a high-growth startup at significant personal cost, that is one specific trade that worked for one specific person in one specific context. It tells you almost nothing useful about your own situation.

Envy is information, not instruction. Notice what you actually want: the recognition, the autonomy, the financial security, the sense of having figured something out. Those are real desires worth examining directly. Chasing someone else's job description as a proxy for them rarely ends well.

The most grounded senior engineers you will meet are almost always the ones who stopped tracking their peers at some point and started tracking their own growth curve instead.

## If You Just Got Let Go

Job loss in the AI sector follows a predictable pattern: funding cycles, product pivots, and the gap between what organisations promise AI will deliver and what it actually does. It also, increasingly, follows the automation of execution work that a significant fraction of the workforce has been hired to provide.

If you are in this situation right now, Chapter 11 addresses it in full, the first 48 hours, the audit, the search strategy, the consulting bridge, and what to do with your sense of self when the job that quietly provided its structure disappears. Turn there now if you need to. This chapter will be here when you come back.

## The Short Version

In Phase 1: Ship something real. One deployed API. One working project. Stop collecting courses.

In Phase 2: Learn MLOps seriously. The model is never the hard part. The pipeline, the monitoring, the reliability, that is what the market pays for.

In Phase 3: Practice problem framing. Write a one-page brief on a business problem and the AI approach you would take. Share it. Get feedback. Repeat until it feels natural.

In Phase 4: Mentor someone two phases behind you. Teaching forces the kind of clarity that solo work does not.

The loop will continue. The tools will change. What a senior AI engineer means in 2029 will look different from what it means today. The real question is whether you can learn to move through the loop, consciously, deliberately, without clinging too tightly to any single version of yourself or your title, not whether you can stop it.

No version of this field ever promised stability. What it has consistently rewarded is the capacity to adapt.

# Chapter 5: The Skills That Actually Matter in 2026

## *What to Learn, What to Build, and How to Tell the Difference*

There is a version of skill-building that feels productive and produces very little. You complete a course on a new framework. You add it to your LinkedIn profile. You start another course. The profile grows longer. The actual capability does not grow at the same rate, because the course gave you vocabulary and the job requires judgment, and those are not the same thing.

There is another version that compounds. You encounter a real problem. You learn what you need to solve it. You build something. You encounter the ways it fails. You learn more. The knowledge sticks because it was acquired in context, applied immediately, and tested against reality.

The difference between these two versions of skill-building comes down to sequencing, not intelligence or effort. Learning the right thing at the right stage of your career, in the right order, applied to a real problem, this is what separates the professional who is genuinely more capable at Year 5 than at Year 2 from the one who has simply accumulated more credentials.

This chapter is a sequenced map of what to learn, when, and how to demonstrate it. It is organised around the four phases from Chapter 4, because the skills that matter in Phase 1 are different from those that matter in Phase 3, and confusing them is one of the most common and costly mistakes in an AI career.

## Before You Learn Anything: The Hype Filter

The AI field generates more noise per square kilometre than any other domain in technology. Every week brings a new framework, a new model, a new architectural pattern, a new certification, a new claim that the previous approach is now obsolete.

Most of it does not require your attention. The fraction that does requires it urgently.

Developing a reliable hype filter is itself a skill, and it is worth developing early. Here is a simple one that works.

Before investing significant time in learning something new, ask three questions. First: is this appearing in actual job descriptions for roles I want, or only in conference talks and Twitter threads? Second: can I find evidence of this being used in production systems, not just in demos and research papers? Third: is this something that solves a real problem I have encountered, or something that sounds impressive in the abstract?

If the answer to all three is yes, it deserves serious attention. If the answer to one or two is yes, it deserves a shallow survey, enough to understand what it is and whether it applies to your situation. If the answer to all three is no, it can wait.

In 2026, the things that pass this filter consistently are: production-grade Python, SQL at depth, MLOps tooling, RAG pipeline design, agentic system architecture, vector database implementation, model monitoring, and the mathematical foundations that underpin all of them. The things that frequently fail this filter are: specific model versions, individual framework releases, certification programmes tied to vendor ecosystems, and anything described primarily in terms of what it will be able to do rather than what it currently does.

## Phase 1 Skills: The Tool User (0–2 Years)

The goal of Phase 1 is to become genuinely competent at a small number of foundational things, and to deploy something real, not to know everything.

### The non-negotiable foundations

Python at production grade is the single most important skill to develop in Phase 1. Not notebook Python, the Python that shows up in production systems. This means writing functions with proper input validation, modules with clear interfaces, unit tests that catch regressions, and code that someone else can read and maintain without your help. The gap between notebook Python and production Python is larger than most early-career professionals realise, and it is one of the most consistent differentiators in technical interviews.

SQL is the second non-negotiable. Not SELECT * from a tutorial. Window functions, CTEs, query optimisation, understanding of indexes and how they affect performance, the ability to write a query that retrieves exactly what is needed from a messy schema without loading the entire table into memory. Data scientists who cannot write solid SQL are dependent on data engineers for work they should be able to do themselves, and this dependency is visible to every hiring manager who reviews their work.

Git from day one. Version control everything, notebooks, scripts, configuration files, data processing code. The professional who has been committing to GitHub since their first project has a demonstrable history of how they think. The one who uploads a zip file of their work has not.

### The mathematical layer

Phase 1 is the right time to build mathematical foundations, not because you will use them immediately but because the time required to build them compounds negatively if you defer. The mathematical literacy required for senior AI work, understanding what attention mechanisms are actually doing, knowing why a particular regularisation choice makes sense, being able to read a paper and evaluate whether the results are credible, cannot be acquired in a weekend when you need it for an interview.

The priority order: linear algebra first (vectors, matrices, dot products, eigenvalues, these are the vocabulary of neural network computations). Probability and statistics second (conditional probability, Bayes theorem, distributions, hypothesis testing, the meaning of precision and recall). Calculus third (gradient descent, backpropagation, understand the mechanics, not just the intuition). Optimisation theory last (relevant once you are working with non-standard model architectures or reinforcement learning).

None of this requires a formal course. MIT OpenCourseWare, 3Blue1Brown's linear algebra series, and Feller's probability textbook cover the relevant ground. What matters is the application: every mathematical concept you encounter should be connected immediately to something you have seen in a model or a dataset.

### The first real project

The milestone that separates Phase 1 completion from Phase 1 continuation is deploying something. Not a notebook. Not a demo that works on your laptop. An actual API endpoint that takes input and returns a prediction or a generated output, hosted on a cloud platform, with documentation that explains what it does, how it works, and what its failure modes are.

The specific technology matters less than the fact of deployment. FastAPI for the endpoint, Docker for containerisation, a free tier on AWS or GCP or Azure for hosting. The project should solve a problem you actually care about, applied to a domain you understand, using data you had to acquire and clean yourself. This last part, dealing with real, messy data, is what most early-career portfolios are missing, because Kaggle datasets are pre-cleaned to a standard that production data never meets.

In the Indian market specifically, the deployed project is what moves a candidate from the ₹4–8 L entry band to the ₹8–20 L high-value entry band. Not the college name. Not the certification. The working, deployed, documented project.

### What to avoid in Phase 1

The most common Phase 1 trap is breadth over depth, learning ten frameworks at a surface level instead of one framework at a production level. Hiring managers can detect framework tourism in about five minutes of technical interview. The person who has built and deployed one serious project with PyTorch understands more than the person who has completed courses in PyTorch, TensorFlow, JAX, and Keras without building anything that ran in production.

The second trap is certification collection. Certifications have some value as signals of commitment and baseline familiarity. They have no value as substitutes for demonstrated ability. The AWS Machine Learning Specialty certification tells a hiring manager you sat an exam. A deployed ML system on AWS tells them you can build something that works.

## Phase 2 Skills: The Builder (2–5 Years)

The transition from Phase 1 to Phase 2 is the most technically demanding shift in an AI career. The work changes from individual model development to system design. The relevant question changes from "does this model work?" to "does this system work reliably, at scale, when the data changes and the user base grows and someone pushes an update at 11pm on a Friday?"

### MLOps: no longer optional

MLOps is the discipline of taking ML from experiment to production and keeping it there. By 2026 it has become the baseline expectation for anyone claiming to do production AI work, not a specialisation.

The core MLOps stack in learning order: MLflow for experiment tracking (track every run, every parameter, every metric, if you cannot reproduce your experiments, you cannot improve them systematically). Docker for containerisation (understand what a container is, why it exists, and how to build images that are small, reproducible, and secure). One cloud ML service in depth, SageMaker on AWS, Vertex AI on GCP, or Azure ML, pick one and stay with it until you understand it properly. Airflow or Prefect for pipeline orchestration. Kubernetes basics, you do not need to be a Kubernetes expert, but you need to understand what it does and why it matters for scaling ML workloads.

At Years 3–4, add model monitoring. Evidently AI for data drift detection. Prometheus and Grafana for infrastructure metrics. The ability to set up an alert that fires when a model's performance degrades before users notice it, this is one of the highest-value skills in the market and one of the least commonly demonstrated in portfolios.

At Years 4–5, add LLMOps tooling specifically: evaluation pipeline design, vector database implementation at scale, agentic workflow frameworks like LangGraph. The Phase 2 builder who has MLOps depth plus LLMOps breadth is positioned at the boundary of what the market most urgently needs.

### RAG before fine-tuning

One of the most practically important things to understand in Phase 2 is when not to fine-tune a model.

Fine-tuning a model on proprietary data is expensive, brittle, and frequently unnecessary. A well-designed RAG pipeline, retrieval-augmented generation, where the model is given relevant context at inference time rather than having that context baked into its weights, outperforms a fine-tuned model on most enterprise tasks at a fraction of the cost and maintenance overhead. Fine-tuned models become stale as the underlying data changes. RAG pipelines update as the knowledge base updates.

This matters for your career because the ability to make this argument, to recommend RAG over fine-tuning based on a clear understanding of the trade-offs, is a Phase 3 skill appearing in Phase 2. It signals the kind of judgment that separates builders from executors. Learning the technical implementation of RAG thoroughly in Phase 2 is the prerequisite for making that argument credibly in Phase 3.

The RAG implementation stack: a vector database (start with ChromaDB for local development, Pinecone or Weaviate for production), an embedding model (understand the difference between embedding models and generative models, and when to use each), a retrieval strategy (dense retrieval, sparse retrieval, hybrid approaches), and an evaluation framework to measure whether retrieval quality is actually improving response quality.

### Model optimisation: the underrated differentiator

The Phase 2 skill that most people skip and most senior hiring managers notice is model optimisation. The ability to take a large model and make it run faster and cheaper, quantisation, ONNX export, efficient inference configuration, is rarer than it should be and more valued than most early-career professionals realise.

The practical case: a company using a frontier model API for a high-volume task is paying per token. A Phase 2 engineer who can replace that frontier model call with a smaller, quantised, locally-hosted model that performs comparably on the specific task can save meaningful money monthly. That is a concrete, measurable business contribution that appears directly in financial reports. It is the kind of work that gets noticed and rewarded in ways that incremental model accuracy improvements often do not.

Start with quantisation basics: understand the difference between FP32, FP16, and INT8 precision, and what the trade-offs are. Learn ONNX export for model portability. Explore smaller models, Llama 3, Mistral, Phi-3, and understand what tasks they can handle well enough to replace frontier model calls.

### The 2026 project for Phase 2

The Phase 2 portfolio centrepiece should be an end-to-end ML system: not just a model but a pipeline. Data ingestion from a real source, preprocessing, model training with experiment tracking, deployment as an API, monitoring for drift, and a retraining trigger when performance degrades.

In the Indian market, Phase 2 projects that solve domain-specific problems, fraud detection for a UPI transaction dataset, crop yield prediction from publicly available agricultural data, clinical text processing using Indian medical records, stand out more than generic projects using standard datasets. Domain specificity signals that you understand the problem, not just the technology.

## Phase 3 Skills: The Translator (5–10 Years)

Phase 3 is where technical competence becomes insufficient on its own. The work that matters at this level is not building, it is framing, deciding, and communicating. The skills required are harder to learn from a course because they are accumulated through the experience of being responsible for outcomes rather than just for deliverables.

### Problem framing

The most underrated and most valuable skill at this level is the ability to convert a vague business question into a precise, solvable ML problem with the right success metric.

This sounds straightforward. It is not. A business stakeholder who says "we need to reduce churn" has not given you a problem statement. They have given you a symptom. The problem statement requires knowing: which customers are churning, over what time horizon, what signals precede churn in the data, what intervention is available if you predict it, what the cost of a false positive is versus a false negative, and what level of model performance is actually required to make the intervention economically worthwhile.

Working through those questions with a stakeholder, asking them in the right order, in language they can engage with, without making them feel interrogated, is a skill that takes years of real stakeholder interaction to develop. It cannot be learned from a course. It can be accelerated by deliberately taking on the problem definition work rather than waiting for someone else to define the problem before you engage.

### AI pruning

Knowing when not to use AI is a Phase 3 skill. Many organisations in 2026 are dealing with AI fatigue, too many tools, too many models, inconsistent interfaces, nothing talking to each other reliably. The most valuable contribution a senior person can often make is: we do not need a custom model here. We need a better schema and a business rule. We do not need an LLM for this classification task. We need a decision tree and a threshold.

This judgment requires genuine technical depth, you cannot credibly argue against an AI solution unless you understand what the AI solution would actually involve and what its failure modes would be. But it also requires organisational courage: recommending a simpler solution when the stakeholder is excited about the sophisticated one is uncomfortable, and most people avoid the discomfort by building what was asked for.

### Communication at altitude

Phase 3 professionals spend increasing time talking to people who do not share their technical vocabulary. The ability to explain model uncertainty to a business leader, to describe the cost of data quality problems in terms of business outcomes rather than statistical metrics, to present a build-versus-buy recommendation on foundation models in language that a CFO can evaluate, these are Phase 3 competencies.

The most practical way to develop them is to write. A one-page brief on a technical decision, written for a non-technical audience, that correctly characterises the trade-offs and makes a clear recommendation, this is harder to produce than a ten-page technical document, and it is what Phase 3 work actually requires. Write one for every significant technical decision you make. Share it. Get feedback. The writing practice accelerates the communication skill more reliably than any amount of presentation training.

## Phase 4 Skills: The Shaper (10+ Years)

Phase 4 skill development is less about learning new technical tools and more about developing taste, the accumulated judgment to see which technical bets are worth making, which architectural decisions will age well, and which problems are worth solving at all.

Two skills deserve explicit mention because they are genuinely learnable rather than simply accumulated.

### Evaluation design

The ability to design a rigorous evaluation framework, for a model, for an AI system, for an organisation's AI strategy, is one of the most consistently undervalued and underdeveloped skills across the entire career arc. Most evaluations are designed to confirm that something works rather than to discover how it fails. A Phase 4 professional designs evaluations that are genuinely adversarial: that probe the specific failure modes the system is most likely to exhibit in production, that measure what the business actually cares about rather than what is easy to measure, and that produce actionable information rather than just a score.

In the LLM era, evaluation design has become more complex and more important simultaneously. Hallucination rates, groundedness scores, factual consistency across different phrasings of the same question, behaviour under adversarial prompts, these require evaluation frameworks that did not exist three years ago and are still being developed. The professional who can design and implement credible LLM evaluations is genuinely rare and genuinely valued.

### Mentoring as skill development

Teaching forces a clarity of understanding that solo work does not require. When you have to explain why a particular architecture choice makes sense, in terms that a Phase 1 professional can understand and apply, you discover quickly whether you actually understand it yourself or whether you have been pattern-matching successfully without genuine comprehension.

Mentoring in the Indian tech community is significantly undersupplied relative to demand. The number of early-career professionals who need good mentorship is enormous; the number of experienced professionals investing time in providing it is small. If you are in Phase 3 or Phase 4, spending two hours a month with someone in Phase 1 or Phase 2 is one of the highest-return investments available to you, for them obviously, but also for your own understanding of what you know and what you only think you know.

## The Full-Stack Shift: Vertical Stack Literacy

If there is one thesis to carry out of this chapter into the interview chapters that follow, it is this: framework fluency is becoming cheap, and systems understanding is becoming expensive. In 2023, saying you had built RAG with LangChain differentiated you. In 2026, the interviewer's response is increasingly a sequence of follow-ups: how did you evaluate retrieval, how was the model served, what happens when five hundred requests arrive at once, where does the KV cache live, what does one request cost, and what breaks first. The shift is from knowing how to assemble AI components to understanding the system beneath and around them.

It helps to picture the modern AI system as a vertical stack. At the top sits the business problem and the product design around it. Below that, evaluation and guardrails. Below that, the application layer: RAG, agents, natural-language-to-SQL, orchestration. Below that, the models themselves, transformers and the smaller specialised models that increasingly sit beside them. Below that, the inference engines that serve those models, vLLM and its peers. Below that, the physical layer of GPU memory, bandwidth, and compute. And underneath everything, the cloud, Kubernetes, and MLOps machinery that keeps it running.

Nobody needs equal depth at every layer, and pretending otherwise turns preparation into a list of forty-seven technologies. What senior candidates increasingly need is vertical literacy: enough understanding at each layer to reason across the boundaries, to say why a retrieval choice affects serving cost, or why a latency target constrains model choice. The useful shape is the T-shaped engineer, deep in one or two layers with working literacy across the rest, and interviews are now explicitly probing the vertical bar of the T, as the drill-down pattern in Chapter 9 shows in detail.

## Evaluation Engineering: Evals Are the New Test Set

Evaluation appears throughout this book as a differentiating competency, but it deserves stating as its own discipline, because it is the layer of the stack most consistently probed at senior level and most consistently underprepared. The days when a single accuracy number settled the question are over; every system type now carries its own evaluation vocabulary, and interviewers notice immediately whether you speak it.

For RAG systems, the vocabulary splits retrieval from generation. Retrieval is measured with recall and precision at k, and rank-aware metrics such as MRR and NDCG@K where the order of results matters, not just their presence. Generation is measured with context relevance, faithfulness or groundedness (does the answer follow from what was retrieved), answer relevance, and hallucination rate. Around both sit latency, cost per query, and end-to-end task success, which is the only number the business actually experiences.

For natural-language-to-SQL systems, syntactic validity (does the query parse) is the weakest signal, execution accuracy (does it run) is stronger, and result-set equivalence against a gold query is the real test, since two syntactically different queries can be equally correct. Beyond correctness sit schema-linking accuracy, handling of ambiguous questions, and the security dimension: forbidden query checks and read-only execution, so a malformed or overly broad query is caught before it reaches the database.

For agentic systems, task completion rate is the headline, but the diagnostic metrics are underneath it: tool-selection accuracy, trajectory quality, number of steps to completion, loop and failure rate, cost per successful task, and human escalation rate. An agent that completes tasks at twice the step count of an alternative is not half as good; it is twice as expensive.

A closely related question is worth flagging on its own, because it recurred across this search far more than any single metric name: what do you do when there is no golden or labelled dataset to evaluate against at all. The answer is not to reach for a single framework and stop, it is to decompose evaluation into layers that need different amounts of ground truth, several of which need none. Faithfulness and answer relevance are reference-free and can run from day one; retrieval quality can be bootstrapped into a synthetic evaluation set built from the corpus itself before any human labels a single example; a human-curated golden set is grown progressively rather than demanded up front; and production behavioural signals, task completion, reformulation rate, escalation rate, run continuously underneath all of it. The worked version of this answer, including the graph-RAG extension, is in Appendix G, and the compact reference table is boxed in Appendix L.

Finally, hold on to a three-way distinction that marks a genuinely senior answer: offline evaluation, online evaluation, and business

KPI are three different things that only sometimes move together. A model can improve on the offline benchmark, degrade in online A/B, and leave the business KPI unchanged, and knowing why that happens, distribution shift, metric misalignment, user adaptation, is precisely the judgment that evaluation design at Phase 4 is about.

## Three Project Blueprints for 2026

The following project blueprints are specific enough to start building from, substantial enough to impress a 2026 hiring manager, and scoped to be completable in three to four weeks of focused work alongside a full-time role.

### Blueprint 1: Domain-Specific RAG System with Evaluation Pipeline (Phase 1–2)

Build a RAG system over a domain-specific knowledge base, Indian legal judgements (available from the Indian Kanoon API), SEBI regulatory filings, or a set of research papers in a domain you know well. The system should answer natural language questions about the documents, cite the specific passages it drew on, and flag when it does not have enough information to answer confidently rather than hallucinating.

The evaluation component is what distinguishes this project. Build a test set of fifty questions with known correct answers, and measure retrieval accuracy (did the right document come back?) separately from generation quality (did the model use the retrieved document correctly?). Document both metrics and how they change as you adjust the retrieval strategy.

Stack: Python, LangChain or LlamaIndex, ChromaDB or Pinecone, an open-source embedding model, FastAPI for the endpoint, a simple Streamlit interface for demonstration.

What this demonstrates: RAG implementation at production depth, evaluation thinking, domain knowledge, end-to-end system design, the ability to separate retrieval quality from generation quality.

### Blueprint 2: Multi-Agent System with DPDP Compliance Checker (Phase 2–3)

Build a multi-agent system that takes a company's privacy policy or data processing document as input and generates a structured compliance assessment against the requirements of India's Digital Personal Data Protection Act. One agent handles document parsing and extraction. A second handles mapping extracted clauses to DPDP requirements. A third generates the assessment report with specific citations and gap analysis.

The interesting technical challenge is designing the handoff between agents, how does Agent 1 pass structured information to Agent 2 in a format that Agent 2 can reason about reliably? How do you detect when an agent has produced an unreliable output and needs to retry or escalate?

Stack: Python, LangGraph for agent orchestration, an LLM API for reasoning, structured output parsing, a simple web interface for document upload and report download.

What this demonstrates: Agentic system design, multi-step reasoning, domain specificity (legal/regulatory), Indian regulatory awareness, evaluation thinking (how do you know when the compliance assessment is correct?).

### Blueprint 3: Production ML System with Full Monitoring (Phase 2)

Build a production-grade ML system for a real prediction problem, credit default prediction using a publicly available Indian banking dataset, flight delay prediction using Indian aviation data, or agricultural yield prediction using publicly available crop and weather data. The system should include: data ingestion pipeline, feature engineering with documented decisions, model training with experiment tracking in MLflow, deployment as a REST API, data drift monitoring using Evidently AI, and a simple dashboard showing model performance over time.

The key constraint: the system should be designed to retrain automatically when drift exceeds a defined threshold. This is the part most portfolio projects skip, and it is the part that most closely mirrors what production ML systems actually require.

Stack: Python, MLflow, FastAPI, Docker, one cloud platform, Evidently AI, Grafana or a simple custom dashboard.

What this demonstrates: Full MLOps lifecycle, monitoring and drift detection, retraining pipeline, production system design, the ability to maintain a system rather than just build one.

## What Not to Learn: The Deprecation List

As important as knowing what to learn is knowing what to deprioritise. The following are skills that were genuinely valuable in recent years and have either been superseded or commoditised to the point where they no longer differentiate.

Standalone prompt engineering without broader LLM system design context. The market has corrected, as the salary data in Appendix C shows, pure prompt engineering now sits at the lower end of the AI compensation spectrum. Prompt engineering as a component of agentic system design remains relevant; as a standalone skill it does not.

Basic data visualisation using standard tools. Tableau, Power BI, standard matplotlib dashboards, these are baseline expectations for data roles, not differentiators. The differentiator is not being able to make a chart but being able to decide what question the chart should answer and whether it actually answers it.

Generic cloud certifications without accompanying project work. The AWS Certified Machine Learning Specialty or the Google Professional Machine Learning Engineer certification has some signal value. Without a portfolio of deployed projects on the relevant cloud platform, it signals that you sat an exam, which is a weaker signal than the exam provider would prefer you to believe.

LSTM and RNN expertise as a primary skill. These architectures have been largely superseded by transformer-based approaches for sequence modelling tasks. Understanding them conceptually is useful for reading older literature. Building expertise around them as a primary skill is not a sound investment in 2026.

## The Compounding Principle

Every skill in this chapter builds on the ones that precede it in the sequence. Production Python enables MLOps work. MLOps work enables agentic system design. Mathematical foundations enable the debugging that makes production systems reliable. The evaluation skills developed in Phase 2 become the evaluation design competence that defines Phase 4.

The professionals who fall behind in this field are almost never the ones who stopped learning. They are the ones who learned in the wrong sequence, acquiring advanced knowledge before they had the foundation to apply it, or staying at the surface of many things rather than going deep enough on any one thing for the knowledge to compound.

Learn in sequence. Build in public. Deploy before you think you are ready. The gap between your current skills and the market's needs is not an obstacle. Closing it deliberately, one real project at a time, is the career.

The specific tools named in this chapter will not survive unchanged for long. The sequence in which you learn them will hold up better. Start where you are, build what you can, and move to the next phase once the current one has taught you what it has to teach.

# Chapter 6: The Psychological Pressures Nobody Talks About

There is a version of the data science career conversation that happens on LinkedIn. It involves someone announcing a new certification, a promotion, a paper accepted at NeurIPS, a move to a company with a better-known name. The comments fill with congratulations. Everyone appears to be accelerating.

There is another conversation that almost never happens in public. It happens at 11pm when the Slack notifications have finally stopped, or on a Sunday afternoon when the anxiety about Monday has already arrived. It is about feeling permanently behind. About not being sure whether you actually understand what you are doing or whether you have just learned to sound like you do. About watching the field move so fast that last year's skills feel like last decade's. About the gap between what your family thinks you do and what you actually spend your time on.

This chapter is about that conversation.

## The Field That Never Lets You Rest

Most professions have a stable core. A lawyer called to the bar in 2010 is still using the same foundational legal reasoning in 2026. A surgeon trained fifteen years ago is still performing surgery recognisably similar to what they trained for. The domain evolves, but the evolution is measured enough that a competent professional can stay current without feeling like they are running to stand still.

Data science and AI are not like this. The transformer architecture that defined the field in 2020 was itself a disruption of what came before. The LLM applications that felt cutting-edge in 2023 are infrastructure by 2026. The skills that made someone hireable three years ago are now the baseline that gets you past the first filter, if you are lucky.

This rate of change is not a temporary condition of an immature field settling down. It appears to be a structural feature of AI development. Each wave of progress obsoletes a portion of the previous wave's skill premium. The professional who spent two years becoming expert in one framework finds that framework either absorbed into a higher-level abstraction or quietly deprecated.

The psychological consequence of this is a chronic low-grade anxiety that is rarely named directly. It is closer to the feeling of trying to read a book while someone keeps tearing out the pages you have not read yet than to outright burnout, though it can turn into that too.

## Imposter Syndrome in a Credential-Heavy Culture

Imposter syndrome, the persistent feeling that you do not deserve your position, that you are less competent than others believe, and that you will eventually be found out, is common across professional fields. In data science, it has specific features that make it particularly corrosive.

The first is the breadth of the field. A genuinely accomplished data scientist is expected to have working knowledge of statistics, software engineering, machine learning theory, domain expertise, communication, and increasingly, the architecture of LLM-based systems. No one is excellent at all of these. Everyone is aware of their gaps. The result is that even highly capable people can always find a dimension on which they feel inadequate, because the field is genuinely too broad for any one person to master completely.

The second is the visibility of other people's competence. The people you see on Twitter, on LinkedIn, on YouTube, are the ones who are confident enough to publish, to speak, to claim expertise. They are not a representative sample. They are a selection of people whose relationship with their own knowledge happens to produce visible output. The vast majority of working data scientists, including very good ones, are invisible in these spaces. When you compare your private uncertainty to other people's public confidence, you are comparing incomparable things.

The third, specific to India, is the credentialing culture. The IIT filter, the GATE score, the postgraduate degree from a ranked institution, these function as proxies for competence in a market where actual competence is hard to assess quickly. The consequence is that people who came through a different path, or the same path but with less prestigious stops along the way, carry a persistent sense of starting behind. And people who came through the prestigious path carry a different anxiety: the fear that the credential will eventually be exposed as having been the most impressive thing about them.

None of this reflects actual ability. It reflects the gap between how competence is signalled in this market and how it is actually distributed.

## The Illusion of Readiness

Online learning platforms have made it genuinely easier to acquire new skills quickly. They have also created a new psychological trap.

The trap works like this. A new technology emerges, say, a framework for building agentic AI systems. Within weeks, there are courses on it. Within months, there are certifications. You complete the course. You pass the assessment. You add it to your LinkedIn profile. You feel ready.

But readiness, in the sense that matters to an employer, comes from having built something with the technology, encountered the ways it fails, debugged it at 2am when it stopped working in production, and developed the intuition that comes from having been responsible for it, not from having completed a course. The course gives you the vocabulary. The experience gives you the judgment. These are not the same thing, and the gap between them is exactly what interviewers are probing when they go deep on your past projects.

The problem is that the proliferation of courses creates the appearance of a clear path to readiness, which makes the gap more disorienting when you encounter it. If you have done the course, completed the certification, and still feel underprepared, the natural conclusion is that something is wrong with you, rather than that the course was never going to be sufficient on its own.

This dynamic has a name in learning science: the Dunning-Kruger effect operates in reverse at the top of the competence curve. The more you actually know about a subject, the more acutely you are aware of what you do not know. Beginners feel confident because they do not yet know enough to see the complexity. Experts feel uncertain because they see it clearly. In a field where expertise is genuinely hard to demonstrate to outsiders, this can manifest as a persistent sense of not being good enough, even among people who are very good indeed.

## Family, Expectations, and the Indian Context

The career anxiety of a data scientist in India does not exist in a vacuum. It exists inside a family context, a social context, and a set of expectations that were formed at a time when the technology landscape looked very different.

For many professionals in their thirties and forties, their family's mental model of a good technology career was formed in the 1990s and 2000s: get into a good company, get a stable job, get promoted regularly, retire with a pension or a comfortable corpus. The concept of a career as a loop, where you periodically become partly obsolete and have to reinvent yourself, is not part of this model.

Neither is the concept of independent research, or portfolio careers, or consulting work that pays well but comes without the security of a permanent position.

This creates a specific kind of pressure. When you tell your parents that you are upskilling in agentic AI frameworks because your current skills are becoming less differentiated, they hear: my child's job is at risk. When you say you are considering leaving a stable GCC role to join a startup or pursue independent work, they hear: my child is making a reckless decision. The conversation about career risk management that feels strategic to you reads as instability to them.

None of this calls for different choices. It does mean understanding that the psychological cost of navigating a non-linear career in India includes the weight of managing other people's anxiety about your choices, on top of your own.

There is also the marriage market dimension, which is rarely discussed in professional contexts but is real for many people in their twenties and early thirties. Employment status, company name, and salary level are visible signals in ways that depth of expertise, quality of work, or long-term career trajectory are not. A person doing excellent independent research at a modest income can find themselves disadvantaged in contexts where a mediocre performer at a brand-name firm appears, on the surface, to be a better prospect.

## Watching Peers Get Promoted

At some point in most careers, someone you started alongside will move ahead of you. A promotion you expected goes to someone else. A peer's LinkedIn update announces a title you were hoping for yourself. Someone who joined after you is now technically your senior.

This is one of the more reliably painful experiences of professional life, and it is almost never discussed honestly because the emotion it produces, a complicated mixture of envy, self-doubt, and something close to grief, is not socially acceptable to express in professional settings.

A few things are worth saying clearly.

The comparison is almost always between your internal experience and someone else's external presentation. You know every doubt you had, every mistake you made, every moment you felt out of your depth. You see only the announcement, the title, the public-facing version of their success. These are not comparable things.

Promotions in technology organisations are not purely meritocratic. They depend on visibility, on having the right manager at the right time, on being in the right team when the organisation decides to invest in that area, on political factors that have nothing to do with technical competence. Someone getting promoted ahead of you tells you something about their situation. It tells you very little about yours.

Envy, when you examine it carefully, is usually information about what you actually want. Not their specific job, the desire is rarely that precise, but something they appear to have: recognition, autonomy, financial security, the sense of having figured something out. These are legitimate desires worth examining directly, rather than through the distorting lens of comparison.

The most grounded senior professionals you will meet are almost always the ones who stopped tracking their peers at some point and started tracking their own growth curve instead. This is easier to say than to do. But it is a more useful orientation than the alternative.

## Sustainable Learning vs Performative Learning

There is a version of continuous learning that is genuinely sustaining. You encounter a problem you cannot solve with what you know. You go and learn what you need. You solve the problem. The learning has a purpose, a context, a moment of application that makes it stick.

There is another version that is performative. You add courses to your profile because the profile needs to look current. You read papers because not reading papers feels like falling behind. You attend webinars because the invitation created a faint anxiety about missing something important. The learning has no particular destination. It is driven by the fear of obsolescence rather than the pull of genuine curiosity.

The performative version is exhausting and mostly ineffective. Skills acquired under anxiety, without application, decay quickly. The course you completed in three weeks to add to your profile will not be there in the interview when someone asks you to go deep on how you actually used it.

The sustainable version requires deliberately limiting what you learn. This sounds counterintuitive in a field where there is always more to know. But attention is finite, and the professional who learns three things well is more capable than the one who has skimmed thirty things anxiously.

A practical question to ask when you encounter a new technology or framework: is this something I need right now for work I am actually doing, or is this something I feel I should know because it is generating noise in my feed? The first category deserves your attention. The second category can wait, or can be addressed with a shallow survey rather than a full course.

## When It Becomes More Than Stress

Most of what has been described so far is the normal psychological texture of a demanding career in a fast-moving field. Uncomfortable, sometimes exhausting, but navigable.

There are situations where it becomes something more. Chronic anxiety that interferes with sleep, concentration, and the ability to function at work is a health problem, not a career management one, and deserves to be treated as such. Burnout, the combination of exhaustion, cynicism, and reduced professional efficacy that follows sustained overload, is similarly not something that resolves through better time management or a longer weekend.

The Indian technology sector has a particular cultural reluctance around mental health. Seeking help is still, in many professional contexts, seen as a sign of weakness rather than a sign of self-awareness. This reluctance has costs that are rarely counted in the career conversation: talented people leaving the field, or continuing in it at significantly reduced capacity, because the stress was never addressed.

If what you are experiencing has moved beyond the ordinary discomfort of a demanding career, the most important thing you can do is talk to someone qualified to help. A therapist, a counsellor, a psychiatrist if medication is appropriate, these are not last resorts. They are first-line resources for a problem that will not resolve on its own.

## The Uneven Playing Field

Most of what this chapter describes is the experience of a particular kind of Indian technology professional: urban, English-medium educated, from a family background where a technology career was a known and respected path. This is the experience the chapter can describe with most accuracy. It is not the whole experience of working in Indian AI.

The credentialling culture described earlier, the IIT filter, the brand-name institution premium, the structured networking that follows from shared educational backgrounds, does not operate neutrally. It systematically advantages people from families that had access to expensive coaching, English-medium schooling, and the social capital to navigate selective admission processes. Far from controversial, this is a structural feature of how AI hiring in India currently works, and acknowledging it is a prerequisite for changing it.

Women in Indian AI face the imposter syndrome described in this chapter alongside additional pressures that are specific to their situation: the marriage market dimension already noted, the workplace cultures in some technology environments that remain genuinely unwelcoming, and a gender pay gap that is documented in the salary data, women earning approximately ₹74–81 for every ₹100 earned by men in equivalent roles, and whose causes are structural rather than individual. The "you are not the only one feeling this" reassurance that closes this chapter is true, but the specific pressures vary meaningfully depending on who you are.

Professionals from non-metro backgrounds, regional-language-medium education, or first-generation technology careers carry a particular form of the credential anxiety described earlier, one that is compounded by genuine information gaps about how hiring actually works, genuine network deficits in the communities where opportunities concentrate, and the particular isolation of being the only person in your immediate circle navigating a career that nobody around you has done before. The portfolio-over-pedigree argument in Chapter 4 is specifically relevant here: the public project that demonstrates real capability bypasses some of the gatekeeping that credential-based hiring perpetuates.

**What Actually Helps**

Name the anxiety specifically. "I am worried that my skills are becoming obsolete" is a manageable problem. "I feel vaguely terrible about my career" is not. The more precisely you can identify what is actually bothering you, the more directly you can address it.

Distinguish between what you can control and what you cannot. The rate of change in the field is not something you control. Whether you spend two hours a week on deliberate, applied learning is something you control. Putting your energy into the second category and accepting the first reduces the background noise considerably.

Build a small community of peers who are willing to be honest. Not the LinkedIn version of their careers, the real version. People who will tell you when they are struggling, when they do not understand something, when they made a mistake. This kind of community is rare and worth investing in.

Protect non-work time genuinely. The professional who reads, practices a contemplative discipline, engages with ideas outside the field, maintains physical health, and invests in relationships outside work is more resilient than the one who optimises every available hour for career advancement. This is a basic condition for remaining a functional human being over a decades-long career, not a productivity hack.

Finally, remember that the loop continues for everyone. The senior person who appears to have it figured out is managing their own version of this uncertainty. The field does not become less demanding as you become more senior. The demands change shape. Learning to live with that uncertainty, rather than waiting for it to resolve, is perhaps the central psychological challenge of a long career in AI.

*The pressure is real and the anxiety is understandable. You are not the only one feeling it, you are simply in a field where almost nobody says so out loud. Specific mental health resources for Indian tech professionals, including helplines, affordable therapy options, and guidance on workplace burnout, are collected in Appendix K if you want them.*

# Chapter 7: Why AI Projects Fail

## *And What It Means for Your Career*

Picture a team six months into an ML project. The model works. In the notebook, on the curated dataset, with the carefully selected evaluation metric, it works well. The accuracy numbers are good enough to present to the stakeholder who approved the budget.

Then it goes into production.

The data arriving in production looks nothing like the data the model was trained on. The preprocessing pipeline that was hand-built for the experiment does not scale. The latency is three times what the product requires. The model's outputs, which looked reasonable in the notebook, are occasionally wrong in ways that are difficult to explain to a non-technical manager and impossible to explain to a user. The team spends the next four months firefighting. The project is quietly shelved. The organisation concludes that ML does not work for this problem. The data scientists involved update their resumes.

This is not an unusual story. It has been estimated that around 80 percent of ML projects fail to make it into the final shipped product. The percentage has not improved meaningfully in the LLM era, if anything, the arrival of generative AI has added new failure modes on top of the original ones, and the gap between what organisations expect AI to deliver and what it actually delivers has widened as the hype has intensified.

Understanding why projects fail matters as much for anyone evaluating whether to join a team as for people already inside one. The questions you ask in an interview, the signals you look for in how a team talks about its work, and the red flags you learn to recognise in job descriptions, all of these depend on knowing what failure actually looks like from the inside.

This chapter maps the seven failure modes. For each one, it describes what the failure looks like from within a team, and what it looks like from outside, what to ask, and what to listen for, before you join.

## Failure Mode 1: Ill-Defined Expectations

The nature of ML and data science projects is that they suffer from too many variables and uncertainties. Unlike conventional software engineering, where a feature either works or it does not, an ML solution exists on a continuum of performance that is always improvable and never definitively complete. This makes expectations management both essential and unusually difficult.

Teams fall into this failure mode in two directions. The first is overconfidence: expecting an ML model to immediately outperform a rule-based solution that has been tuned over years, without accounting for the time and iteration required to reach comparable performance. The second is vagueness: starting a project without precise agreement on what success looks like, which metrics matter, and what level of performance is actually required for the solution to be useful.

In the LLM era, this problem has become more acute. Large language models produce fluent, confident-sounding outputs even when they are wrong, which makes it harder for non-technical stakeholders to assess whether a system is actually working. Teams now need to define not just accuracy metrics but hallucination rates, groundedness scores, factual consistency measures, and user trust indicators as part of their success criteria from the start. Projects that skip this definition phase produce systems that look impressive in demos and fail in deployment.

In Indian organisational contexts, this failure mode has a specific shape. GCC teams often receive requirements from headquarters that are vague by design, the parent company knows it wants "an AI solution" for a problem but has not done the work of specifying what that means precisely. The GCC team, eager to demonstrate capability and reluctant to push back on a headquarters mandate, accepts the vague brief and begins building. Six months later, the deliverable does not match what the stakeholder had in mind, because neither party had made their mental model explicit.

What to look for before you join: Ask the interviewer to describe a recent ML project's success metrics in concrete terms. If they struggle to give you specific numbers, not "we improved accuracy" but "we improved precision from 0.71 to 0.84 on this specific task, which reduced support ticket volume by 23 percent", the organisation may not yet have the discipline to define success before building. Ask what happens when a model's performance does not meet expectations. The answer tells you how the organisation handles the inherent uncertainty of ML work.

## Failure Mode 2: Lack of a Qualified Team

Many organisations new to ML make the mistake of hiring one or two ML specialists and expecting them to deliver production-grade systems without adequate support. This reflects a fundamental misunderstanding of what ML work actually requires.

A production ML system needs data engineers to build reliable data pipelines, software engineers to integrate the model into existing systems, ML specialists to develop and iterate on the model itself, domain experts to validate that the outputs make sense, and product or project managers who understand ML well enough to make sensible decisions about scope and timeline. Expecting a single data scientist to cover all of these roles produces systems that work in notebooks and break in production.

The LLM era has added a new version of this problem. Because anyone can use ChatGPT, some organisations have concluded that anyone can build a production LLM system. This has led to systematic underestimation of the expertise required for prompt engineering at scale, RAG pipeline design, evaluation pipeline construction, fine-tuning, and the ongoing monitoring and maintenance that production LLM systems require. The team qualification problem has not gone away. It has shifted to a different and equally scarce set of skills.

In India, this failure mode intersects with the GCC model in a specific way. A GCC may have a large team of technically qualified people, but if the team's mandate is execution rather than research, the people with the deepest ML expertise may be underutilised on the work that actually requires their skills, while spending most of their time on integration, testing, and maintenance work that does not develop their capabilities further. Headcount is not the same as qualified team.

What to look for before you join: Ask who you would be working with on a typical ML project, not just the data science team, but the data engineering, software engineering, and product functions. Ask who the most senior ML person on the team is, and what their background is. Ask whether the team has shipped production ML systems before, and what the path from model development to deployment actually looks like. A team that has never shipped anything to production will teach you different things than one that has shipped and maintained production systems for three years.

## Failure Mode 3: Scope Creep

ML projects are particularly vulnerable to scope creep because the objectives are often not well-defined at the outset, the technology is novel enough that stakeholders do not know what to ask for until they see something working, and the gap between a promising prototype and a production-ready system is much larger than most organisations anticipate.

Scope creep in ML manifests in specific ways: the problem being solved shifts partway through development, the performance threshold required for production keeps rising, new data sources are added that require rebuilding the pipeline, or the integration requirements expand as the product team understands more about what the model can and cannot do.

The solution is disciplined incremental delivery. Getting the simplest end-to-end solution into a testing environment as quickly as possible, even if its performance is modest, provides the concrete reference point around which stakeholder expectations can be anchored and refined. A model in production, however imperfect, generates real data about real failure modes. A model in development generates speculation.

In the Indian technology context, scope creep has an additional source: the difficulty of pushing back on scope changes when the person requesting them is a senior stakeholder at headquarters. Indian GCC teams often operate in a culture where disagreeing with headquarters is uncomfortable, and the path of least resistance is to absorb the new requirement and work harder rather than renegotiate the timeline or the scope. The result is teams that are permanently behind on a target that keeps moving.

What to look for before you join: Ask how the team handles it when a stakeholder changes requirements midway through a project. Ask whether the team uses agile methods, and if so, how sprints are actually managed in practice. Ask what the last project looked like at the six-month mark versus what it looked like at the start. A team that gives you a specific, honest account of how scope changed and how they managed it is more trustworthy than one that describes only smooth, on-plan delivery.

### Failure Mode 4: Lack of Data, and the Mechanisms to Create Usable Training Data

Data is the foundation of any ML system. This is widely understood in principle and consistently underestimated in practice.

The problems are several. Good labelled data in useful volumes is difficult to obtain. The data that is available may not reflect the distribution the model will encounter in production. The labelling process introduces its own errors and biases. The mechanisms for measuring model performance, the evaluation datasets, the ground truth labels, the user feedback loops, must be built before the model goes into production, not after, because without them there is no reliable way to know whether the model is actually working.

In the LLM era, the data problem takes a different shape. Instead of labelled training data, teams need high-quality evaluation datasets to measure whether model outputs are accurate, safe, and useful. Building a good evaluation set is unglamorous work that is frequently skipped, which means teams have no reliable way of knowing whether their prompt changes are making things better or worse. This is one of the most common causes of LLM project failure in 2026, and it is almost never discussed in the job description or the interview process.

In the Indian context, data access is also shaped by organisational boundaries in ways that are specific to the GCC model. The data that would be most useful for training or evaluation may sit with the parent company, subject to data governance restrictions that make it difficult or slow to access from an Indian subsidiary. Teams end up building models on the data they have rather than the data they need, and the performance ceiling is set by the data constraint rather than the model capability.

What to look for before you join: Ask what data the team currently has access to, and what the process is for accessing additional data when needed. Ask whether the team has evaluation datasets for the systems they are building, and how those datasets were constructed. Ask what happens when the model is deployed and its performance in production differs from its performance in evaluation. A team that has thought carefully about evaluation is significantly more likely to ship systems that actually work.

## Failure Mode 5: The Trust Gap

Even technically sound ML systems fail to reach production when the organisation is not ready to trust them.

This trust gap can run in either direction. The more familiar version is under-trust: a business function that has established ways of working pushes back on an ML recommendation because it conflicts with existing intuitions or threatens existing processes. The people who would need to change their behaviour to accommodate the model's outputs resist the change, and the model is quietly sidelined.

In the LLM era, the trust gap also runs in the opposite direction. Some teams over-trust LLM outputs, treating confident-sounding responses as authoritative without verification, and ship systems that produce plausible misinformation at scale. The failure mode of over-trust is newer and in some ways more dangerous because it is less visible, the system appears to be working until a high-stakes error surfaces.

Building appropriate trust requires two things: transparency about what the model can and cannot do, and visible mechanisms for human oversight. Systems that include human review steps for high-stakes decisions, that surface their own uncertainty rather than hiding it, and that have clear escalation paths when the model's confidence is low, tend to earn trust more reliably than systems that present themselves as authoritative.

In Indian organisational contexts, the trust gap often has a specific cultural dimension. ML teams are sometimes positioned as separate from the business functions they are serving, physically and organisationally. The lack of daily interaction between the data scientists building the model and the people whose work it is meant to support creates distance that makes trust harder to build. Solutions imposed from a distance, without genuine involvement of the people who will use them, encounter resistance that is not really about the technology.

What to look for before you join: Ask how the data science team interacts with the business functions it supports. Ask whether the team has shipped systems that are actually being used by the people they were built for, or whether previous projects have been technically delivered but not adopted. Ask what the process is for getting business stakeholder input during model development, not just at the requirements stage and the delivery stage.

## Failure Mode 6: No Postmortem When Projects Fail

Every failed project contains information that is valuable for future projects. Teams that do not systematically capture and learn from that information are condemned to repeat the same failures with different names.

The reluctance to conduct proper postmortems is understandable. Failure is uncomfortable to examine, organisational cultures often make it difficult to discuss what went wrong without assigning blame, and the team is usually already under pressure to move on to the next project. The postmortem gets scheduled, then postponed, then quietly dropped.

This is a significant waste of what is genuinely valuable data. The specifics of why a particular project failed, the exact point where the data pipeline broke down, the specific stakeholder misalignment that derailed the scope, the particular model behaviour that eroded user trust, are exactly the information needed to design the next project more successfully.

In the Indian IT context, there is an additional barrier: a culture in some organisations where admitting failure is treated as a career risk rather than a learning opportunity. Teams that operate in this culture tend to reclassify failures as partial successes, which preserves short-term comfort at the cost of long-term learning.

What to look for before you join: Ask the interviewer to describe a project that did not go as planned, and what the team learned from it. The quality of the answer, whether it is specific, honest, and demonstrates genuine reflection, tells you a great deal about the organisation's learning culture. An organisation that can only describe successes has either been very lucky or has not been honest with itself about its failures.

## Failure Mode 7: No Plan for Model Drift and Ongoing Maintenance

A model that performs well at launch can degrade quietly over time as the data it encounters in production drifts away from its training distribution. User behaviour changes. The underlying system it is connected to evolves. The world changes in ways the training data did not anticipate.

For LLM-based systems, this can happen faster than for traditional ML models, because the world changes and the model's knowledge becomes stale. A customer service LLM trained on data from 2024 will encounter product questions in 2026 about features and policies that did not exist when it was trained. Its responses will be confidently wrong in ways that are difficult to detect automatically.

Teams that do not plan for ongoing evaluation, monitoring, and periodic retraining or updating are building systems with an implicit expiry date that no one has acknowledged. The planning for maintenance needs to happen before deployment, not after performance problems appear, because by the time the degradation is visible to users it has usually been happening for longer than the team realises.

In Indian GCC environments, maintenance planning is complicated by the question of ownership. If the model was built by a GCC team against a specification from headquarters, it is not always clear who is responsible for retraining when the model drifts, the GCC team that built it, the headquarters team that specified it, or a separate operations function that was not involved in the original development. Ambiguous ownership produces delayed responses to degradation that is obvious to users long before anyone takes responsibility for fixing it.

What to look for before you join: Ask who is responsible for monitoring and maintaining production ML systems after they are deployed. Ask how often models are retrained and what triggers a retraining decision. Ask whether the team has explicit model drift detection in place, or whether performance degradation is identified through user complaints. The answers reveal how seriously the organisation takes the long-term reliability of the systems it builds.

## Reading the Room Before You Join: A Summary Checklist

The failure modes described in this chapter are detectable before you accept a role, if you know what to look for. The following questions, asked across multiple interviews with different people in the organisation, will give you a reliable picture of where a team sits on each dimension.

On expectations: Can you describe the success metrics for a recent ML project in concrete, quantitative terms? What happened when the model's performance did not initially meet the target?

On team qualification: Who are the key people I would be working with on ML projects, across data engineering, software engineering, and domain expertise? Has this team shipped production ML systems before?

On scope management: How do you handle it when stakeholder requirements change midway through a project? Can you describe a time when that happened and how the team responded?

On data: What does your current data infrastructure look like? How do you build evaluation datasets for LLM-based systems? What is the process for accessing data that currently sits outside the team?

On trust: How does the data science team interact with the business functions it supports? Can you describe an ML system that is actively being used by the people it was built for?

On learning: Can you describe a project that did not go as planned, and what the team learned from it?

On maintenance: Who owns the ongoing monitoring and maintenance of production ML systems? How do you detect and respond to model drift?

No single answer is definitive. The pattern of answers, the honesty, the specificity, the evidence of genuine reflection, tells you what kind of organisation you are evaluating. A team that answers all of these questions fluently and specifically has probably built and maintained real systems through real difficulties. A team that can only describe smooth successes is either very new to production ML or not being fully honest with you.

## The Connection to What Comes Next

The failure modes described in this chapter are not just technical problems. They are organisational problems, and they are directly related to the structural dynamics of the GCC environment that the next chapter addresses.

The Coordination-Context Gap, the distance between where decisions are made and where work is done, makes several of these failure modes more likely. Ill-defined expectations are harder to resolve when the people who understand the business context are in a different time zone and a different organisational layer from the people building the system. The trust gap is wider when business stakeholders and data scientists have never been in the same room. Data access problems are compounded by the governance boundaries that separate a GCC from its parent company's data infrastructure.

Understanding why projects fail, and what the organisational conditions that produce those failures look like, is the preparation for understanding what to look for in any organisation you consider joining. Chapter 8 provides the framework for doing exactly that.

# Chapter 8: The GCC Trap

***How to Tell If Your Role Has Real Context Density, Before You Join***

There is a particular kind of professional frustration that is hard to name. You are qualified. You are working hard. The company is prestigious, a global name, a Bengaluru or Hyderabad address, a salary that impressed your family. And yet, six months in, you feel like a very expensive pair of hands.

You are not solving problems. You are processing them. Someone else decided what the problem was. Someone else designed the architecture. Someone else will decide what to do with the output. Your job is to sit in the middle of that chain and move things along it efficiently.

This is not imposter syndrome. This is not a skill gap. This is the GCC trap, and it is structural, not personal.

## What a GCC Actually Is

Global Capability Centres, you will also see them called GCCs, captive centres, or offshore development centres, are the Indian arms of multinational companies. They employ roughly 1.9 million technology professionals in India and generate around USD 64 billion annually. The industry narrative describes them as innovation hubs, transformation engines, centres of excellence.

The reality, for the majority of people working in them, is more complicated.

A GCC is typically established for one of two reasons: cost arbitrage (accessing Indian talent at a fraction of the cost of equivalent talent in the US or Europe) or capacity scaling (building a large team quickly to handle volume that the parent company cannot absorb at home). Both of these founding logics share something important: they are about execution, not strategy.

The parent company sets the direction. The GCC delivers against it. This is less a moral failing than an organisational design choice, made rationally, with consequences for everyone working inside it.

## The Coordination-Context Gap

To understand why the GCC trap exists, it helps to think about something called context density. This is not a term you will find in most career guides, but it describes something every working data scientist intuitively recognises.

Context density is how close you are to the things that actually matter in an organisation: the risk, the decisions, the customers, the strategic debates, the moments when the company has to choose one direction over another. High context density means you are in the room where those choices get made, or at least close enough to understand why they were made. Low context density means you receive the output of those conversations as a requirements document.

The gap between where the decisions get made and where the work gets done is the Coordination-Context Gap. In most GCCs, this gap is wide and structurally maintained.

Here is why it persists. The knowledge that enables good strategic decisions, what the customer actually needs, what the competitive landscape looks like, what risks the company is willing to take, is mostly tacit. It lives in relationships, in conversations over coffee, in the institutional memory of people who have been at headquarters for fifteen years. It does not transfer easily across time zones and organisational hierarchies. It cannot be written into a Jira ticket.

So the parent company retains it. Not out of malice, but because the mechanisms for sharing it do not exist at the scale required. And the GCC, however talented its workforce, operates on the downstream side of that gap.

## Governance Debt: Why Good Organisations Stay Stuck

Software engineers are familiar with technical debt: the accumulated cost of shortcuts taken for short-term convenience that must eventually be paid back if the system is to remain functional.

Organisations accumulate something similar. Call it Governance Debt: the deferred cost of structural reforms that would allow a GCC to operate with genuine strategic authority, but which keep getting postponed because the current model is delivering acceptable results.

The current model works well enough for the parent company. Code gets written. Tickets get resolved. Quarterly targets are met. The incentive to change the governance relationship, to actually delegate decision-making authority, to let the Indian team own the architecture, to measure output by strategic impact rather than execution throughput, is low, because the pain of not changing it falls mostly on the people inside the GCC, not on the parent company's balance sheet.

This is why the gap between what GCCs are described as and what they actually do has persisted even as the sector has grown more sophisticated. Industry bodies call for cognitive arbitrage and innovation mandates. The underlying governance relationship remains asymmetric. The description changes; the structure does not.

For you, as a working professional, this matters because the Governance Debt of your organisation is effectively your problem.

You are the one whose qualifications go underused. You are the one whose performance review measures ticket velocity rather than intellectual contribution. You are the one who leaves after three years, slightly hollowed out, wondering why a role that looked so good on paper felt so thin in practice.

## The Context-Bandwidth Matrix: Where Does Your Role Actually Sit?

Not all GCC roles are the same. Some have genuine authority, real product ownership, and meaningful strategic involvement. Others are execution roles dressed in innovation language. The challenge is telling them apart before you join.

Think of any role as sitting somewhere on two axes. The first is execution bandwidth: how much well-defined, high-volume work the role involves. The second is context density: how close the role is to real decisions, real risk, and real strategic information.

Most GCC roles sit in the lower-right of this space: high execution bandwidth, low context density. You process a lot of well-defined work efficiently. This is not without value, but it is not where careers compound.

The upper-right is where you want to be: high execution bandwidth and high context density. You are building at scale and you understand why. These roles exist in GCCs, but they are not the default. They require specific governance conditions, local authority over research direction, performance measured by outcomes rather than throughput, genuine embeddedness in the product or platform, that most GCCs have not established.

The upper-left, high context density, low execution bandwidth, is the research lab model. You are close to the strategic conversation but not shipping much. This exists in a few specialised GCCs and in academic research roles.

The lower-left is where careers go to die slowly: low context density, low execution bandwidth. Maintenance work on legacy systems with no connection to anything that matters.

## How to Identify Context Density Before You Join

The language in job descriptions is almost useless for this purpose. Every GCC role in 2026 mentions innovation, strategic impact, and frontier technology. The words are not the signal. Here is what to look for instead.

Who owns the architecture? Ask directly in the interview: who makes the final call on system design decisions? If the answer involves headquarters, an offshore architecture team, or a senior person in another country who reviews and approves, the role is downstream. If the answer is the local team, that is a meaningful signal.

Where does the roadmap come from? Product roadmaps that originate entirely from headquarters indicate low context density. Roadmaps where the Indian team has contributed to or challenged the direction indicate something closer to genuine mandate.

What does the performance review actually measure? Ask what success looks like at the twelve-month mark. Answers involving delivery metrics, sprint completion, and utilisation rates point to execution orientation. Answers involving product outcomes, customer impact, or strategic contributions suggest higher context density.

Who do you present results to, and can they act on them? If your work goes into a report that goes to a manager who summarises it for someone in another country who may or may not read it, you are far from consequential outcomes. If you are presenting directly to people who make decisions based on what you show them, the context density is real.

What happened to the last person in this role? If they were promoted internally, into roles with broader scope and more authority, the organisation has a track record of developing people. If they left after two years, find out why.

Is there a research budget that the local team controls? Local control over even a small research budget is a strong signal. It means the organisation trusts the team to make decisions about where to invest intellectual effort, which is the minimum condition for genuine innovation work.

## The AI Transition: Pressure Without Guaranteed Reform

The current wave of AI adoption is creating pressure on the GCC model from below. If agentic AI tools can automate routine execution work, code generation, test running, ticket triage, basic data pipelines, the financial logic of establishing a large Indian team to do that work weakens.

Industry data from early 2026 suggests this pressure is already materialising. Indian IT firms reduced more jobs in the first quarter of 2026 than in all of 2025, with cuts concentrated in execution-oriented teams. The automation is coming first for the work GCCs were originally built to provide, not for the innovative work.

This creates a narrow window of opportunity. The argument for governance reform, for actually moving GCCs up the context density axis, becomes not a values claim but a financial one. The lower-right quadrant is becoming less economically viable. Companies that want to retain their Indian operations have an incentive to change the governance relationship, because the alternative is replacing the entire execution layer with software.

Whether this leads to genuine reform or simply to smaller and equally constrained workforces depends on choices being made right now, in boardrooms that most GCC employees will never see.

For you, as an individual, the implication is this: the window for repositioning yourself from execution to strategy is open, but it will not stay open indefinitely. The roles that survive the automation of routine work are the ones with real context density. Now is the time to move toward them, whether inside your current organisation or outside it.

## When to Stay, When to Leave

Not every GCC role is a trap. Some organisations have built genuine innovation capacity in their Indian operations. The conditions that make this possible are identifiable: full product ownership from design through deployment, local authority over research direction and resource allocation, performance measured against strategic outcomes, and a track record of promoting from within into roles with broader scope.

If your current role has these conditions, or is plausibly moving toward them, staying and deepening your position makes sense. The relationships you have built, the institutional knowledge you have accumulated, and the credibility you have established with local leadership are assets that take years to rebuild elsewhere.

If your role has none of these conditions, and the organisation shows no sign of changing its governance model, the most honest advice is to treat your current position as a platform for repositioning rather than a destination. Use the stability and the salary to build the portfolio, the skills, and the external visibility that will allow you to move into a role with genuine context density. Then move.

The trap is not the GCC itself. The trap is staying in a low context density role past the point where it is teaching you anything, because the name on the building still sounds impressive.

## A Practical Checklist

Before accepting any role, GCC or otherwise, run through these questions:

- Who owns the architecture and the roadmap?
- What does success look like at twelve months, in concrete terms?
- What are the performance metrics used in annual reviews?
- Who do you present results to, and can they act on them?
- Is there a local research or innovation budget?
- What happened to the last two people in this role?
- Has anyone at this centre been promoted into a role with significantly broader scope in the last two years?
- Does the Indian team have the authority to push back on requirements from headquarters?

No single answer is definitive. The pattern of answers tells you where the role sits in the matrix. Trust the pattern more than the job description. None of this is inevitable, but it is the default, which is exactly why escaping the GCC trap starts with knowing it exists and asking the right questions before you sign anything.

# Chapter 9: The Interview Landscape in 2026

### *What Has Changed, What to Expect, and How to Prepare*

The data science and machine learning interview has changed more in the last three years than in the previous decade. The formats are different. The tools being used in the room have changed. The questions being asked have shifted. And the context in which all of this happens, a market where candidates are screened by AI before a human sees their name, where the interview itself may involve using AI tools, and where the role you are interviewing for might be automated within two years, is unlike anything that career guides written before 2024 can adequately prepare you for.

This chapter maps the 2026 interview landscape: what formats you will encounter, what is being tested in each, how to prepare at each phase of the loop, and what the India-specific patterns look like across product companies, GCCs, MNCs, and startups. It draws on the accumulated interview experience of someone who has been on both sides of the table, updated for a market that would be largely unrecognisable to its 2019 version.

## What Has Actually Changed Since 2019

The skills being tested have shifted in content but not in structure. Interviewers still want to know whether you can code, whether you understand the mathematics behind what you are building, whether you have shipped something real, and whether you can communicate clearly with people who do not share your technical vocabulary. These requirements have not changed.

What has changed is the specific content within each of these categories, the tools available during the interview, and the formats used to assess applied competence.

**The content shift:** In 2019, a strong ML interview required depth in classical algorithms, SVMs, decision trees, ensemble methods, CNNs, RNNs, plus solid statistics and Python. In 2026, that foundation is still necessary but no longer sufficient. Interviewers now also expect familiarity with transformer architecture and attention mechanisms, RAG pipeline design, agentic system architecture, model evaluation for LLM outputs, MLOps tooling, and increasingly, the regulatory and ethical dimensions of AI deployment. The interview has not replaced the old content. It has added a substantial new layer on top of it.

**The tools shift:** AI coding assistants are now frequently available and sometimes expected in technical interviews. GitHub Copilot, Cursor, and similar tools are present in some interview formats, not as a crutch but as a test of how well you can work alongside AI tools rather than independently of them. The candidate who can use these tools effectively, verify their outputs critically, and catch the subtle errors they introduce is demonstrating exactly the kind of human-AI collaboration that production roles require.

**The format shift:** Take-home projects, system design questions, and agentic coding interviews have grown in prominence relative to pure algorithmic coding rounds. The LeetCode-style interview has not disappeared, but it is increasingly accompanied by formats that test applied ML judgment rather than just algorithmic fluency.

## The Format Landscape

### The screening call

Almost universally the first step. Typically thirty minutes with a recruiter or a junior technical person. The goal is to establish basic fit, role, experience level, compensation expectations, availability, and a first pass at technical vocabulary.

Prepare for this by being able to describe your most recent project in two minutes or less, in plain language, ending with the business outcome rather than the technical implementation. Recruiters at this stage are not evaluating your technical depth. They are evaluating whether you can communicate clearly and whether your experience level matches what the role requires.

In the Indian market, this call often also covers notice period, current CTC, and expected CTC. Have clear, prepared answers for all three. The notice period question is particularly important, Indian technology companies typically expect 30 to 90 days, and candidates who have thought through whether and how they can negotiate this are better positioned than those who have not.

This is also the right point to raise scheduling conflicts honestly. A coding round I was scheduled for this year landed in the same week as two other final-stage interviews. I told the recruiter exactly that and asked whether it could move by ten days. It moved without friction. Companies running a deliberate process generally have more scheduling flexibility than candidates assume, and naming the real conflict reads as someone managing a serious search, not someone being difficult.

### The online assessment

A timed coding or mixed assessment, typically 60 to 90 minutes, administered through platforms like HackerRank, Codility, or company-specific portals. The content varies significantly by role.

For ML Engineer and Data Scientist roles, expect: Python coding questions at medium difficulty (sorting, searching, dynamic programming, graph problems), SQL queries involving window functions and CTEs, and increasingly, short ML-specific questions, implementing a metric from scratch, explaining a model choice for a given problem, identifying an error in a training loop.

For GenAI and LLM roles, some assessments now include prompt engineering tasks, RAG implementation questions, or short evaluation exercises, given a set of model outputs, rank them and explain your reasoning.

The most consistent mistake candidates make in online assessments is attempting hard questions before completing easy ones. Time management matters more than it appears to. Solve everything you can confidently before spending time on what you cannot.

## The technical interview: coding round

Still present at most companies, though its weight varies. Product companies and global tech firms weight it heavily. GCCs and service companies weight it less. Startups are inconsistent, some run rigorous technical interviews, others are more focused on past project discussion.

The canonical preparation resources remain relevant: LeetCode, InterviewBit, HackerRank for algorithmic practice. Aim for comfortable fluency with sorting and searching algorithms, dynamic programming patterns, graph traversal, hashing, and recursion. For most ML roles, medium difficulty is the expected level, you do not need to solve hard graph problems to get an ML Engineer role, but you do need to solve medium array and string problems cleanly and explain your reasoning while you do it.

One change worth noting: many companies now allow or encourage solving in Python specifically rather than a choice of language, because Python is the de facto language of production ML work. If you have been practising in another language, switch.

A pattern worth noting from the real, anonymised interview log in Appendix G: the coding round was consistently the most common point of elimination across that search, more often than the ML depth round, the system design round, or the project deep dive, even in cases where those other rounds went well. If preparation time is limited, weighting it toward coding fluency specifically, ahead of further conceptual study, reflects where candidates following this pattern actually lost ground.

### The technical interview: ML and data science depth

This is where the 2026 content shift is most visible. The interviewer will probe your past projects in depth, do not list anything on your resume that you cannot explain fully, including the internal mechanics of the algorithms you used, the specific data challenges you encountered, and the limitations of the approach you chose.

Beyond past projects, expect questions covering:

Statistics and probability, conditional probability, Bayes theorem, hypothesis testing, A/B test design, the meaning of p-values and confidence intervals, the distinction between correlation and causation. These have not changed and remain consistently tested.

Machine learning fundamentals, bias-variance tradeoff, regularisation techniques and why they work, how decision tree splits are selected, kernel functions in SVMs, the mechanics of gradient descent including vanishing and exploding gradients, when to use CNNs versus RNNs versus transformers, how to handle class imbalance, cross-validation approaches, feature selection methods.

Modern ML systems, transformer architecture and attention mechanisms (understand the key-query-value formulation, why positional encodings are needed, how pre-training and fine-tuning differ), RAG pipeline design (how retrieval quality affects generation quality, how to evaluate each separately), fine-tuning approaches (LoRA, QLoRA, when fine-tuning is preferable to RAG and when it is not), vector databases and similarity search.

LLM-specific, hallucination detection and mitigation, evaluation frameworks for LLM outputs including LLM-as-a-Judge approaches, prompt engineering at a systems level rather than a single-call level, RLHF fundamentals.

MLOps, model monitoring and drift detection, experiment tracking, CI/CD for ML pipelines, the retraining decision (what triggers it, how it is implemented, how you validate that the new model is actually better).

### The ML system design interview

One of the fastest-growing interview formats and one of the least well-prepared for by candidates. You are given a real-world problem and asked to design an end-to-end ML solution, architecture, data requirements, model choice, evaluation strategy, deployment approach, monitoring plan.

Examples that appear regularly: design a content recommendation system for a streaming platform, design a fraud detection system for a UPI payment provider, design a customer churn prediction model for a telecom company, design a search ranking system for an e-commerce platform, design a document question-answering system for an enterprise knowledge base.

The assessment cares less about arriving at the "correct" answer, there often is no single correct one, than about demonstrating structured thinking: how you define the problem before proposing a solution, how you reason about data availability and quality, how you make and justify trade-offs between model complexity and deployment simplicity, and how you think about what could go wrong and how to detect it.

### A reliable framework for ML system design interviews:

First, clarify the problem. What is the business objective? What does success look like? What are the constraints, latency, cost, explainability requirements, regulatory requirements? Spend five minutes here before drawing anything.

Second, frame the ML problem. What exactly is being predicted or generated? What is the input and output? What evaluation metric aligns with the business objective?

Third, discuss the data. What data is available? What needs to be collected or engineered? What are the data quality risks?

Fourth, propose a model architecture. Start simple, what is the simplest approach that could work? Then discuss what more sophisticated approaches would add, and whether the added complexity is justified.

Fifth, address deployment. How does the model get served? What is the latency requirement? How does it integrate with the existing system?

Sixth, discuss monitoring and maintenance. How do you know when the model is degrading? What triggers retraining? Who owns this over time?

Practice this framework out loud. System design interviews reward people who think out loud clearly, not people who think in silence and then present conclusions.

The examples used to teach this framework are usually invented for the purpose: a streaming recommender, a generic fraud model. Real 2026 system design questions increasingly come from infrastructure scale and domain-specific territory that invented examples do not prepare you for, training and scoring ten thousand models against hundreds of millions of records, or designing a RAG and knowledge graph system to translate a custom quality measure definition into a live computation over hospital data. Appendix G works through two such questions end to end, taken from real 2026 assignments rather than constructed for the book.

### The take-home project

Common across all company types in India, particularly for mid-to-senior roles. You receive a dataset and a problem, and you have 24 to 72 hours to produce a Jupyter notebook with analysis, a model, an evaluation, and a short write-up explaining your approach and findings.

This format rewards people who treat it as a communication exercise rather than a pure technical exercise. The technical work matters, but the write-up is often what differentiates candidates. A clear explanation of what you tried, why you tried it, what worked, what did not work, and what you would do next with more time, this demonstrates exactly the kind of reflective, communicative technical judgment that senior roles require.

Common mistakes: over-engineering the model at the expense of the explanation, not addressing the business question clearly in the write-up, submitting without any discussion of model limitations or failure modes, failing to explore the data before jumping to modelling.

The actual assignments I have been given this year fall into two recognisable types. One was a take-home RAG pipeline: build a working retrieval system over a mixed set of PDFs, spreadsheets, and IoT sensor exports, with no further specification of architecture. The other was a written system design case study: design an MLOps platform to train ten thousand models and run batch inference on hundreds of millions of records, with no live coding at all, just a structured document and a follow-up conversation about it. Two worked examples from real 2026 system design assignments, including one drawn directly from a healthcare RAG and knowledge graph problem, are in Appendix G. Read them before you assume you know what a take-home in this market actually looks like.

### The agentic coding interview

The newest format, appearing most frequently at companies building AI-first products. You are given a problem and asked to solve it using AI coding tools, GitHub Copilot, Claude Code, Cursor, with the interviewer watching how you work.

The evaluation is about judgment, not tool access. Specifically: do you verify the tool's output critically, or do you accept it without checking? When the tool produces subtly incorrect code, do you catch it? Can you prompt effectively to get useful output? Can you iterate when the first attempt does not work?

The preparation for this format is different from traditional coding interview preparation. The most useful practice is to spend time building real things with AI coding tools, paying deliberate attention to where the tools fail and how you detect those failures. The candidate who has caught a dozen AI-generated bugs in real projects is better prepared than the one who has only used the tools to generate tutorial code.

### The vertical drill-down and the resume depth trap

A pattern worth formalising, because it now shapes senior interviews more than any single question format: the vertical drill-down. It begins with one innocent bullet on your resume, say, built a natural-language-to-SQL RAG system using Mixtral. The interviewer descends: what problem did it solve, why RAG, how did retrieval work, how did you evaluate it, how did you evaluate SQL correctness specifically, why Mixtral, where was it hosted, on what GPU, with how much VRAM, how did it fit, was it quantised, which inference engine, why vLLM, how does PagedAttention work, what is the KV cache. Fifteen questions later, a conversation that began in business analytics has arrived at GPU architecture, and every step of the descent was licensed by a noun you chose to put on the page.

Call this the resume depth trap, and state the rule plainly: every noun on your resume creates a possible drill-down tree, and you own the whole tree, not just the root. The preparation that follows is mechanical and unglamorous. Before an interview, take each major project on your resume and build its tree five levels deep, from the business problem down through the design decisions to the infrastructure it actually ran on. Where you hit a level you cannot answer, either learn that level or reword the bullet so it no longer claims territory you cannot defend. The real interview log in

Appendix G contains a full example of what happens when the descent reaches layers the candidate has not prepared.

### The hardware sanity check

One specific drill-down deserves its own warning. If you claim you deployed a model, an experienced interviewer may calculate in their head whether your claimed hardware could actually run it, and the arithmetic is short enough to do while you are still talking. The estimate is parameter count times bytes per parameter (four for FP32, two for FP16 or BF16, one for INT8, half for INT4), plus the KV cache, plus perhaps ten to twenty percent for activations and overhead. A 7B model in FP16 is about 14 GB of weights and fits a 24 GB card with room for cache; a 70B model in FP16 is about 140 GB and requires either multiple GPUs or 4-bit quantisation to roughly 35 GB; Mixtral 8x7B carries about 47 billion total parameters, so at FP16 it is roughly 94 GB and does not fit a single 80 GB A100 without quantisation, whatever a confident resume bullet implies. Being able to walk this arithmetic aloud converts what looks like trivia into reasoning, and failing it while claiming the deployment is one of the most damaging single moments an interview can contain.

### AI system design is replacing ML system design

The system design framework earlier in this chapter still applies, but the canonical architecture being drawn on the whiteboard has changed. Classical ML system design was a pipeline: data, features, training, deployment, monitoring. Modern GenAI system design is a request path: a user request enters through a gateway, passes an intent classifier or router, gathers context through retrieval and tool calls, has its context window constructed, reaches the LLM, and the output passes through guardrails, evaluation hooks, and observability before returning. Beneath that path sits the serving layer, the inference engine, GPU capacity, autoscaling, and caching, and beside it runs a security and governance column: identity and access management, PII handling, prompt injection defence, audit logging, and cost controls. Practise drawing this shape until it is automatic, because it is the skeleton under almost every GenAI design question now being asked, and the worked designs in Appendix G all reduce to instances of it.

## Who is actually interviewing you

Most advice written for this market still assumes a human being from the hiring company is on the other end of every screen. In a growing share of 2026 processes, that assumption no longer holds, and it is worth naming directly because almost nothing else written about interviewing addresses it.

I went through two AI-administered screens this year, one for an MLOps role and one for a coding round, on platforms of a kind that a number of large Indian IT services firms now use for early-round screening, companies such as Berribot and others building similar autonomous interviewing systems. The format is the same each time: it pulls your resume, captures you on camera, asks you to introduce yourself, and then asks questions generated directly from whatever you listed as projects and tools, before moving into a coding exercise inside its own browser environment. There is no one to read in real time, no pause that signals interest, no tone of voice to calibrate against. Candidates who go through this format consistently report the same experience afterward: a generic status update, and no individual feedback, because the system queues the recording for a human panel to review later rather than scoring it live in front of you.

A separate round went through one of the interview-outsourcing services that several Indian IT and product companies now use to hand off first-round technical screening to a pool of vetted freelance interviewers rather than running it in-house, companies such as Risebird and similar platforms in that category. The person on that call was a working engineer somewhere else, paid per session and rated on how well they ran it, not necessarily briefed on the specific team or project behind the role. He was professional and technically sharp. He also could not answer a single question I had about the actual position, because his job that day was to score me against a rubric, not to represent the company hiring for it.

Neither format is a fringe case. Companies facing hundreds or thousands of applications per posting, the volume problem described earlier in this book, are adopting both AI-administered screening and interview outsourcing specifically to manage that volume at the first round, before a human at the actual hiring company ever sees you. Two adjustments follow from this, and they pull in slightly different directions.

Against an AI interviewer, treat your resume as the literal question bank. The system is generating questions from it nearly line by line, with no inclination to skim past something you cannot actually support. If a tool, a project, or a number appears on the document, expect to be asked about it directly and expect to need the depth this chapter described earlier under resume probing. A model has no social reason to let a vague claim pass.

Against an outsourced human interviewer, the absence of shared context cuts the other way. Insider references, company-specific framing, anything that depends on the listener already knowing your target team's stack or history, will not land, because the person asking often does not have that context either. What scores well here is a complete, self-contained technical answer, closer in feel to a structured certification exam than a conversation with a future colleague.

Ask the recruiter directly, before the round, what kind of interview it is and who or what will be evaluating it. Companies running AI-administered or outsourced screens rarely volunteer this upfront, and it changes how you should perform. Time spent trying to build rapport with a system that has none to offer is time taken from demonstrating the depth that the resume-driven questions will actually probe.

## The Core Question Bank: What They Will Ask

Knowing the format is half the battle. The other half is knowing the specific questions. The 2026 interview draws from a predictable core of problem types, even as the surface details change. What follows is a representative map of the question categories you will encounter, with the underlying pattern being tested in each. The full practice bank with sample answers and preparation hints is in Appendix G.

Transformer and LLM questions now appear at every seniority level, not just research roles. You will be asked about attention mechanics, positional encodings, the difference between fine-tuning and RAG, and how you would evaluate an LLM output in production. These are not trivia questions: they are checking whether you can reason about the systems you are building rather than just using them.

Agentic system questions are emerging as the distinguishing topic for 2026 senior roles. Interviewers want to know whether you understand how to design systems where an LLM calls tools, routes between agents, and handles failure states. The ReAct framework, multi-agent orchestration, and loop prevention are specific areas to prepare.

Coding remains non-negotiable, but the emphasis is on pattern recognition over memorisation. The fifteen patterns that underlie most coding interviews (sliding window, two pointers, binary search on answer space, BFS/DFS, dynamic programming, heaps, backtracking, and their variants) give you more coverage per hour of preparation than grinding individual problems randomly.

ML system design is where senior candidates separate themselves. Interviewers are not looking for the correct answer. They are watching whether you define the problem before proposing a solution, reason about data quality and latency constraints, make explicit trade-offs, and think about monitoring and failure modes. The framework matters as much as the content.

SQL and database questions are the most consistently underestimated preparation area. Window functions, CTEs, and query optimisation appear across every role type. Vector database concepts (ANN search, HNSW, hybrid retrieval) are now expected for any GenAI-facing role.

Behavioural questions run through every interview, even when not labelled as such. The candidate who can describe a production failure honestly, explain a disagreement with a stakeholder without blame, and give a specific rather than performed answer to the weakness question is demonstrating exactly the self-awareness that senior roles require.

Finally, the questions you ask the interviewer reveal your judgment as much as your answers do. The list of red-flag signals at the end of Appendix G gives you a framework for reading whether a company genuinely has a production AI strategy or is chasing capability without context.

A real, anonymised log of interview questions actually encountered, organised by context rather than by employer, is in Appendix G under Real Interview Logs. The pattern that held across that search is worth internalising here: very few interviews probed deep mathematics, most included system design or architecture, nearly all wanted a genuine deep dive into actual project work, and coding rounds were the single most common point of elimination, even when the technical conversation itself had gone well. That ordering, coding fluency first, project deep-dive narratives second, system design third, conceptual theory last, is a reasonable default for anyone whose preparation time is limited.

## How to Prepare by Phase

### Phase 1 (Tool User, 0–2 years)

Your interview profile is mostly potential rather than demonstrated production experience. What you can control: the quality of your portfolio projects, your foundation in statistics and ML basics, your

Python fluency, and your ability to articulate clearly what you built and why.

Prioritise: one deployed project you can discuss in depth, comfortable fluency with medium-difficulty LeetCode problems in Python, solid understanding of the most common ML algorithms and when to use them, basic familiarity with RAG concepts and vector databases.

Do not try to fake depth you do not have. Interviewers at product companies probe hard on anything listed on a resume. If you mention a framework, you will be asked how it works internally. Only list what you can genuinely discuss at depth.

**Phase 2 (Builder, 2–5 years)**

Your interview profile should show production experience. The key differentiator at this level is demonstrating that you have shipped ML systems that ran in production, not just built models that worked in notebooks.

Prioritise: system design preparation (use the framework above, practice out loud), MLOps depth (be ready to discuss monitoring, retraining, drift detection from your own experience), RAG and agentic system familiarity, cost and latency optimisation experience.

The question that separates Phase 2 candidates is: "Tell me about a time a production ML system failed and how you handled it." Have a specific, honest answer. The candidate who has never seen a production failure is not a candidate who has never worked in production, they are a candidate who has not been paying attention.

**Phase 3 (Translator, 5–10 years)**

At this level, technical depth is necessary but not sufficient. Interviewers are assessing whether you can shape a technical strategy, not just execute one.

Prioritise: preparing for problem framing questions (given a vague business problem, how do you convert it into a solvable ML problem?), ML system design at architectural scale, build-versus-buy arguments for foundation models, team structure and process questions, and your views on AI governance and ethics in your domain.

Expect questions that have no correct answer: "How would you decide whether to build a custom model or use a foundation model for this use case?" The assessment is the quality of your reasoning, not the conclusion you reach.

### Phase 4 (Shaper, 10+ years)

Interview formats at this level are less standardised. Expect more conversational technical discussions with senior leadership, a presentation of a technical strategy or past project at scale, and significant time spent on cultural and organisational fit.

The preparation is more about articulating a coherent point of view on the direction of the field and your role in it than about demonstrating specific technical skills. It is tempting to add that the technical skills are assumed at this level, and older versions of this advice said exactly that. My own recent interviews are evidence that this is no longer safe. Senior candidates face fewer textbook questions but much deeper vertical probes into any system they claim to have built, down to serving engines and GPU memory, and seniority makes an interviewer less forgiving of architectural ignorance rather than more, because a Shaper is expected to understand what the teams beneath them are building. The question beyond that is whether your judgment, taste, and communication make you someone who will shape the organisation's approach to AI or merely execute within it.

## India-Specific Patterns

### Indian product companies (Zomato, Swiggy, Flipkart, PhonePe, CRED, Razorpay and equivalents)

These companies run among the most rigorous technical interviews in the Indian market. Expect strong algorithmic coding rounds, deep ML fundamentals, and system design at scale, their systems handle hundreds of millions of users and the interview reflects that reality.

The domain specificity matters here. A candidate interviewing for a fraud detection role at PhonePe who has studied UPI transaction patterns, imbalanced classification techniques, and the specific regulatory requirements of Indian fintech is significantly better positioned than a candidate with strong general ML skills who has not thought about the domain. Research the company's public technical blog before any interview at this level, Swiggy, Zomato, and Flipkart all publish technical content that reveals exactly the kinds of problems their teams are working on.

### Global tech firms in India (Google, Microsoft, Amazon, Meta)

Interview processes here are largely identical to the global standard. Strong algorithmic coding (LeetCode hard is not unusual), deep ML fundamentals, system design at very large scale, and behavioural interviews using the STAR framework.

The preparation investment is significant, typically three to four months of serious preparation for a competitive candidate. The compensation ceiling justifies this investment for the right person, but be realistic about the probability-weighted return before spending four months on LeetCode at the expense of other opportunities.

### GCC environments

Interviews at GCCs vary enormously depending on whether the hiring is being driven from India or from headquarters, and whether the role is execution-oriented or innovation-oriented.

Execution-oriented GCC roles typically have lighter technical interviews, a coding screen, a past project discussion, and a behavioural round. The bar is set for competence in well-defined work rather than for the judgment required to frame and solve ambiguous problems.

Innovation-oriented GCC roles, where they exist, can run interviews comparable to product companies. Use the context density checklist from Chapter 8 to understand which kind of role you are interviewing for before you calibrate your preparation level.

One India-specific pattern: many GCC interviews include a "manager round" that functions as a cultural fit assessment. Be prepared to discuss how you handle feedback, how you work across time zones, how you manage ambiguity in requirements from remote stakeholders, and how you have pushed back on direction you disagreed with. These questions are assessing whether you will function effectively in the specific context of a subsidiary reporting to a distant headquarters, understanding that context helps you answer authentically.

**Startups**

Early-stage startup interviews in India are highly variable. Some run rigorous technical processes; others move primarily on referrals and cultural instinct. The most consistent pattern is that startups at Series A and earlier care most about end-to-end ownership and scrappiness, can you build something that works with limited resources and without extensive support infrastructure?

The most effective preparation for a startup interview is a genuinely working project that you built yourself from scratch, deployed yourself, and can discuss including the compromises you made and why. The startup interviewer is not looking for perfection. They are looking for evidence that you can ship.

For later-stage startups (Series C and beyond) that have grown their engineering organisations, the interview process increasingly resembles that of a mid-market product company. The technical bar rises with the headcount.

## The Hour Before

What you do in the hour before an interview matters more than most candidates treat it. This is not the time to learn anything new. If a concept is not solid by now, an hour of last-minute reading will not fix it and mostly adds anxiety. Use the time instead for logistics, warm-up, and calm.

Confirm the practical basics first. For a video interview, join the platform itself, not just check that it is installed, five minutes early, test camera and microphone, close every other application and browser tab that could notify or crash mid-call, and keep water within reach. For an in-person interview, confirm the exact address and floor in advance and build in real buffer for Bengaluru traffic specifically. Arriving stressed from a commute costs more than arriving twenty minutes early and waiting in the lobby.

Warm up rather than cram. Read through, do not solve from scratch, two or three problems in whichever pattern you are weakest in, and read your two-minute project pitch and two or three prepared anchor stories, a production failure, a disagreement handled well, a specific technical decision with a clear tradeoff, once each, ideally out loud. The goal is retrieval practice on material you already know, not new coverage.

Spend a few minutes on physiological calm before you join. Slowing the exhale relative to the inhale, four seconds in and six to eight out, for a couple of minutes has a real, well-documented effect on acute stress. This is not about eliminating nerves, some activation sharpens performance, it is about keeping the stress response described later in this chapter from tipping into the kind of freeze that costs you material you actually know.

Finally, reread the job description and your own resume one last time. Interviewers, human or AI-administered, draw questions directly from both, and having the specific wording active in memory minutes before the call is worth more at that point than any new preparation.

## The Behavioural Dimension

Every interview includes a behavioural component, even when it is not explicitly labelled as such. How you describe your past work, how you handle a question you cannot answer, how you respond to being pushed back on, all of this is being assessed throughout.

A few principles specific to the Indian interview context.

Disagreeing with an interviewer is acceptable and sometimes actively valued. A candidate who has a well-reasoned position and can defend it respectfully is demonstrating exactly the kind of intellectual confidence that Phase 3 and 4 roles require. The candidate who immediately capitulates when pushed is demonstrating the opposite. Distinguish between updating your view because you have been shown something you had not considered, which is good, and capitulating because the interviewer seemed confident, which is not.

Gaps in knowledge should be acknowledged directly, not papered over. "I have not worked with that specific tool, but my experience with X is relevant because..." is a better answer than a vague response that implies familiarity you do not have. Interviewers are testing honesty as well as knowledge, and the candidate who cannot say "I do not know" is difficult to trust in a production environment where admitting uncertainty quickly is a safety mechanism.

The question about weaknesses is not a trap. The interviewer is not looking for performed humility ("I work too hard"). They are looking for self-awareness, evidence that you understand your own development edges and are actively working on them. A specific, honest answer about a real limitation and what you are doing about it is significantly more compelling than a deflection.

## When You Go Blank

At some point in a live interview, on a question you can answer perfectly well outside the room, you will freeze. This is not a rare failure specific to underprepared candidates. It happens to people who know the material cold, because acute stress activates a threat response that temporarily degrades working memory and recall, exactly when an interview demands both. Treating a blank as evidence you did not really know something, rather than as evidence you were under stress in that moment, is usually the wrong diagnosis, and drawing that wrong lesson from it tends to make the next blank more likely, not less.

Two things help more than additional content review once the material is actually known. First, narrate your process before you have the answer: restating the question in your own words, or saying out loud what you are about to try, buys a few seconds for recall to catch up and keeps the interviewer engaged with your reasoning rather than sitting in silence while you visibly search. Silence reads as not knowing; narrated searching reads as working through a problem, which is closer to the truth. Second, for live coding specifically, pick whichever language you have the least syntax-recall risk in under pressure, not necessarily the one you are most senior in generally. Exact method names and boilerplate are exactly the kind of detail that stress erodes fastest, so reducing how much of that you need to hold in working memory during a stressful round is worth more than proving fluency across every language you know.

If a blank happens anyway, the honest recovery beats the performed one: "give me a second, I want to think this through properly" is a normal, well-regarded thing to say, and it buys real time without pretending you were not affected. Interviewers who have run many rounds recognise the difference between a candidate who does not know something and one who knows it but needs a moment, and they reward the second far more than candidates assume.

## After the Interview

Follow up within 24 hours with a brief note to the recruiter or hiring manager thanking them for the time and reiterating one specific thing that made the role compelling. This is not standard practice in the Indian market but is consistently remembered, and in a hiring process where the decision is close, being the candidate who followed up thoughtfully is a meaningful differentiator.

If you receive a rejection, ask for feedback. Most companies will not provide it, but some will, and even a brief response is useful information for the next interview. The candidate who treats each interview as data, what worked, what did not, where the questions caught you unprepared, compounds their interview performance over time in a way that the candidate who moves immediately to the next application does not.

If you receive an offer, negotiate. This is uncomfortable for many Indian professionals, particularly those from backgrounds where negotiating feels presumptuous or ungrateful. It is neither. The offer you receive is the company's opening position, not their final one. A straightforward, respectful request for more, citing a competing offer if you have one, or market data from Appendix C if you do not, is appropriate and expected. The worst realistic outcome is that they say no. The best is ten to twenty percent more over the life of the role, which compounds significantly over time.

## If You Get Feedback At All

Explicit feedback is rare in the Indian interview market. Across dozens of applications and interviews in this search, exactly one company returned substantive round-by-round feedback rather than silence or a generic rejection notice, and it arrived, as it usually does when it arrives at all, secondhand through a staffing vendor rather than from the hiring company directly. Treat this as a genuine exception, not something to expect or build a strategy around. Most processes end in silence regardless of how the interview actually went, and the absence of feedback says nothing about your performance.

On the rare occasion you do get it, two things are worth knowing. Read brief, secondhand feedback for the pattern rather than the exact wording, since it has usually passed through at least one layer of paraphrasing between what an interviewer actually said and what reaches you. And if the same theme repeats independently across separate rounds with separate interviewers, that repetition is a stronger signal than any single comment and worth prioritising in whatever preparation time remains.

It is also worth separating two kinds of gap that feedback like this tends to blur together. A knowledge gap is not knowing the material: you never learned confidence intervals properly, or you have not designed an A/B test. A delivery gap is knowing the material but not presenting it well live: needing prompts to arrive at an answer you actually have, or giving a correct answer wrapped in enough hedging that it reads as uncertain. The fix for a knowledge gap is study. The fix for a delivery gap is a rehearsed structure for how you open every technical answer, not more content.

## The Point-First Answer

The structure that fixes a delivery gap is simple to describe and takes real repetition to make automatic under pressure: state the direct answer in one sentence first, give two or three supporting points or the underlying mechanism, then stop, elaborating further only if asked. Candidates with strong underlying knowledge often do the opposite instinctively, building up to the answer through the mechanism first, and by the time they reach the conclusion the interviewer has already lost the thread and asks a clarifying question, which then reads as the candidate needing help to reach an answer they, in fact, already had. Practising this out loud against a timer, cutting yourself off at roughly forty-five seconds unless asked to continue, does more for how you come across in a live round than an additional week of content review once your fundamentals are already solid.

## A Note on Rejection

You will be rejected. More than once, probably significantly more than once, and some of the rejections will be for roles you were well-qualified for. This is a feature of the market, not information about your worth.

The signal-to-noise ratio in the Indian AI job market in 2026 is extremely poor. Roles get hundreds of applications. Screening is partly automated and imperfect. Hiring decisions involve timing, internal politics, and candidate comparisons that have nothing to do with your absolute quality. A rejection is evidence that you did not get this particular role at this particular time. It is not evidence of what you are capable of.

Earlier this year I went through two full rounds with a company I was genuinely excited about, technical and panel, with what felt like positive signals after each, and then nothing. No rejection email, no closing note, just silence I eventually had to read as a no. That silence says something about how that particular process was run. It says nothing about the two rounds I actually passed to get there.

What is worth paying attention to: if you are consistently getting rejected at the same stage, passing the screen but failing the coding round, or passing the technical rounds but failing the behavioural, that is a signal worth acting on. The pattern tells you where to focus preparation. The individual rejection tells you almost nothing.

Preparation pays off when it is aimed at the interview format you are actually going to face, at the level you are actually at, for the kind of organisation you are actually targeting. Most of what is left over is noise.

# Chapter 10: The Interview as Organisational X-ray

***What the Process Reveals About Who You Would Be Working For***

Most job-search advice treats the interview as a one-way street. The company evaluates you, and your job is to pass. That framing isn't wrong, but it is incomplete. An interview is also a noisy, imperfect, but genuinely useful signal about how an organisation actually operates: what it values, how it treats people under pressure, and how decisions get made once you are inside it.

There is an important caveat. A single interviewer is one sample, not a verdict. One rude interviewer does not prove a toxic company, and one brilliant, generous interviewer does not guarantee a great workplace. People have bad days, and individuals do not always represent the system they work in. But interviews rarely happen in isolation. Across multiple rounds, multiple interviewers, and enough companies over time, patterns emerge, and patterns are data.

This chapter is about learning to read that data, treating the interview process as a kind of organisational X-ray that reveals structure you cannot see from the job posting alone.

## What Different Signals Tend to Mean

Certain patterns recur often enough across companies to be worth naming directly.

| **Interview Behaviour** | **Possible Organisational Value or Culture** |
|---|---|
| Interesting real business problems, live problem-solving | Values applied reasoning over rehearsed answers |
| Open-ended case questions, thinking on the fly, not necessarily coding | Values analytical ability itself, not just speed |
| Mostly LeetCode-style gatekeeping, sometimes a large fixed battery of problems before design rounds | Coding proficiency treated as a hard filter, often a large, standardised hiring pipeline |
| Deep, sustained questioning on ML/DL fundamentals, transformers, LLM internals | Expects engineers to reason from first principles, not just apply libraries |
| Research discussion, walking through your own work | Encourages innovation, curiosity, end-to-end ownership |
| Pair programming | Collaborative engineering culture |
| Only trivia questions | May value credentials over practical thinking |
| Respectful rejection, with feedback | Values candidates as professionals, likely reflects internal psychological safety |
| Dismissive or curt rejection ("you failed, that's it") | Possible low psychological safety internally |

| Interview Behaviour | Possible Organisational Value or Culture |
| --- | --- |
| AI interview bots, or visibly disengaged, part-time interviewers | Role or team may be under-resourced or a low hiring priority |
| Ghosting after several rounds | Weak recruiting process, unclear ownership of the req, or internal indecision |
| Interviewers arrive unprepared | Internal coordination problems |
| Refuses to discuss team, project, or client | Lack of transparency |
| Won't disclose office location or basic logistics | Common in staffing or bench arrangements, potential organisational dysfunction |
| Interviewers seem exhausted | Possible workload or burnout issues |
| Everyone talks enthusiastically about their projects | Higher engagement and ownership |
| Every answer is "it depends on the client" | Consulting or service-driven, client-first culture |

No single row is a dealbreaker or a green light on its own. It is the accumulation across rounds and across companies that turns this into signal instead of noise.

## A Few Patterns From the Field

A few real patterns, stripped of any identifying detail, make this concrete.

One company built an entire technical round around solving an ML problem together, live, and asking about actual past research. That is a company that values applied reasoning and real experience over rehearsed answers.

Another asked genuinely hard ML questions that needed thinking on the spot, with no coding involved at all. That is a company that values raw analytical ability on its own terms.

A few large employers, mostly in regulated industries, went deep and stayed deep on ML and DL theory, transformers, and LLM internals, round after round. That is a company that wants engineers who understand first principles, not just applied fluency.

One large employer required dozens of algorithmic coding problems solved correctly before a candidate could even reach a design round. That is a company treating coding speed as a hard, non-negotiable filter, usually a mark of a big, standardised hiring pipeline.

Several employers, across different industries, simply went quiet after multiple rounds with no explanation either way. That pattern points to recruiting friction, shifting priorities, or nobody clearly owning the hiring decision.

A handful of consulting and staffing-style firms would not say where the office was or which client the role served, even late in the process. That is usually a sign the role is a bench placement rather than a direct hire, and that candidate experience is not a priority.

None of this is a moral judgement about any company. It is inference, built from repeated exposure to the same behaviour, about what daily life inside that organisation is probably like.

## When Interviewer Depth Is Role-Relevant, and When It Is Not

Sometimes an interview goes technically deeper than anything the JD describes, and you leave wondering whether you were being tested against the role or against the interviewer's personal specialty. The honest answer is that you usually cannot know for certain in the room, and accusing an interviewer, even privately, of showing off is a less useful habit than reading the pattern of the questions. Three signals help.

**A coherent drill-down is usually legitimate.** If the descent follows the structure of your own project, from what it did, to how it was deployed, to how it was served, to what hardware it ran on, the interviewer is testing whether your claimed system actually existed at the depth you claim. That is fair examination, and the resume depth trap in Chapter 9 is the preparation for it.

**Disconnected trivia suggests interest bias.** If the questions jump between an obscure paper, a niche CUDA fact, and an unrelated research corner without following any thread through your work or the role, you are more likely watching an interviewer tour their own bookshelf. It still has to be answered gracefully, but it says less about the job.

**Role mismatch is the strongest signal, and it is a question you can ask.** If the JD describes an applied data science role in forecasting and RAG and seventy percent of the interview is spent on inference optimisation, ask directly: does this team own model serving infrastructure? If the answer is yes, the depth was role-relevant and the JD was incomplete, which is itself useful information. If the answer is no, you have learned something about how the organisation interviews, and either way the question marks you as someone who thinks about role fit rather than just passing rounds. The answer becomes part of the X-ray this chapter is about.

## Building Your Own Company Radar

To turn scattered impressions into something usable, score every interview round on a consistent set of dimensions right after it happens, while the details are still fresh: respect, technical depth, relevance to the actual job, transparency, organisation of the process itself, communication speed, intellectual stimulation, professionalism, whether you learned something, and whether you would enjoy working with these people.

None of these need false precision. A quick gut number, logged consistently, is more useful than a perfect rubric applied once. Over several interviews, even a handful of companies, the scores start to cluster, and the clusters tell you something a job description never could.

## A Simple Field-Note Template

After each round, two minutes is enough to capture the signal before it fades.

Company or role (anonymised if you like):

[write here]
What depth level did they probe? Theory, applied reasoning, or raw coding speed?

[write here]
How did they behave under a "no," or under ambiguity?

[write here]
What did they volunteer versus withhold? Location, team, project, client?

[write here]
Scores across the ten dimensions above:

[write here]
One line, gut reaction:

[write here]

Kept across a job search, this becomes a small but genuinely useful dataset, one you built yourself from direct experience, that no review site or LinkedIn post can match.

## The Shift in Mindset

The deeper value of this chapter is not the scoring system. It is the shift in posture it produces. Most candidates walk into an interview thinking only: please hire me. That framing puts all the power, and all the anxiety, on one side of the table.

A more useful posture holds both questions at once. Am I a fit for them, and are they a fit for me? Every question they ask, every delay, every act of courtesy or discourtesy, every unwillingness to answer a simple logistical question is information, whether or not they intend it to be.

An interview does not just reveal whether you are a fit for the company. It reveals whether the company is a fit for you. Every question they ask, every delay, and every decision reflects something about how they work, and cumulatively, whether it is somewhere you would want to work at all.

# Chapter 11: If You Just Got Let Go

## *What to Do in the First Six Weeks*

This chapter is written for a specific moment: the one where you have just been told your role is being eliminated, your contract is not being renewed, or the company is restructuring and you are on the wrong side of the line. It is also written for the moment just before that, when the signs are clear enough that you can see what is coming but it has not happened yet.

If neither of these describes your situation right now, read it anyway. The AI job market in 2026 makes this chapter relevant to almost everyone working in the field. Layoffs in technology follow funding cycles, product pivots, and the gap between what organisations promise AI will deliver and what it actually does. They also, increasingly, follow the automation of the execution layer that a significant fraction of the Indian technology workforce has been hired to provide. This is a structural feature of the moment we are in, not a remote possibility.

Knowing what to do before you need to know it is one of the more useful forms of career preparation available.

The conversation that prompted me to write this chapter happened in a one-on-one, not a formal notice. A manager told me that I should start looking outside based on some metrics and it felt unfair to me. What mattered more, in the weeks after, was treating the fairness argument and the job search as two separate projects rather than one. The first is worth having, through whatever internal process exists for it, because a sloppy metric deserves to be challenged on principle and because the record matters. The second does not wait for the first to resolve. Both can be true at once: that you were measured unfairly, and that the search starts now regardless of how that argument turns out.

## The First 48 Hours

Be upset. Be angry. Be confused. Let yourself feel whatever you actually feel, without immediately converting it into LinkedIn networking or resume updating or the performance of resilience.

This is practical, not self-indulgent. The people who skip the emotional processing and go straight into search mode tend to make reactive decisions, applying everywhere indiscriminately, accepting the first offer out of relief rather than judgment, projecting an urgency that interviewers can sense and that works against them. The 48 hours you spend being human about what happened will cost you nothing in the search and may save you from decisions you will regret for years.

After 48 hours, something needs to shift. Not to optimism necessarily, but to function. You are now solving a problem. The problem is real and it is solvable and you are the person who has to solve it. Everything that follows is structured around that shift.

## What Just Happened: An Honest Assessment

Before you update your resume, before you tell LinkedIn you are open to opportunities, before you do anything visible externally, spend time understanding what actually happened. This is the step most people skip because it is uncomfortable, and skipping it is one of the main reasons people end up in the same situation again two years later.

Ask yourself four questions honestly.

**Was this structural or situational?** Structural means the kind of work you were doing is becoming less economically viable, execution-oriented roles being automated, a skill set that has been commoditised, a domain that is contracting. Situational means the company had specific problems that had nothing to do with your value in the market: a funding round that did not close, a product that failed, a reorganisation driven by leadership politics. The distinction matters because structural displacement requires repositioning, while situational displacement requires patience and momentum. Treating a situational problem as structural leads to unnecessary panic and premature pivots. Treating a structural problem as situational leads to waiting for a market that is not coming back.

**Was I doing commodity work?** Be honest about this. Commodity work is work that is increasingly automatable, increasingly offshorable, increasingly substitutable by someone with less experience and lower salary expectations. If your role consisted primarily of tasks that a well-prompted LLM can now perform adequately, routine code generation, standard data cleaning, templated reporting, basic pipeline maintenance, the displacement you just experienced is the beginning of a trend, not an anomaly. Treat it as information, not a moral judgment.

**Was I too dependent on a proprietary stack?** Some skills transfer across organisations. Others are deeply embedded in a specific company's tools, codebase, or internal processes and have limited external value. If your expertise is primarily in technologies that are not widely used outside your former employer, the job search will be harder than your years of experience suggest it should be. The lesson for the future is to ensure that a meaningful fraction of your skill development happens in transferable, publicly recognised technologies.

**Did I see this coming and not act?** Sometimes layoffs are genuinely sudden. Often they are not. There were signs, a change in how leadership talked about the team, a round of performance management that felt different from previous ones, a budget conversation that went quiet, a headcount freeze that lasted longer than explained. If you saw the signs and hoped they would resolve themselves, the lesson is not about the layoff but about decision-making under uncertainty. The next time you see those signs, act earlier.

## What They Called It: The Corporate Mechanics

Before the practical steps, one thing needs to be said plainly: the vocabulary companies use to describe what happened to you is almost never accurate.

No company calls it a layoff if it can avoid doing so. The vocabulary is: Performance Improvement Plan. Managed exit. Mutual separation. Role realignment. Resource optimisation. Fitment issue. Project starvation. Skill currency gap. Each term has been chosen to locate the problem in you rather than in the organisation's financial decisions. Each term has a legal function: to create a paper trail that avoids severance obligations, prevents the clustering of terminations that would invite scrutiny, and frames economic redundancy as individual failure.

The Performance Improvement Plan deserves special attention because it is the most widely misunderstood instrument in the Indian technology sector. In the United States and Europe, PIPs are occasionally genuine development tools, associated with termination rates of 30 to 50 percent. In India, research into HR practice suggests termination rates following a PIP of 80 to 90 percent. This gap has nothing to do with Indian employees underperforming at higher rates. It comes down to design intent: the Indian PIP is typically constructed to be failed. Timelines of 30 to 45 days, insufficient for genuine skill development. KPIs set unilaterally and vaguely. No assigned coach. The manager who initiated the PIP serving as sole evaluator. Severance denied on "performance cause" grounds. The PIP functions as a termination mechanism that avoids the legal and reputational costs of a transparent layoff, not as a development intervention.

The forced resignation variant is structurally similar. You are called into a room, without prior notice, without agenda, with HR and your manager present. A pre-drafted resignation letter may already be on the table. Refusal is technically your right. Practically, refusal means a PIP designed to fail, a "for cause" exit letter, and the very real possibility of a negative background verification entry, which in India, where a relieving letter is mandatory to join any organised-sector employer, can end a career in the organised tech sector entirely. The legal right to refuse is real. The practical ability to exercise it without career consequences is close to zero for a mid-career professional with dependants and a mortgage in Bengaluru or Hyderabad.

Variable pay weaponisation is the least visible mechanism and may affect the largest number of people. In large Indian IT firms, variable pay constitutes 10 to 30 percent of total compensation. For bench employees, those between projects, variable pay is routinely zeroed before any formal PIP begins. A 20 to 30 percent effective pay cut, applied silently, with no paper trail, and no legal remedy. It functions as resignation by starvation: make the financial pressure great enough that the employee leaves voluntarily, which avoids even the minimal ex gratia that a managed exit would require.

The AI narrative deserves its own category. Multiple large technology and consulting firms have publicly attributed workforce reductions to AI efficiency gains, positioning cuts as technological inevitability rather than financial decision. Analysts describe this as AI-washing. Two questions help separate genuine AI displacement from AI-washed cost-cutting. First: was the work being eliminated genuinely automatable by current AI tools? Junior coding, testing, templated reporting, yes. Senior architecture decisions, client relationship management, novel problem definition, no. Second: were the exits concentrated at higher salary bands? If so, the driver is more likely margin pressure than automation. AI disproportionately substitutes for junior execution work. When senior engineers are exiting in large numbers, the more probable explanation is salary cost, corrected overhiring, or ageism, not AI capability.

### Was It You or the Macro? A Brief Diagnostic

Three signals suggest your exit was primarily structural rather than performance-based, regardless of how it was framed.

Your OKRs were met or close to met in the period immediately before the exit. Genuine performance failures leave a trail of missed targets. Structural exits under performance framing frequently happen to people whose recent evaluations were adequate or positive. If your last three performance reviews were fine and then you were suddenly on a PIP, the PIP is not about your performance.

Others in similar roles at similar seniority levels left at the same time. Individual performance problems produce individual exits. Structural exits cluster. If five people in your team or department left within a three-month window, that is not a performance coincidence. That is a headcount reduction.

The stated reason shifted across conversations. In a genuine performance exit, the reason is consistent: here is the specific gap, here is what was required, here is where you fell short. In a pretextual exit, the reason changes between the HR conversation, the written notice, and the reference that is eventually provided. Shifting stories are the clearest indicator that the original stated reason was not the real one.

This matters not because the distinction changes your immediate situation, you still need to find a new role, but because it changes how you should interpret what happened. Internalising a structural exit as a personal failure produces the wrong conclusions about what needs to change. If the exit was structural, you do not need to become a different professional. You need a different context for the professional you already are.

The shame dimension is worth naming directly, because it is the part nobody talks about. Being let go in the Indian professional context is not a private event. It has a social dimension: the family member who asks how work is going, the former colleague who sees your LinkedIn status change, the specific humiliation of being "available for opportunities" after years of seniority. None of this is trivial and pretending it is would not serve you. The shame is real. It is also not information about your competence. It is information about how your culture has organised status and identity around employment, a structural problem that has been personalised, in the same way that the structural exit was personalised. Recognise it for what it is. Name it to someone you trust. Then set it aside and get to work.

### Stabilise First

Before strategy, stability. This is not the sequence that feels natural, the instinct is to move immediately, to be seen to be moving, to demonstrate to yourself and others that you are handling it. But movement without a stable base tends to be frantic and misdirected.

**Know your financial runway precisely.** Savings divided by monthly expenses. Not an estimate, the actual number, calculated from your actual accounts. This number determines everything else about how you run the search. A person with eighteen months of runway can afford to be selective. A person with six weeks cannot. Both of them need to know which situation they are in, because the search strategy is different.

If the number is uncomfortably small, address it immediately rather than hoping the search will resolve before it matters. This may mean reducing expenses, drawing on savings that were earmarked for something else, having a difficult conversation with family about finances, or taking on short-term consulting work to extend the runway while the main search proceeds. None of these are pleasant. All of them are preferable to making a bad career decision because you were desperate.

**File for whatever you are entitled to.** In India, this includes PF withdrawal or transfer, gratuity if applicable, and any notice period payment or severance that was agreed. Many people delay this because it feels like accepting the situation or because the administrative process is unpleasant. It is money you are owed. Handle it in the first week.

**Restore a basic structure to your days.** This is more important than it sounds. Employment provides structure invisibly, a reason to be up at a certain time, a sequence of tasks that organises the day, a social context that creates a sense of belonging and purpose. When employment disappears, the structure disappears with it, and the resulting formlessness is psychologically corrosive in ways that are distinct from the financial stress.

A fixed wake time, some form of physical activity, and a clear separation between focused search-related work and personal time will do more for the quality of your search than any amount of optimising your LinkedIn headline. The search is a cognitive task. Cognitive tasks are done better by people who are sleeping, moving, and maintaining some sense of routine.

## The Audit: What the Market Actually Wants From You

Once you are stable, the next step is an honest audit of where you sit in the market as it currently exists, not as it existed when you last looked for a job, not as you would like it to be, but as it actually is right now.

Pull up twenty to thirty current job descriptions for roles you are realistically qualified for. Not aspirational roles, realistic ones, based on your actual experience and skills. Read them carefully, not for the specific requirements but for the patterns. What skills appear repeatedly? What level of experience is being asked for? What domains are hiring and which ones have gone quiet? What titles are being used for work that resembles what you have done?

Compare what you find to what you actually have. The gap between the two is your audit result. It tells you whether your search is primarily a positioning problem (you have the skills but are not presenting them in the language the market uses), a skills problem (there are genuine gaps between what you offer and what is being asked for), a domain problem (your expertise is in an area that is contracting while adjacent areas are growing), or a level problem (you are applying at the wrong level for your experience).

Each of these problems has a different solution, and applying the wrong solution wastes time you may not have in abundance.

A positioning problem is solved by rewriting your resume, LinkedIn profile, and cover letters in the language the market is currently using, not dishonestly, but accurately. If you have been doing retrieval-augmented generation under an internal project name that no one outside your former company would recognise, call it RAG. If you have been doing LLMOps work under a generic data engineering title, make that explicit.

A skills problem requires an honest decision about whether the gap is bridgeable in the time available. A gap of one or two skills that can be demonstrated through a project built over two to three weeks is bridgeable. A gap that requires twelve months of learning before you are genuinely competitive is not bridgeable within a job search, it requires a longer-term repositioning plan, which is compatible with continuing the search at your current level while building toward the next one.

A domain problem may require a lateral move into an adjacent domain that is hiring. This is uncomfortable because it often means taking a role that feels like a step sideways rather than forward. It is almost always preferable to waiting for your contracting domain to recover.

A level problem is the most delicate. If you have been applying at senior level and not getting traction, consider whether a principal or lead role with a smaller scope might be more accessible and might, paradoxically, accelerate your trajectory by giving you a track record in a new context that a larger senior role might not.

## Choose One Direction

The most common mistake in a job search is applying everywhere. It feels productive. It produces very little.

The person applying to twenty different kinds of roles, data scientist, ML engineer, AI researcher, analytics lead, product manager for AI products, presents to each hiring manager as someone who does not know what they want. Hiring managers are not looking for candidates who are open to anything. They are looking for candidates who want this specific thing and have a credible reason for wanting it.

Choose one direction. Make every visible surface, resume, LinkedIn, GitHub, cover letters, coherent around that direction. Then move toward it deliberately.

The direction should be chosen at the intersection of three things: what the market is actually hiring for right now, what you have genuine experience doing, and what you find sufficiently interesting to do well. The first without the second produces applications you cannot back up in interview. The first without the third produces a role you will leave within eighteen months. All three together produces a search with a real chance of ending in a role that compounds.

In practical terms for the 2026 market, the directions with the strongest demand in India are: AI engineering with a focus on systems, infrastructure, and LLMOps; applied AI with a focus on end-to-end problem solving using RAG and agentic workflows; AI plus domain, combining technical skills with deep expertise in a specific sector; and AI governance, ethics, and compliance, which is a newer category but growing as regulation increases.

Pick the one that fits your actual profile most closely. Then stop looking at the others.

## Build One Thing

The most effective thing you can do during a job search, alongside the applications themselves, is build something visible.

This does not mean a portfolio of ten projects assembled hastily from Kaggle datasets. It means one thing, built properly, that demonstrates how you actually approach a problem. An end-to-end application that solves a real problem using current tools. A well-documented GitHub repository that shows not just the code but the thinking behind the decisions. A Medium article that explains what you built and what you learned.

The reason this matters is that the interview process for technical roles in 2026 increasingly asks candidates to demonstrate current, applied competence rather than just describe past experience. A working project that uses RAG, or agentic workflows, or LLMOps tooling, or whatever is central to your chosen direction, is evidence in a way that a resume entry is not.

It also keeps your skills current during a search that may take longer than you hope. The professional who spends six weeks applying and waiting, versus the one who spends six weeks applying and building, arrives at interviews in very different states of technical confidence.

Choose the project based on what is most relevant to your chosen direction, and on what you can complete to a demonstrable standard in two to three weeks. Completion matters more than ambition. A finished, working, documented project of moderate scope is more valuable in an interview than an impressive but incomplete one.

## The Consulting Bridge

A layoff is a legitimate moment to consider whether fractional or consulting work might serve as a bridge, both financially and professionally.

Many organisations in India, particularly mid-sized companies and startups, cannot afford a full-time senior AI hire but will pay reasonable rates for ten to fifteen hours a week of expert help: setting up a RAG pipeline, evaluating a model architecture, building a monitoring dashboard, advising on AI strategy. This kind of work keeps income flowing, keeps skills current in a real-world context rather than just a personal project context, and frequently generates referrals or full-time opportunities.

The practical challenge is finding the first engagement. The most effective source is your existing network, former colleagues, former managers, people you have collaborated with professionally who know the quality of your work. The second most effective source is the community you have built through writing, speaking, or open source contribution, which is another reason why building in public over the long term pays dividends precisely when you need them most.

If you have not built that network or that community, the consulting bridge is harder to access quickly. This is useful information for what you build in the next phase of your career, whether or not you use consulting as a bridge this time.

Do not underprice consulting work significantly below what the market pays for full-time equivalents. Consultants are paid for expertise and flexibility, not just time, and clients who pay properly tend to take the engagement more seriously than those who negotiate aggressively on rate.

## The First Offer

The first offer matters more than it logically should, and it is worth understanding why.

Before the first offer arrives, the search feels like scarcity. Every rejection is evidence that the market has closed. Every week without an offer is a week of eroding confidence. The internal narrative, whatever you are telling yourself about your value and your prospects, tends to darken progressively in the absence of external validation.

After the first offer, the search feels like options. The same market, the same candidacy, but the internal narrative has shifted. Subsequent conversations happen differently because you are no longer negotiating from need.

This asymmetry means that the first offer is worth more than its face value suggests. An offer that is decent but not perfect may be worth accepting if it restores the psychological footing that makes everything else easier. Delivered well over twelve to eighteen months, it generates a track record and relationships that can be leveraged into a better role. That is not settling. That is strategy.

The exception is an offer that would actively damage your positioning, a role so misaligned with your chosen direction that taking it would make subsequent moves harder rather than easier. These are rarer than the fear of them suggests, but they exist, and it is worth being clear in advance about where your line is.

## The Job Was Never You

The hardest part of a layoff is rarely the logistics. It is the sudden absence of something that quietly provided your days with structure, your identity with an anchor, and your sense of self with a context in which your skills had a place to matter.

You were not just employed. You were embedded. The company name on your email, the team Slack channel, the Monday morning standup, the colleagues who understood what you were working on without needing it explained, these formed a context that you inhabited, and losing it is a genuine loss that deserves to be treated as one.

In the Indian context this loss has particular weight, because professional identity is often deeply intertwined with social identity. The question "what do you do?" is asked early and answered often. The company you work for is a signal that others read. When that signal disappears, the social dimension of the loss compounds the professional one.

What is worth remembering, and keeping close during the weeks when it is hardest to believe, is this: the job was never you. It rented your identity for a while. It gave your capabilities a context in which to be useful. But the capabilities themselves, the years of learning, the judgment accumulated through real problems, the ability to think clearly about complex systems, the domain knowledge that took a decade to build, none of that left with the job.

The desk was the least interesting part of you. What you need now is a new context in which what you actually are can be useful again, not a recovery of what you had. That is a smaller problem than it feels like in week two.

## A Note on Telling People

Tell people you are looking. This feels vulnerable and many people resist it. It is also one of the most practically effective things you can do.

The majority of roles in the Indian technology market are filled through referrals or through networks rather than through applications to advertised positions. The person who quietly applies to job boards while telling no one they are searching is competing in the most crowded part of the market while leaving the least crowded part entirely uncontested.

Tell former colleagues. Tell your professional network. Tell people outside the technology sector who might know of organisations building AI capability. Update your LinkedIn status to signal openness. Write a post, not a desperate one, a confident one, that says clearly what you are looking for and why someone should want to work with you.

The framing matters. "I am between roles and looking for my next opportunity" is a statement of fact that invites referrals. "I was recently let go and really need to find something" is an invitation to pity that rarely produces useful responses. The former is vulnerable in the appropriate amount. The latter gives away the negotiating position you need to protect.

## The Loop Continues

A layoff feels like an interruption of the career. It is more accurately a feature of it, an accelerated version of the periodic reinvention that the loop requires of everyone working in a field moving this fast.

The professionals who come through it well are not the ones who avoided it. They are the ones who moved through it with clarity about what happened, honesty about what needs to change, and enough structural stability, financial, psychological, relational, to make good decisions rather than reactive ones.

The loop does not end here. The tools will change again. The market will shift again. The skills that make someone valuable in 2026 will be partly obsolete by 2029, just as the skills that made someone valuable in 2022 are partly obsolete now. Rather than a reason for despair, treat it as a reason to build the habits, of continuous learning, of building in public, of maintaining optionality, that make each reinvention faster and less destabilising than the last.

You have been through this before, in smaller ways, every time the field shifted and you had to shift with it. This is a larger version of the same thing. You know how to do it. Now do it.

The job was never the whole of who you are, even though it can feel that way for a while after losing it. The loop continues regardless, and the most useful thing available to you right now is to keep moving through it.

# Chapter 12: Playing the Long Game

## *What a 20-Year AI Career Could Actually Look Like*

Most career advice is written for the short term. How to get the next job. How to negotiate the next salary. How to pass the next interview. This is understandable, the short term is where the anxiety lives, and anxiety is what drives people to pick up career guides.

But the decisions that shape a career most significantly are rarely the ones made under pressure. They are the ones made quietly, over years, about what to learn, what to build, who to spend time with, and what kind of work to say no to. These decisions compound. The professional who makes them well looks, from the outside, like someone who got lucky. From the inside, it feels more like a series of small choices that gradually became a direction.

This chapter is about the long view. Not a prediction, the field will look different in 2036 in ways that are genuinely impossible to specify today, but a set of principles that have held across previous waves of technological change and are likely to hold across the next ones.

### The Compounding That Nobody Measures

There is a version of career compounding that is easy to measure: salary increases, title progression, the size of the teams you manage. These are real, and they matter. But they are not the most important kind.

The compounding that matters most is harder to see. It is the accumulation of judgment: the ability to look at a new problem and draw on ten years of pattern recognition to understand where the real difficulty lies. It is the depth of domain knowledge that allows you to see what a model is missing, not just whether its accuracy metric is acceptable. It is the network of relationships with people who trust your work and will vouch for it. It is the reputation that means interesting problems find their way to you rather than you having to hunt for them.

None of this shows up on a resume in the way that certifications do. None of it can be acquired in a three-week course. It accumulates slowly, through sustained engagement with real problems over real time, and it becomes the most durable asset you have when the next wave of technological change makes specific technical skills temporarily less valuable.

The implication for the early and middle parts of a career is counterintuitive: optimise for depth of engagement with real problems over breadth of credential acquisition. The professional who spent three years genuinely owning a production ML system, debugging it, retraining it, explaining its failures to stakeholders, watching it drift and fixing it, has accumulated something that a portfolio of online course certificates cannot replicate.

## Domain Depth as Career Insurance

The data scientist who understands credit risk, or clinical trial methodology, or supply chain dynamics, or agricultural yield modelling, is harder to replace than the one who knows only the technical stack.

The reason has less to do with domain knowledge being more valuable than technical skill in the abstract, and more to do with the combination being rare, and rarity commanding a premium. There are many people who can implement a gradient boosting model. There are fewer who can implement one and also understand why the features that matter for predicting loan default are different in the Indian microfinance context than in a Western retail banking context. The second person is solving a harder problem and is correspondingly harder to substitute.

Domain depth also provides resilience against technical obsolescence. When the framework you specialised in gets deprecated, or the approach you mastered gets superseded, domain knowledge transfers. The understanding of what credit risk actually means, what drives it, how it is regulated, and what the consequences of getting it wrong are, this does not become less valuable because a new model architecture emerged. The technical implementation changes; the domain understanding persists.

The question of which domain to go deep in is worth thinking about carefully. The most useful heuristics are: go where the data is genuinely complex and consequential, go where regulation creates a sustained need for human judgment, and go where your existing interests or background give you a head start. In the Indian context, domains with particularly strong long-term prospects include healthcare and diagnostics, financial services and insurance, agriculture and climate, urban infrastructure, and legal and regulatory compliance.

## Building in Public: The Indian Context

The professional who writes about their work, speaks at conferences, publishes on GitHub, and contributes to open source projects is building something that transcends any single employer: a public record of how they think.

This matters more than it used to, for two reasons. The first is that the signal-to-noise ratio in hiring has collapsed. Recruiters are inundated with applications, many of them generated or polished by AI tools, and the ability to distinguish genuine competence from well-packaged mediocrity has become harder. A body of public work, a GitHub repository that shows how you actually approach a problem, a Medium article that demonstrates you understand the implications of what you are building, a conference talk that shows you can communicate technical ideas to a non-technical audience, cuts through that noise in a way that a resume cannot.

The second is that building in public creates serendipity. Opportunities find you in ways that systematic job searching does not produce. A paper you wrote gets cited by someone at a company you would never have thought to apply to. A GitHub project attracts a collaborator who becomes a professional relationship that matters for years. A conference talk leads to a consulting engagement. These are not predictable outcomes. They are the kind of lateral connections that a career built entirely inside organisational hierarchies rarely produces.

The Indian professional context has some specific friction around building in public. There is a cultural tendency toward privacy about work, partly because intellectual property concerns at employers are often communicated in ways that make people uncertain about what they are allowed to share, and partly because the professional culture has traditionally been less oriented toward public intellectual contribution than, say, the American technology culture.

The practical resolution is to build in public on problems that are clearly not proprietary: open datasets, general methodological questions, career reflections, domain analysis that does not touch employer data. The corpus of public work does not need to reveal anything confidential to be useful. It needs to demonstrate how you think.

In the Indian market specifically, LinkedIn remains the most professionally consequential platform for most people. Medium and Substack are valuable for longer-form technical and reflective writing. GitHub is essential for anyone doing technical work. Speaking at meetups, Bangalore, Hyderabad, Pune, and Mumbai all have active data science communities, is underutilised by people who would benefit from it most.

## The Independent Path

At some point in a long career, many professionals begin to wonder whether there is a version of their work that does not require an employer's permission structure. Consulting, independent research, writing, teaching, these are not alternatives to a career so much as different configurations of the same underlying skills.

The independent path is genuinely difficult in ways that are often underestimated. The financial irregularity is real: income that comes in project-shaped chunks rather than monthly salary transfers requires a different relationship with money and risk. The absence of colleagues, institutional affiliation, and the daily structure that employment provides is a psychological adjustment that many people find harder than they expected. The requirement to find your own work, to maintain relationships, to be visible, to pitch, is a skill set that is separate from technical competence and takes time to develop.

It is also genuinely freeing in ways that are hard to describe to someone who has not experienced it. The ability to choose which problems to work on, which collaborators to work with, and which clients to say no to is not a small thing. The absence of performance review cycles, organisational politics, and the particular indignity of being managed by someone less capable than you are, these matter more than they appear to from the inside of a conventional employment relationship.

The most sustainable version of the independent path, particularly in the Indian context, is not a clean break from employment but a gradual shift. A consulting engagement on the side that grows into a significant income stream. A writing practice that builds an audience before it needs to generate revenue. A research collaboration that establishes credibility in a new domain before you need to depend on it financially. The people who make the independent path work over the long term are rarely the ones who leapt dramatically. They are the ones who built the foundations while still employed, and then stepped across when the foundations were solid enough.

## The Academic-to-Industry Transition

For those moving from PhD or postdoctoral research into industry, a path that a meaningful fraction of this book's readers are navigating, the following observations are based on research and direct professional observation rather than theory.

The PhD is an asset in some contexts and a liability in others, and knowing which context you are entering matters more than the degree itself. Product companies at Series A and beyond, and global tech firms with genuine research functions, value PhD depth, particularly in machine learning, NLP, and systems. They are hiring for the ability to read and implement frontier research, to think rigorously about novel problems, and to push against existing approaches rather than just implementing them. For these roles, your publications, your thesis work, and your research instincts are genuine differentiators. Service companies and execution-oriented GCCs are more ambivalent. A PhD signals potential but also, sometimes, a mismatch with the pace and defined-ness of delivery work. Be honest with yourself about which kind of environment you are targeting before you pitch your research background as a primary asset.

On framing publications: list the work that is most relevant to the roles you are applying for, and be prepared to explain it in plain language to a hiring manager who may not share your domain. The ability to translate a technical contribution into a business implication, "this work reduced inference latency by 40 percent on sequence-to-sequence tasks, which is relevant to the production serving challenges you described", is more valuable in an industry interview than the paper's citation count. Curate rather than list everything. Three papers you can discuss in depth are more useful than twelve you mention in passing.

The culture shock is real and worth naming. Research moves on timescales of months to years; product development moves on timescales of weeks to months. The careful, thorough, revision-oriented pace that produces good research is not the pace that ships products. This is not a deficiency of industry, it is a different mode of work with different values, and adjusting to it takes time. The most common failure mode for PhDs entering industry is not technical: it is the unwillingness to ship something imperfect, or the impulse to keep refining when the organisation needs to move. The academic instinct to get it right and the product instinct to get it out are both legitimate, and the most effective industry researchers develop both.

One practical note: arXiv preprints, conference paper submissions, and even thesis chapters can be shared as portfolio work in industry interviews where they are relevant, they demonstrate that you can produce substantial technical writing, think through a problem systematically, and engage with the literature. A well-explained research paper is stronger interview evidence than a generic GitHub repository, for the roles where research depth is what is being assessed.

## What the Money Is Actually For

The Indian technology sector has a complicated relationship with compensation. Salary is a measure of status in ways that go beyond the purely financial: it signals success to family, positions you in social hierarchies, and functions as a proxy for worth in a culture that does not have many other publicly visible measures of professional achievement.

This creates a tendency to optimise for salary in ways that are not always aligned with long-term career development. The 40 percent increment that comes with a move to a brand-name company may be genuinely worth taking. It may also come with a role that is narrower, more execution-oriented, and less developmental than what you were doing before, a trade that looks good on the bank statement for a year and costs you two years of learning.

The more useful frame is to think about what the money is actually for. Financial security, the ability to weather a period of unemployment, to take a career risk, to support family obligations without desperation, is genuinely important and worth building deliberately. Beyond a certain threshold, however, incremental increases in salary produce diminishing returns in actual wellbeing, while the opportunity cost of chasing them can be substantial.

The professional who, by their mid-thirties, has built a financial buffer of twelve to eighteen months of expenses, has no high-interest debt, and has some savings compounding in index funds, has bought themselves something more valuable than a higher salary: optionality. The ability to say no to a bad role, to take time between jobs without panic, to pursue an interesting opportunity that pays less than the market rate, this is a form of career capital that does not show up on a compensation benchmarking survey but shapes the entire trajectory of what follows.

## Mentoring as a Compounding Investment

At some point in a long career, the most valuable thing you can do for your own development is to help someone else with theirs.

This sounds altruistic. It is also entirely self-interested, in the best sense. Teaching forces a clarity of understanding that solo work does not require. When you have to explain why a particular approach to feature selection matters, in terms that a junior colleague can understand and apply, you discover very quickly whether you actually understand it yourself or whether you have just been pattern-matching successfully. The gaps that emerge in that process are the most useful learning you will do.

Mentoring also builds a network in the most durable way: through genuine contribution to someone else's development. The people you help when they are early in their careers become, over time, colleagues, collaborators, hiring managers, and advocates. Mentoring works precisely because it is not approached as a transaction, though it is not purely selfless either: it is one of the most reliable long-term career investments available.

In the Indian context, formal mentoring structures are underdeveloped relative to the size of the talent pool. The demand for good mentorship from early-career professionals is enormous; the supply of experienced people willing to invest time in providing it is insufficient. If you are ten or more years into a career in data science or AI, the marginal value of one more certification is low. The marginal value of spending two hours a month with someone five years behind you is high, for them, obviously, but also for you.

## Staying Human in a Machine-Shaped Field

There is something worth saying, at the end of a book about navigating an AI job market, about what it means to remain fully human inside a field that is increasingly shaped by non-human intelligence.

The risk is quieter than that. It has nothing to do with AI making you obsolete or replacing your thinking wholesale. The risk is subtler: that the pace of the field, the pressure to stay current, the emphasis on measurable outputs and quantifiable skills, will gradually crowd out the parts of you that are not optimisable.

The capacity for genuine curiosity, following an idea because it is interesting, not because it is on the skills gap list. The ability to sit with a difficult problem without immediately reaching for a tool. The practice of reading widely, across fields and centuries, because the connections that form between disparate ideas are often the source of the most original thinking. The investment in relationships that are not professionally instrumental. The attention to whatever contemplative or creative practice sustains your inner life.

These are not soft additions to a technical career. They are the source of the judgment, the taste, and the ethical sensibility that distinguish a career that matters from one that merely accumulates credentials. The most impressive technical professionals you will encounter over a long career are almost never the ones who knew the most frameworks. They are the ones who thought most clearly, communicated most honestly, and brought genuine human judgment to problems that required it.

The machines are getting better at the technical parts. The human parts are becoming more valuable, not less. Investing in them is your career, at its deepest level, not a distraction from it.

## A Letter to Your Future Self

Imagine the professional you want to be in 2036. Not the title, not the salary, those are outcomes, not intentions. The kind of work you want to be doing. The kind of problems you want to be known for solving. The kind of person you want to have become through the doing of that work.

Now work backwards. What would that person have spent the intervening decade learning? What would they have built? What would they have said no to? What relationships would they have invested in? What practices would they have sustained?

The gap between where you are now and where that person is, is the career, not an obstacle to it. The loop continues, the tools change, the problems evolve, and through all of it, if you navigate it well, you become someone whose judgment is worth having, whose work is worth doing, and whose presence in the field made it slightly better than it would have been without you.

That is enough. In a field moving this fast, in a world this uncertain, it is more than enough.

Playing the long game will not guarantee the outcome you want. It remains, even so, the only game worth playing.

# Chapter 13: The Reputation Economy

In 2015, your CV found jobs. You applied; companies reviewed; someone decided. The job posting was the mechanism, and the resume was the proof. The sequence was linear, and the direction was clear.

In 2026, this model still works. But a parallel model has emerged that is faster, higher-signal, and increasingly how the most interesting opportunities are filled. In the parallel model, jobs find you. A recruiter at a company you have never heard of opens your GitHub and sees a project that solves the exact problem their team is wrestling with. A hiring manager at a Series B startup has been reading your Substack for three months before your name ever appears in their ATS. An engineering lead at a database company notices the bug report you filed, sees how you diagnosed it, and messages you on Discord asking if you are open to a conversation. None of these require an application. None of them appear in a job posting. All of them happen through reputation.

This appendix is for readers who have not started building that reputation yet, or who have started but are not doing it systematically. Forget personal branding in the LinkedIn-advice sense. This is about making your work visible, consistently and honestly, so that people who need someone who thinks the way you do can find you.

## Why the CV Signal Has Weakened

The volume problem is real. A senior ML engineer role at a known company in Bengaluru in 2026 receives hundreds of applications within the first twenty-four hours, many of them polished to similar surface quality by similar AI tools. The recruiter has a fixed amount of time. The signal-to-noise ratio has collapsed.

At the same time, the information available to a motivated recruiter has expanded dramatically. Your GitHub commit history, your writing, your open-source contributions, your conference talks, your Stack Overflow answers, your Discord participation in technical communities, all of this is publicly legible to anyone who looks. The recruiter who spends five minutes on your public profile before your application ever reaches them is increasingly common. The recruiter who discovers your application via your public profile, rather than the other way around, is becoming common too.

The practical implication is not to stop applying for jobs, but to build, continuously, a public record of how you think, so that the people worth working for can find you before you need to find them.

## The Platforms, in Order of Leverage

### GitHub: the primary technical signal

GitHub is where technical hiring managers actually look first. Your commit history, your repository quality, the problems you have chosen to work on, and the way you document your work all communicate something that a resume cannot. The signal is in the specifics.

A repository that contains a RAG pipeline over Indian legal documents, with a clear README explaining the design decisions, the evaluation approach, and the known limitations, tells a hiring manager more about your judgment in five minutes than a bullet point on a resume claiming RAG experience.

A few principles for making GitHub count. READMEs matter more than code quality for initial impressions: a well-explained project with adequate code is more compelling than a technically impressive project that is opaque. Commit messages matter: a history of meaningful commit messages signals how you work, not just what you built. Stars are a weak signal; genuine utility is a strong one. One well-maintained project is worth more than twenty abandoned experiments.

The highest-leverage GitHub activity in 2026 is contributing to the tools that the field actually uses: FalkorDB, vLLM, LangGraph, the Model Context Protocol, Ragas. A genuine contribution to an open-source project that practitioners depend on, even a small one, a bug report with a reproducible case, a documentation fix that resolves a genuine ambiguity, a feature addition that addresses a real use case, puts your name in front of the maintainers and the community in a way that no application can replicate.

### Writing: the medium-term compounding investment

Writing is where most technical professionals leave the most value on the table. The gap between how much people know and how much they write about what they know is enormous in the Indian technology community, for cultural reasons (privacy about work, uncertainty about intellectual property) and practical ones (it takes time, and the return is not immediate).

The return is not immediate. But it compounds. An article you write today about a specific failure mode in RAG retrieval for multilingual documents will still be findable in three years, and the person who finds it and finds it useful will remember you. The technical writing you produce over two years creates an asset that works for you while you are sleeping, while you are in your current job, and long after you have moved on from it.

On platforms: LinkedIn remains the most professionally consequential platform for visibility in the Indian market. Posts that describe a specific technical problem and how you thought through it, not tutorials, not definitions, but genuine working-through of something real, consistently outperform generic commentary and motivational content. Medium and Substack are better suited for longer-form technical and analytical writing that builds a sustained readership. arXiv and technical blogs establish credibility in research-adjacent roles in ways that LinkedIn cannot.

What to write about: your own work, including what did not work. A post that says here is what I tried, here is why it failed, here is what that revealed is significantly more interesting to a technical reader than a post that presents a polished solution. The thinking is the signal. The thinking is what a hiring manager is evaluating when they read your public work.

## Community participation: where serendipity lives

The highest-leverage but lowest-utilised reputation-building activity for most Indian AI professionals is active participation in the technical communities where practitioners actually gather. Discord servers for open-source AI tools. GitHub Discussions on repositories they use. Technical Slack groups for practitioners in their domain. The Python India community. Bangalore's data science meetups.

The mechanism is simple but requires consistency. When you encounter a problem in a tool, file a detailed bug report rather than a vague complaint. When you solve something that took you a day, post the solution in the community forum so the next person does not spend a day on it. When you have a genuine question, ask it publicly rather than in a DM, because the answer benefits everyone and the question demonstrates what you are working on.

The direct career consequence of this: in 2026, several of the most significant AI infrastructure tools are actively recruiting from their own contributor and community base. The engineers who maintain vLLM, LangGraph, and the Model Context Protocol know who the engaged community members are by name, because they interact with them regularly. When a role opens, the first outreach goes to people they already know and trust. That is not a pipeline you can enter by applying.

## Speaking: lower volume, higher impact

Giving a talk at a technical meetup is uncomfortable for most people and valuable in ways that are disproportionate to the discomfort. A twenty-minute talk on something you have actually built and learned from reaches an audience that is specifically interested in that topic, gives them a face and a voice to associate with your name, and creates a social context for the kind of conversation that LinkedIn DMs rarely produce.

The Indian AI meetup ecosystem in Bengaluru, Hyderabad, Pune, and Mumbai is more active than most people realise, and consistently under-subscribed for speakers. The person who has shipped a production system and can talk honestly about what they learned has material that organisers actively seek. Start with a local meetup. The talk does not need to be polished. It needs to be honest and specific.

## The Compounding Timeline

Building a reputation is slow for the first year and then faster than you expect. The typical trajectory: months one through six, you are producing content and participating in communities that almost no one sees. Months six through twelve, you start to see evidence that people have found it, a comment on a post, a GitHub star, a DM from someone who read your article. Year two, the network effects begin to work. People share your work with each other. Opportunities appear through introductions you did not engineer.

Begin now, before you need the results, because the infrastructure you build in the next year is what will find you opportunities in the year after that. Waiting for the compounding to start first defeats the purpose.

> *The professionals who attract interesting opportunities are rarely the ones who applied most aggressively. More often, they made it easy to be found long before they needed to be, simply by doing real work visibly and consistently over time.*

# Chapter 14: When Full-Time Is Not the Answer

The conventional career script assumes that the goal is a full-time role at a company with a salary, a title, and a career ladder. For a growing number of AI professionals in India, the better question is not how to get that job, but whether that job is the right vehicle for the kind of work they want to do and the kind of income they need to generate.

Treat it as an increasingly practical option, one that the structure of the AI market in 2026 makes viable in ways that were not true five years ago, more than a lifestyle choice. The combination of global remote work norms, the growing market for senior AI expertise on a project basis, the infrastructure for finding and serving clients, and the AI tools that allow one person to do work that previously required a team, has made independent work a realistic path for people who could not have pursued it in the previous decade.

It is also a path that will become necessary for a significant fraction of experienced AI professionals, not as a preference but as a reality. The execution layer contraction described in Chapter 3 reaches well past junior professionals. It is restructuring how senior expertise gets deployed: fewer permanent headcount positions, more project-based engagements, shorter contracts, fractional arrangements. Understanding the independent path is not optional for anyone thinking seriously about a 20-year career in this field.

## The Models, and What Each Actually Requires

### Project-based consulting

The most common independent model: a company has a specific AI problem and hires you for a fixed period to solve it. This could be designing a RAG pipeline for an internal knowledge base, evaluating a foundation model for a specific use case, auditing an existing ML system for production readiness, or leading an AI capability assessment. The engagement is typically two to six months, the deliverable is specific, and the relationship ends when the work is done.

What this model requires: a clear service offering that you can describe in one sentence, a method for finding clients (referrals from your network, visibility through writing and GitHub, direct outreach to companies in your domain), and the ability to scope and price a project. Pricing in India ranges widely for this kind of work. Senior AI consulting rates for technical work start at approximately Rs 8,000 to 15,000 per day for experienced professionals and go significantly higher for genuinely specialised expertise, with international clients.

The first client is always the hardest. The practical path to the first client is almost always through a previous employer, a colleague who has moved somewhere, or a direct connection who knows a company with a problem you can solve. Do not begin by building a website and waiting. Begin by telling the ten people who know your work best that you are available for project engagements.

### Fractional roles

A fractional arrangement is a part-time senior role: you work for a company two or three days per week, typically in a senior technical capacity, while working for other clients the rest of the time. The company gets senior expertise they cannot afford or do not need full-time. You get stability and variety simultaneously.

Fractional arrangements are more common in the West than in India, but they are growing in the Indian startup ecosystem, particularly for roles like fractional CTO, fractional Head of AI, or fractional ML Architect. The companies that use these arrangements are typically post-seed startups that have raised enough money to need senior guidance but are not yet at a scale that justifies a full-time senior hire.

The practical challenge with fractional work in India is that most employment contracts are structured for full-time commitment. Negotiating a fractional arrangement that is clearly defined, with boundaries around other work you are doing, requires the kind of explicit conversation that Indian professional culture sometimes makes awkward. Have the conversation explicitly, in writing, before starting.

### Expert networks and advisory

Expert networks like GLG, Guidepoint, and AlphaSights connect professionals with deep domain knowledge to clients, typically institutional investors, strategy consultants, and corporate strategy teams, who pay for one-hour expert calls. The rates are typically Rs 15,000 to 50,000 per hour for genuine experts in specific domains.

For AI professionals with deep domain expertise in a specific industry (Indian fintech, healthcare AI, GCC operations, telecom network intelligence), expert network work is among the highest income-per-hour activities available. The barrier to entry is demonstrating genuine domain specificity; generalist AI knowledge is less valued than narrow, deep expertise in a context the client actually cares about.

### Teaching, writing, and digital products

Courses, workshops, technical writing, and digital products (evaluation frameworks, prompt libraries, system design templates) represent a genuinely scalable income stream for people with both technical depth and the ability to communicate it clearly. The Indian AI education market is substantial and undersupplied with genuinely high-quality technical content.

The honest caution here: building a course or digital product audience takes time, typically one to two years of consistent output before the income becomes meaningful. Approach it as a long-term compounding investment that works best as a parallel track to other income, not a replacement for it, rather than as a bridge income strategy for an urgent financial situation.

## The Financial Reality of Independence

The income volatility of independent work is real, and the cultural context of Indian professional life, family expectations, mortgage obligations, and the social weight of employment status, makes it harder to navigate than the equivalent situation might be in a Western context.

A practical framework: before pursuing independent work as a primary income model, aim to have twelve to eighteen months of expenses saved, at least one client relationship in place before you exit employment, and a specific service offering that you have tested at least once. The people who make independent work sustainable over the long term are almost never those who leapt into it without infrastructure. They built the foundations first.

## Tax and compliance for Indian freelancers and consultants

Section 44ADA of the Income Tax Act allows professionals and consultants to pay tax on 50 percent of their gross receipts as presumptive income, up to a gross of Rs 75 lakh per year. This is a significant simplification of tax accounting for independent consultants and effectively reduces the tax burden relative to salaried income in the same bracket. Consult a CA who understands freelance and consulting income before filing.

GST registration is mandatory once your annual turnover exceeds Rs 20 lakh (Rs 10 lakh in some states). Most consulting engagements with corporate clients require a GST invoice. Register early and include GST compliance costs in your pricing. The administrative overhead of GST filing is real but manageable with accounting software.

Invoicing and contracts: use a written service agreement for every engagement, regardless of how well you know the client. Define the scope, deliverables, timeline, payment terms, and intellectual property ownership explicitly. Payment terms of net 30 are standard; insist on a percentage (30 to 50 percent) upfront for new client relationships. Late payments are common in the Indian market and erode the financial benefit of higher day rates.

## When to Make the Move

Independent work is the right primary model when: you have a specific expertise that is valuable enough that clients will pay a premium for it, you have enough financial runway to survive a slow first year, you have at least one client relationship that will likely generate work, and you have a genuine tolerance for income variability and the absence of institutional structure.

It is the wrong model when: you are in the early phases of your career and still building foundational skills (you learn faster inside good organisations than independently at Phase 1 or early Phase 2), when you are in a financial situation where income variability would create real harm, or when you are pursuing independence as an escape from a difficult employment situation rather than as a positive choice about how you want to work.

> *The independent path is a different configuration of the same underlying skills as employment, with different trade-offs around stability, autonomy, variety, and risk, neither better nor worse on its own terms. Making the choice deliberately, based on an honest assessment of your situation, matters more than making it early.*

# Chapter 15: Decoding the Offer and Negotiating It

Salary benchmarks exist. Chapter 9 of this book references the negotiation conversation, and Appendix C gives you the numbers. What does not exist, in most career guides written for the Indian context, is a practical account of how to actually use that information in a live negotiation with a company that has more experience in this conversation than you do.

This appendix covers the offer letter in detail, the specific mechanics of Indian compensation structures that routinely mislead candidates, and the negotiation conversation itself including scripts, timing, and what to do when you have a competing offer versus when you do not.

## Decoding the Offer Letter: What CTC Actually Means

The Cost to Company figure in an Indian offer letter represents the total cost the company incurs employing you, including components you will never see as spendable money, not your salary. Understanding the difference between CTC and take-home is the first skill in offer evaluation, and the gap is larger than most candidates expect.

### Components that inflate CTC without proportionally increasing take-home

Provident Fund employer contribution: typically 12 percent of basic salary. This goes into your PF account and is genuinely yours, but it is not spendable in the short term and is often omitted from mental calculations of actual income.

Gratuity: typically 4.8 percent of basic salary included in CTC calculations, but only payable after five continuous years of service. If you leave before five years, you receive nothing. A significant fraction of people who stay less than five years at a company are implicitly discounting money they listed in their CTC.

Variable pay: presented as part of CTC but subject to company performance, individual performance ratings, and manager discretion. At many Indian IT firms and GCCs, variable pay disbursement for average performers is 60 to 80 percent of the stated amount. For people on benches, on PIPs, or in restructuring scenarios, it is routinely zeroed. A CTC that is 20 percent variable pay is meaningfully different from a CTC where 80 percent is fixed, even if the headline number is identical.

Medical insurance: included at face value in some CTC disclosures even though it is a group policy with limited individual benefit.

Meal vouchers, transport allowance, LTA: genuine tax benefits, but often inflated in CTC comparisons between companies that handle them differently.

### The calculation that actually matters

Before accepting any offer, calculate your actual monthly in-hand. Take the fixed basic salary. Add fixed allowances (HRA, special allowance). Apply income tax at your slab (account for HRA exemption if you pay rent, and Section 80C investments you will actually make). Subtract your PF employee contribution (12 percent of basic). The result is your real monthly income. Compare this number across offers, not the CTC headline.

> *A common scenario: Offer A shows CTC of 30 LPA with 25 percent variable and modest basic. Offer B shows CTC of 28 LPA with no variable and higher basic. Offer B produces more in-hand every month and certainty of income. The candidate who compares only the headline chooses Offer A and is surprised every quarter when variable payout falls short of expectation.*

## ESOPs and Equity in Indian Startups

Employee Stock Ownership Plans are a significant component of compensation at many Indian startups and some product companies. They are also widely misunderstood, and the misunderstanding reliably advantages employers over employees.

The basics: you are granted options to buy shares at a strike price (the exercise price), typically the fair market value at the time of grant. These vest over a period, usually four years with a one-year cliff, meaning nothing vests until you have been at the company for a year, then 25 percent vests, then monthly or quarterly thereafter. When you exercise the option, you buy shares at the strike price. The gain is the difference between the strike price and the current fair market value.

The tax reality most employees do not know until they experience it: in India, you pay income tax at your marginal slab rate on the difference between the strike price and the fair market value at the moment of exercise, even if you cannot sell the shares yet (because the company is private and there is no market). This means you may owe lakhs of rupees in tax on paper gains that you cannot convert to cash until a liquidity event that may or may not happen.

The liquidity reality: most Indian startup ESOPs produce zero financial return. The company must either be acquired or IPO for the shares to become sellable. Of companies that issue ESOPs, a significant fraction are acquired at valuations below the strike price (making the options worthless), never reach a liquidity event, or produce terms in the acquisition that protect founders and lead investors while diluting employee option pools. ESOP as a real compensation component is statistically the exception, not the rule.

How to evaluate an ESOP offer: ask for the current strike price, the most recent 409A valuation (or equivalent fair market value determination), the total number of shares outstanding, and your grant as a percentage of fully diluted shares. Then apply significant discount: a 0.1 percent stake in a company with a current valuation of 100 crore is worth 10 lakh on paper, before tax, before dilution from future funding rounds, before the discount for illiquidity and uncertainty of a liquidity event. A reasonable working assumption for financial planning purposes is that startup ESOPs are worth zero until proven otherwise.

## Notice Period: the Negotiating Leverage Nobody Uses

Indian technology employment contracts typically specify notice periods of 30 to 90 days. The 90-day notice period has become standard at larger IT firms and GCCs. Far from a neutral operational requirement, this is a structural constraint that reduces employee bargaining power and, in practice, significantly limits the ability to move between employers.

What candidates do not negotiate: the notice period itself. In most cases, a notice period can be negotiated down at the time of offer, not after you have joined and signed the contract. A company that wants you will frequently agree to a shorter notice obligation, particularly for a senior role, because they are calibrating for future hiring flexibility as much as for your specific case. Ask. The worst answer is no.

Notice period buyout: many companies offer to buy out part of a candidate's notice period from a current employer. The new employer pays a sum equivalent to your current salary for the period being bought out, which you then use to compensate your current employer for the shortened notice. Not all companies offer this, but it is standard enough to be worth asking for explicitly, particularly for roles where the hiring manager has a specific start date in mind.

Garden leave: if your current employer asks you to serve full notice but places you on garden leave (paid but not working), treat this as personal time. You are entitled to the salary, your employment status continues, and you can use the period to prepare for the new role. Some employers use the garden leave period as a cooling-off mechanism for employees with access to sensitive information. The garden leave period does not reduce your notice obligation unless explicitly agreed otherwise.

## The Negotiation Conversation

Most Indian professionals are uncomfortable negotiating compensation. This discomfort is culturally real: in a professional context where gratitude for the offer is expected and pushing back can feel presumptuous, the negotiation conversation requires fighting against an instinct that has been reinforced by years of social conditioning.

The discomfort is understandable. The practical cost of not negotiating is high. A 10 percent increment on a base offer, compounded over three years at the same company, is a significant sum. The first year you leave on the table is not recovered later.

### The basic script, without a competing offer

Wait for the written offer before negotiating. Do not negotiate verbally in the final interview when numbers are first mentioned. Ask for the written offer, review it against your calculation of actual in-hand, and then respond.

A direct, professional response: 'Thank you for the offer. I have reviewed it carefully and I am very interested in the role. Based on the market for this skill set in Bengaluru and my specific experience with [name one or two relevant areas], I was hoping we could get closer to [specific number]. Is there flexibility on the base?' Name a number. Do not give a range. Giving a range means the company hears the bottom number.

What to do if they say the offer is fixed: ask whether there is flexibility on the joining bonus, the variable pay structure, the start date for salary review, or the notice period buyout. These are often more flexible than base salary, particularly at companies with rigid salary bands. A joining bonus is a one-time cost to the company; a base increase is a permanent commitment. Companies often have more room on the former.

### The script, with a competing offer

A competing offer is leverage. Use it directly but professionally: 'I want to be transparent with you. I have received an offer from another company at [number]. My preference is to join your team, because [genuine reason: specific about the role, the team, the problem]. Is there anything you can do to reduce the gap?'

Two rules for using a competing offer. First, it must be real. Using a fictional offer that gets called is worse than negotiating without one. Second, be prepared to walk away if the gap is not bridgeable, or to accept the original offer if the preference for the role genuinely outweighs the compensation difference. Negotiating with a competing offer and then not acting on it when the offer is not matched signals either bluffing or poor decision-making, neither of which helps the new employment relationship.

### Justifications to Recognise During the HR or Manager Round

The final stage before an offer, sometimes called the HR round or the manager round, is where compensation gets discussed in person rather than through a portal. It is also where a few standard scripts show up, often enough across companies that they are worth naming in advance.

The first is highlighting the CTC number while pushing a large share of it into variable pay. A stated CTC of 25 LPA sounds attractive; a CTC that is 30 percent variable, dependent on ratings you do not control yet, sounds different once you say it back in those terms. Before agreeing to a heavier variable component, ask directly what the actual payout percentage has been for the team over the last two review cycles, not the target figure.

The second is the comparison to an unnamed average: "this is more than what most people at this level get," or "our average tenure here is 20 years, people stay a long time." Neither claim is verifiable in the room, and neither addresses whether the number reflects your market value, your specific skills, or the specific role you are being hired for. A tenure claim describes a different generation of the Indian IT industry and is not evidence about your situation.

The general principle: come into this round with your own justification prepared, not just a number. State it in terms of what you specifically bring, the market rate for that combination of skills in your city (Appendix C has current benchmarks), and any competing signal you have. A number without a reason invites a counter-number. A number with a specific reason is harder to negotiate against, because it requires the other side to argue with the reason, not just the figure.

## The Background Verification Stage

After you accept an offer, most companies run a background verification check before your final joining date. This typically covers employment history, education credentials, and sometimes criminal record and address verification, carried out by a third-party BGV agency on the company's behalf.

Two areas are worth knowing about in advance.

The first is EPFO access. Some verification processes ask you to log into the EPFO portal, or a UAN-linked service, to confirm your employment history, since your PF contributions record which employers you have worked for and when. Logging in yourself and sharing what the portal shows is different from handing over your login credentials or a screenshot that exposes more than employment dates, such as your PF balance or other personal details unrelated to the check. You are entitled to share only what is relevant to the verification being run, and a request that goes beyond employment history is worth pushing back on or asking the agency to clarify in writing.

The second is moonlighting checks. Several large IT employers have become more attentive to whether a candidate held a second undisclosed job, particularly around the pandemic-era remote work period. Where this comes up, some verification processes ask for Form 26AS, the tax credit statement showing salary TDS from every employer that deducted tax against your PAN in a financial year, as evidence of a single declared income source. If your 26AS shows one employer per year, this step is usually a formality. If you did hold overlapping employment at any point, understand that 26AS is a definitive record of who paid you and when, and factor that into your decisions before the verification stage, not during it.

### Red flags in offer letters

Non-compete clauses: Indian courts have consistently held broad post-employment non-compete clauses to be unenforceable. A clause that says you cannot work in AI for two years after leaving is legally near-meaningless. However, clauses that protect specific clients (non-solicitation) or specific confidential information are enforceable and worth reading carefully.

IP assignment clauses: most employment contracts assign to the employer all intellectual property created during employment, including work done on personal time with personal equipment if it relates to the company's business. Before joining, ask for clarity on whether side projects or open-source contributions in adjacent areas require disclosure or approval. Get the answer in writing. Many companies are reasonable about this; the ones that are not reveal something about how they regard employee autonomy.

Training bond clauses: some companies include clauses requiring you to repay training costs if you leave within a specified period. These are enforceable in India. Understand the amount and the duration before signing.

Bench clauses: in some IT services contracts, the employer reserves the right to reduce or eliminate pay during bench periods. This should be explicitly negotiated before joining, particularly for consulting or services roles where bench periods are common.

# Appendix A: AI Skills Map

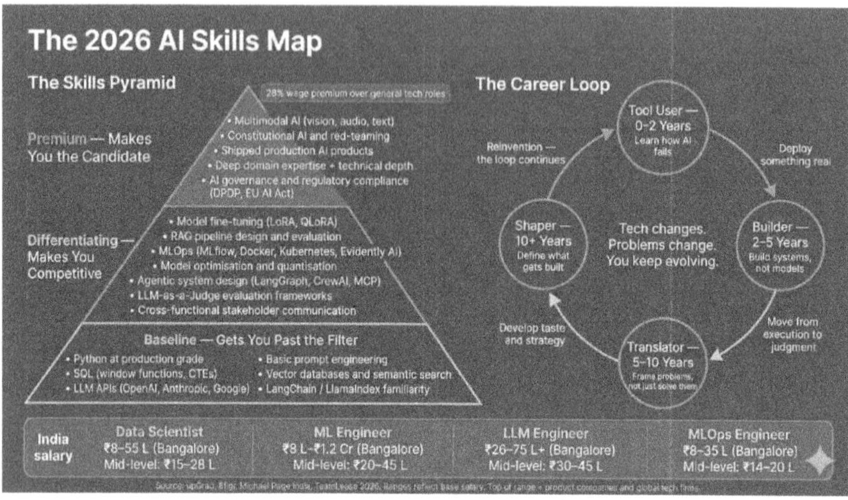

# Appendix B: Resources by Career Phase

### *What to Read, Watch, and Build at Each Stage of the Loop*

A note on how to use this appendix. The resources listed here are selected for practical utility at each phase, not comprehensiveness. The internet contains more AI learning material than any person can consume in a lifetime. The constraint is not access to resources, it is choosing the right ones at the right time and applying them to real problems rather than collecting them.

Every resource listed here passes the hype filter from Chapter 5: it appears in actual hiring contexts, it addresses production realities rather than tutorial scenarios, and it has demonstrated staying power rather than being tied to a single framework release. Where tools and frameworks have changed since a resource was written, the foundational thinking remains applicable even if the specific syntax has moved on.

## Phase 1: The Tool User (0–2 Years)

The goal at this phase: Build genuine foundations. Deploy one real thing. Understand how AI fails, not just how it works.

### Core technical learning

*Hands-On Machine Learning with Scikit-Learn, Keras, and TensorFlow* by Aurélien Géron, the clearest path from ML concepts to working code. Read this before you take any online course. The 2026 editions have shifted focus toward PyTorch and the Hugging Face ecosystem.

*fast.ai courses* (fast.ai), the gold standard for top-down practical learning. You build before you fully understand, which is uncomfortable and effective. Free.

*Python for Data Analysis* by Wes McKinney, pandas from the person who built it. Essential if your Python data manipulation is not yet fluent.

*Introduction to Probability* by Blitzstein and Hwang, available free online. The most readable probability textbook for working practitioners. Build this foundation in Phase 1, not Phase 3 when you need it in an interview.

3Blue1Brown's *Essence of Linear Algebra* and *Neural Networks* series on YouTube, visual, intuitive, free. Watch these before reading technical papers about attention mechanisms.

### Platforms for practice

Kaggle, competitions for model-building practice, notebooks for learning from others' approaches. Do not treat winning as the goal. Treat understanding what the top solutions did and why as the goal.

LeetCode, algorithmic coding practice. Aim for comfortable fluency with medium-difficulty problems in Python. Do this consistently rather than in a pre-interview panic.

roadmap.sh/ai-data-scientist, a visual map of the skill ecosystem that helps you understand what is adjacent to what you currently know.

### First deployment

FastAPI documentation (fastapi.tiangolo.com), the cleanest path to a deployed ML API endpoint. Read the tutorial section, build the project from Chapter 5.

Docker Getting Started guide (docs.docker.com), understand containers before you need them in an interview.

One cloud platform free tier, AWS, GCP, or Azure. Pick one. Deploy your first project on it before you finish Phase 1.

**India-specific communities**

Analytics Vidhya (analyticsvidhya.com), the largest Indian data science community. Forums, competitions, and learning resources with an Indian audience context.

Kaggle India community, active on LinkedIn and in regional meetups.

DataHack Summit (organised by Analytics Vidhya), the largest data science conference in India. Attend if you can; watch recorded sessions if you cannot.

NASSCOM AI community, relevant particularly for understanding the GCC and enterprise AI context.

Bengaluru, Hyderabad, Pune, and Chennai all have active data science and AI meetup groups on Meetup.com and LinkedIn. Attending one meetup per month in Phase 1 is more valuable than completing one additional certification.

## Phase 2: The Builder (2–5 Years)

The goal at this phase: Move from notebooks to systems. Learn MLOps seriously. Build something that runs in production and stays running.

**Core technical learning**

*Designing Machine Learning Systems* by Chip Huyen, the essential Phase 2 book. It teaches you to stop thinking about models and start thinking about data loops, monitoring, and real-world reliability. Read this before you call yourself an ML engineer.

*Made With ML* (madewithml.com), a project-based curriculum covering the full ML lifecycle from data engineering to deployment and testing. Fills the gap between knowing ML and knowing how to ship ML.

*Building LLM Apps* by various authors on the Hugging Face blog and LangChain documentation, the practical documentation for RAG pipeline implementation is better than most books on the subject. Read the official documentation rather than tutorials that may already be outdated.

Andrej Karpathy's *Neural Networks: Zero to Hero* series on YouTube, the clearest explanation of how transformers actually work, built from first principles. Watch this in Phase 2 when you have enough context to appreciate what is being explained.

### MLOps tooling

MLflow documentation (mlflow.org), start here for experiment tracking. The official documentation is genuinely well-written.

Evidently AI documentation (evidentlyai.com), the clearest introduction to model monitoring and drift detection.

Made With ML's MLOps course, project-based, covers the full pipeline from data to deployment to monitoring.

The Full Stack Deep Learning course (fullstackdeeplearning.com), covers the production engineering aspects that most ML courses skip.

### Agentic systems

LangChain documentation and LangGraph documentation, read the source documentation rather than third-party tutorials, which age quickly.

*Agentic AI, explained*, MIT Sloan Management Review, 2026. The clearest non-technical explanation of what agentic systems actually are and why they matter.

The Model Context Protocol documentation (modelcontextprotocol.io), understanding MCP is becoming a Phase 2 requirement. Read the specification.

### India-specific

iMocha AI Skills Report India, annual survey of AI skills demand in the Indian market. Useful for understanding which specific skills are being asked for in Indian JDs.

NASSCOM AI Adoption Index, published annually. Cuts through some of the narrative to provide actual adoption data by sector and organisation type.

AI4Bharat (ai4bharat.org), the primary research initiative for Indic language AI. Relevant if you are interested in the domestic AI opportunity described in Chapter 3. Their models and datasets are publicly available.

## Phase 3: The Translator (5–10 Years)

The goal at this phase: Develop problem framing and communication skills. Build domain depth. Learn to make and defend technical decisions in business terms.

### Core thinking

*Thinking in Systems* by Donella Meadows, not an AI book. The clearest introduction to systems thinking available. Phase 3 work is fundamentally systems work, and this book provides the vocabulary for it.

*The Crux* by Richard Rumelt, on strategy and problem diagnosis. The core skill of Phase 3 is identifying what the actual problem is rather than what presents as the problem. This book teaches that skill explicitly.

*Prediction Machines* by Ajay Agrawal, Joshua Gans, and Avi Goldfarb, the clearest economic framework for thinking about what

AI actually does and where it creates value. Essential for the build-versus-buy conversations that Phase 3 professionals are expected to lead.

*Working in Public* by Nadia Eghbal, about open source but more broadly about building a public technical presence. Relevant for the building-in-public practices described in Chapter 12.

### AI frontier

Anthropic's research blog, OpenAI's research blog, Google DeepMind's research blog, read at least one of these regularly. Not every paper, but the major releases and the explanatory posts about what is changing and why.

arXiv.org cs.LG (Machine Learning) and cs.CL (Computation and Language), the primary venue for AI research. You do not need to read every paper. Learn to read abstracts efficiently and identify the five to ten papers per quarter that are worth reading in full.

Papers With Code (paperswithcode.com), connects papers to implementations. Useful for understanding what is actually being used in production versus what is only in research.

### Domain depth

At Phase 3, the most important resources are domain-specific rather than AI-specific. If you are working in fintech, read the RBI's fintech regulatory framework and SEBI's guidelines on algorithmic trading. If you are in healthcare, read the National Digital Health Mission documentation and the DPDP Act's specific provisions for health data. If you are in agriculture, read ICAR's research on precision agriculture in Indian conditions.

The AI knowledge is table stakes at Phase 3. The domain knowledge is what differentiates you.

### India-specific

The DPDP Act full text and the draft regulations, if you are working on any system that processes Indian personal data, you need to understand this directly, not through summaries.

iSpirt (ispirt.in), the software product industry think tank for India. Publishes policy analysis and industry research that is more honest about the Indian technology sector's actual state than NASSCOM communications.

The Ken (the-ken.com), the best Indian technology journalism. Paywalled but worth it for Phase 3 professionals who need accurate information about what is actually happening in the Indian tech sector beyond the press releases.

## Phase 4: The Shaper (10+ Years)

The goal at this phase: Develop taste. Build institutional knowledge. Mentor. Think about legacy.

### Core thinking

*The Innovator's Dilemma* by Clayton Christensen, still the clearest framework for understanding why established organisations struggle to respond to disruptive technology. Relevant for understanding both the GCC sector's structural challenge and your own organisation's response to the current AI wave.

*An Elegant Puzzle* by Will Larson, on engineering management. The most practical book available on building and leading technical teams. Phase 4 professionals are building organisations, not just systems.

*Thinking, Fast and Slow* by Daniel Kahneman, the research foundation for understanding human decision-making under uncertainty. Phase 4 work involves making decisions about AI systems that affect human decisions. Understanding the psychology of decision-making is directly relevant.

*The Manager's Path* by Camille Fournier, the clearest guide to the IC-to-management transition and the specific challenges of managing technical teams.

## AI governance and ethics

The EU AI Act full text, the most consequential AI regulation currently in force. Even if you are working primarily in India, the systems you build will encounter this regulation if they touch European users or are deployed by European companies.

NIST AI Risk Management Framework (nist.gov/aiRMF), the American standard for AI risk management, widely referenced in enterprise contexts globally.

ISO/IEC 42001, the international standard for AI management systems. Becoming a baseline requirement in regulated industries.

AI Now Institute annual reports (ainowinstitute.org), the most rigorous academic analysis of AI's social and institutional impacts. Phase 4 professionals making consequential decisions about AI deployment should be reading this.

## India-specific

MeitY (Ministry of Electronics and Information Technology) publications on AI policy, India's AI governance framework is developing rapidly. Phase 4 professionals in India need to track this directly.

NITI Aayog's National Strategy for Artificial Intelligence, the foundational document for India's AI policy direction. Read the original, not summaries.

Indian Journal of Artificial Intelligence and Statistics (emerging publication venue), for Phase 4 professionals who want to contribute to the domestic research conversation rather than just consume it.

## Across All Phases: Communities Worth Being Part Of

### Online

Hugging Face community (huggingface.co/spaces), the most active practical AI development community globally. Build in public here.

LessWrong (lesswrong.com), the best community for thinking carefully about AI alignment and the longer-term implications of the technology. Not directly career-relevant but important for Phase 3 and 4 professionals who want to think seriously about what they are building.

LinkedIn, in the Indian market, LinkedIn is still the most professionally consequential platform. Post one piece of original thinking per month at minimum.

Medium / Substack, for longer-form writing. Analytics Vidhya's Medium publication remains the largest Indian data science writing community.

### In-person (India)

Bengaluru: BangPypers (Python community), Bengaluru Data Science meetup, FOSS United Bengaluru.

Hyderabad: Hyderabad Data Science meetup, PyData Hyderabad.

Pune: Pune Data Science meetup, NASSCOM AI community Pune chapter.

Chennai: Chennai Data Science meetup, iSPIRT Chennai community.

Pan-India: DataHack Summit (Analytics Vidhya), NASSCOM AI + Data Science Forum, PyData India conference.

Attending one in-person community event per month, at whatever phase you are at, produces more career-relevant connections than an equivalent time spent on online courses. The Indian AI community is smaller than it appears from the outside and more interconnected than it appears from the inside.

# Appendix C: Salary Benchmarks for AI Roles in India, 2026

## A Note on These Figures

The ranges in this appendix are drawn from multiple sources: Michael Page India's 2026 Salary Guide, TeamLease EdTech's Career Outlook Report (Jan–June 2026), upGrad's salary surveys, IIT Kharagpur's industry compensation data, Intellipaat, and 6figr. A note on sources: 6figr is a user-submitted platform whose figures skew toward self-reported high earners and should be read as upper-bound indicators rather than market averages. Michael Page and TeamLease figures are based on employer surveys and recruiter data and are the most reliable indicators of what companies are actually offering. All sources were accessed in 2026. Where sources conflicted, the more conservative figure was used as the midpoint. The figures represent the market across the four primary technology clusters, Bangalore, Hyderabad, Pune, and Chennai, and should be read as ranges rather than precise figures.

A few important qualifications before you use these numbers.

The top of any range reflects product companies, high-growth startups, and global tech firms with significant India presence. The bottom of the range more accurately represents service companies, smaller GCCs, and organisations new to AI hiring. Most people reading this book will find their current or target compensation somewhere in the middle of each band, not at the ceiling.

Bangalore commands a consistent premium of 25–30 percent above the national average across all roles. Hyderabad is close behind, typically 15–20 percent above average. Pune and Chennai are more moderate, though both offer meaningfully lower costs of living that partially offset the salary differential.

These figures cover base salary only unless otherwise noted. Total compensation at senior levels often includes signing bonuses of ₹5–15 lakh (most common in Bangalore and Hyderabad for GenAI specialists), ESOPs or RSUs that can constitute 30–50 percent of total compensation at unicorns and global tech firms, and performance multipliers that further widen the gap between the stated range and what top performers actually take home.

One macro figure worth keeping in mind: AI-focused roles command a wage premium of approximately 28–30 percent over equivalent general technology roles. This premium is real and it is scarcity-driven, the talent gap in AI is estimated at 50–55 percent of demand, meaning qualified people are consistently being hired before the market has time to equilibrate. That gap will narrow over the next three to five years as education catches up. The premium is highest now and will compress over time, which is one of several reasons why building differentiated skills matters more than chasing the current peak salary for a role that is becoming commoditised.

## Master Salary Table: AI Roles by City and Experience (2026)

All figures in Lakhs Per Annum (LPA). Ranges reflect base salary. Total compensation at senior levels can be 30–60 percent higher when equity and bonuses are included.

### Data Scientist

| Experience Band | Bangalore | Hyderabad | Pune | Chennai |
|---|---|---|---|---|
| Entry (0–2 years) | ₹8–15 L | ₹7–14 L | ₹6–12 L | ₹6–12 L |
| Mid-Level (2–5 years) | ₹15–28 L | ₹14–26 L | ₹12–24 L | ₹12–22 L |
| Senior (5–10 years) | ₹28–55 L | ₹26–50 L | ₹24–45 L | ₹22–42 L |
| City Average | ₹15.7 L | ₹15.2 L | ₹14.2 L | ₹14.6 L |

Domain matters significantly here. Data Scientists in Software Products (average ₹16.9 L) and Financial Services (average ₹16.7 L) consistently earn more than those in consulting or traditional manufacturing. Principal Data Scientists at Tier-1 product companies can reach ₹96 L at the upper end of the senior band.

### Machine Learning Engineer

| Experience Band | Bangalore | Hyderabad | Pune | Chennai |
|---|---|---|---|---|
| Entry (0–2 years) | ₹8–12 L | ₹7–11 L | ₹6–10 L | ₹6–9 L |
| Mid-Level (2–8 years) | ₹20–45 L | ₹18–40 L | ₹16–36 L | ₹14–32 L |

| Experience Band | Bangalore | Hyderabad | Pune | Chennai |
|---|---|---|---|---|
| Senior (8+ years) | ₹45 L–₹1.2 Cr | ₹40 L–₹1 Cr | ₹36–88 L | ₹32–80 L |
| City Average | ₹19–22 L | ₹18–20.4 L | ₹17.4–19.2 L | ₹13.8–15.2 L |

ML Engineers command a 20–30 percent premium over standard software engineering roles at equivalent experience levels. GenAI specialisation within ML engineering frequently attracts signing bonuses of ₹5–15 L in Bangalore and Hyderabad. The mid-level band shows the steepest salary growth of any role type, a reflection of how scarce production-grade ML experience remains.

### LLM Engineer / GenAI Specialist

| Experience Band | Bangalore | Hyderabad | Pune | Chennai |
|---|---|---|---|---|
| Junior (1–3 years) | ₹26–36 L | ₹25–37 L | ₹22–32 L | ₹20–30 L |
| Mid-Level (3–6 years) | ₹30–45 L | ₹28–42 L | ₹25–38 L | ₹22–35 L |
| Senior (6+ years) | ₹45–75 L+ | ₹40–70 L+ | ₹35–65 L | ₹32–60 L |

LLM Engineers earn a 30–40 percent premium over traditional ML roles, reflecting the current scarcity of professionals who can build, fine-tune, and deploy production LLM systems reliably. LLM fine-tuning specialists, those with hands-on RLHF, LoRA, and QLoRA experience, command an additional 45–65 percent premium over base AI salaries. Staff or Principal AI Engineers with 10+ years focused on LLMs and distributed AI systems can exceed ₹1 crore in total compensation at top-tier firms.

Note that the junior range here reflects product companies and AI-first startups. The same role title at a service company or traditional GCC will sit significantly lower, often in the ₹12–18 L range for 1–3 years of experience. The LLM Engineer title is being applied inconsistently across the market, use the context density checklist from Chapter 8 to evaluate whether the role involves genuine LLM engineering or API integration dressed in current terminology.

### MLOps Engineer

| Experience Band | Bangalore | Hyderabad | Pune | Chennai |
|---|---|---|---|---|
| Entry (0–2 years) | ₹8–12 L | ₹7–11 L | ₹6–9 L | ₹6–9 L |
| Mid-Level (2–5 years) | ₹14–20 L | ₹13–18 L | ₹10–15 L | ₹9–14 L |
| Senior (5+ years) | ₹14–35 L+ | ₹12–30 L+ | ₹11–25 L | ₹11–22 L |
| City Average | ₹14–20 L | ₹13–18 L | ₹10–15 L | ₹9–14 L |

MLOps salaries are rising faster than traditional DevOps equivalents. The skill combination that commands the strongest premium is cloud platform depth (AWS, GCP, or Azure) combined with Kubernetes, Docker, MLflow, and model drift monitoring. Adding each of these competencies to a base software engineering profile produces measurable salary jumps, from a starting point of ₹6 L for a Python-only fresher to ₹10–12 L in Bangalore or Hyderabad with cloud, Docker, and MLflow competence demonstrated through deployed projects.

## Emerging and Specialised Roles

| Role | Salary Range (India, 2026) | Notes |
|---|---|---|
| Agentic AI Engineer / Lead | ₹30–55 L (mid); ₹55–90 L+ (senior), extrapolated from posted JD ranges; verified data sparse given role's novelty | Fastest-growing category; significant supply shortage |
| AI Product Manager | ₹10–20 L (entry); ₹20–45 L (senior) | Highest-paying accessible non-engineering AI role |
| AI Governance / Safety Researcher | ₹30–80 L | Growing with regulatory pressure; DPDP Act driving Indian demand |
| Prompt Engineer | ₹4–8 L (entry); ₹14–35 L (experienced) | Premium has compressed significantly since 2024 peak |

| Role | Salary Range (India, 2026) | Notes |
|---|---|---|
| AI Solutions Architect | ₹35–70 L | Bridge between technical depth and client-facing work |
| Analytics Head / AI Director | ₹40–66 L base; ₹60 L–₹1.5 Cr total comp | Leadership premium; equity-heavy at this level |

The Prompt Engineer row is worth pausing on. In 2024 this role was attracting salaries that bore no relationship to the underlying skill requirement. By 2026 the market has corrected substantially, and standalone prompt engineering without broader LLM system design skills sits at the lower end of the AI salary distribution. This is the clearest example in the current market of a skill moving from differentiating to baseline, and then below baseline, within a two-year window.

## The GCC vs Product Company vs Startup Differential

The tables above reflect the overall market. The type of organisation you join produces systematic adjustments to these ranges that are worth understanding explicitly.

**GCC environments** typically sit 15–25 percent below the ranges above for equivalent role titles (based on recruiter data from Michael Page India and TeamLease 2026, corroborated by the EY GCC Pulse Report's finding that GCC average increments run at 10.4 percent annually, roughly a third of the 30 percent available through external job changes). As discussed in Chapter 8, the compensation gap between staying in a GCC and moving to a product company compounds significantly over five to seven years.

A professional who stays in the same GCC for seven years while their peers move to product companies at each market cycle will find themselves 40–60 percent below market rate for their experience level, with a title that no longer accurately reflects what the market is paying for that work.

**Product companies** (Indian unicorns, mid-market SaaS firms, domestic tech companies) generally sit within the ranges above, with equity components that can meaningfully increase total compensation at senior levels.

**Global tech firms** (Google, Microsoft, Amazon, Meta India operations) sit at or above the top of each range, with RSU packages that often double the base salary figure over a four-year vesting cycle. These are the roles driving the upper bounds in the tables.

**Early-stage startups** are the most variable. Cash compensation can be at or below market rate; the equity upside is where the potential lies, and it is genuinely uncertain. Joining a Series A startup at 20 percent below market rate with meaningful ESOP allocation is a reasonable bet for someone with high risk tolerance and five to seven years of experience. Joining at pre-seed for any title below founding team level is usually a poor trade unless the equity allocation is exceptional.

## The Tiered Entry System

For those entering the market or making a first transition into AI roles, the 2026 market has developed a visible tiered structure that determines starting compensation more than credentials alone.

**High-value entry (₹8–20 L):** Reserved for candidates from Tier-1 institutions or those with exceptional portfolios of production-grade AI work, deployed RAG systems, agentic workflows, documented MLOps implementations. The portfolio matters more than the institution for candidates from Tier-2 colleges.

**Standard entry (₹4–8 L):** Common for candidates entering IT service firms with solid coding skills and working knowledge of ML frameworks. This band has strong growth potential but requires deliberate skill-building and portfolio development to escape within two to three years.

**Stagnant entry (₹3–4 L):** Generic IT roles without AI specialisation. Salary growth in this band has largely flatlined. The cost of staying in this band for more than two years is significant, not just in current compensation but in the compounding effect on where you are positioned at Year 5.

The investment required to move from standard entry to high-value entry is a deployed project, not a credential. One well-documented production-grade AI project, built with current tools, applied to a real problem, hosted publicly, explained clearly in an interview, moves a candidate from the standard band to the high-value band more reliably than any certification.

## Interpreting These Numbers for Your Situation

A few principles for using this data practically rather than anxiously.

The 30 percent job-switching premium is real and persistent, but it compounds differently depending on where you start. Moving from ₹12 L to ₹15.6 L is a meaningful increment. Moving from ₹35 L to ₹45.5 L at the same percentage is life-changing. The premium rewards those who have already built differentiated skills, which is another way of saying that the time to build those skills is before you need them for a negotiation.

The salary figure you should actually be optimising for is not your next offer but your offer in five years. A role at ₹18 L that involves genuine production ML work, real ownership, and regular exposure to difficult problems will produce a five-year trajectory that a role at ₹22 L doing well-defined execution work will not. This is the salary number game discussed in Chapter 12, looking at the next increment rather than the compounding arc.

The gender pay gap documented in this data, women earning approximately ₹74–81 for every ₹100 earned by men in equivalent Data Science roles, traces back to the same structural factors that the rest of this book describes: credential gatekeeping, informal network effects, and the concentration of high-context-density roles in hiring pipelines that remain less accessible to women. None of this is inevitable, but awareness of it is not sufficient to close it either; it is a prerequisite for negotiating against it.

Finally: these numbers will date. The specific figures here reflect the market in 2026. The structural relationships, the Bangalore premium, the GCC discount, the product company differential, the compounding effect of differentiated skills, are more durable than the specific rupee figures. Use the numbers for calibration and negotiation. Use the structural relationships for strategy.

# Appendix D: The Red Flag Checklist

## *Questions to Ask Before You Accept Any Role*

This checklist consolidates the interview questions and evaluation criteria from Chapters 7 and 8 into a single, usable tool. Use it before accepting any offer, GCC, product company, startup, or MNC.

The questions are organised by the failure mode or structural issue they are designed to surface. No single answer is definitive. The pattern of answers across multiple conversations with multiple people in the organisation is what tells you the truth.

Score each question on a simple scale: Green (answer is clear, specific, and reassuring), Amber (answer is vague or inconsistent with other signals), Red (answer is alarming or the question is avoided). Count your colours before you sign.

### On Expectations and Success Definition

"Can you describe the success metrics for a recent ML project in concrete, quantitative terms?"

Green: Specific numbers, specific timeframes, specific business outcomes. "We improved fraud detection precision from 0.71 to 0.84, which reduced manual review volume by 23 percent over six months."

Amber: General claims of improvement without specifics. "We significantly improved our model performance."

Red: Unable to name any metrics, or metrics are purely technical with no connection to business outcomes.

"What happens when a model's performance does not initially meet the target?"

Green: A clear process, debug the data, revisit the problem framing, adjust the timeline, communicate to stakeholders with evidence.

Amber: Vague reassurance that the team "iterates."

Red: Implication that the team would be blamed, or that the target would be quietly moved rather than acknowledged.

"What does the stakeholder expect from AI that AI cannot currently deliver?"

Green: A thoughtful answer that acknowledges the gap between hype and reality and describes how the team manages stakeholder expectations actively.

Amber: Claim that stakeholders are well-calibrated without specific evidence.

Red: Inability to name any gap, suggesting either that stakeholders are not consulted or that the interviewee is also operating under inflated expectations.

## On Team Qualification

"Who are the key people I would be working with on ML projects across data engineering, software engineering, and domain expertise?"

Green: Specific names or roles, clear description of how functions interact, evidence of genuine cross-functional collaboration.

Amber: Vague description of "a strong team" without specifics.

Red: The ML team appears to operate in isolation from data engineering and software engineering, or domain expertise is entirely absent.

"Has this team shipped production ML systems before? What does the path from model development to deployment actually look like?"

Green: A specific, detailed description of a past deployment, the technical steps, the timeline, what went wrong, how they handled it.

Amber: General claims of production experience without a specific example.

Red: "Production" means a notebook shared with stakeholders, or the team has never actually deployed anything to a live system.

"Who is the most senior ML person on the team, and what is their background?"

Green: A clear answer with a credible background, production experience, research depth, or both.

Amber: The most senior person is a generalist manager rather than a technical specialist.

Red: No clear answer, or the technical leadership is entirely remote and inaccessible to the Indian team.

## On Scope and Process

"How do you handle it when a stakeholder changes requirements midway through a project?"

Green: A specific process, sprint renegotiation, scope documentation, timeline adjustment communicated to all parties.

Amber: "We are agile" without specifics about what that means in practice.

Red: The team absorbs all requirement changes without negotiation, suggesting a culture of acceptance over delivery integrity.

"Can you describe a time when the scope of an ML project changed significantly after it started, and how the team responded?"

Green: A specific story with a specific outcome, including an honest account of what was hard.

Amber: A general claim that scope changes are managed well.

Red: The question is deflected, or the answer implies that the team simply worked harder rather than renegotiating the scope.

"What is the relationship between the Indian team's technical decisions and the requirements coming from headquarters or the client?"

Green: The Indian team has genuine input into requirements and can push back on technical decisions.

Amber: The Indian team implements requirements but can escalate concerns through a defined process.

Red: Requirements arrive as fixed specifications with no negotiation expected or possible.

## On Data

"What data does the team currently have access to, and what is the process for accessing additional data when needed?"

Green: Clear data governance, accessible pipelines, a defined process for data requests that takes weeks rather than months.

Amber: Data access is possible but slow and bureaucratic.

Red: The team cannot describe what data they have access to, or data access requires approval from a distant team with no defined timeline.

"How do you build evaluation datasets for LLM-based systems?"

Green: A specific process, human annotation, adversarial examples, domain expert review, ongoing expansion.

Amber: Reliance on automated metrics only, without human-curated evaluation sets.

Red: No evaluation datasets for LLM systems, or the team is relying on model self-evaluation without external ground truth.

"What happens when the model is deployed and its performance in production differs from its performance in evaluation?"

Green: A monitoring system that detects this automatically, a defined escalation process, a recent example of how it was handled.

Amber: The team monitors manually and responds to user complaints.

Red: The team does not monitor production performance, or "performance in production" is not a concept they have operationalised.

## On Trust and Adoption

"Can you describe an ML system that is actively being used by the people it was built for?"

Green: A specific system, specific users, specific evidence of adoption and impact.

Amber: Systems that have been "delivered" without clear evidence of adoption.

Red: The team can only describe systems that were built and handed over, with no information about whether they were used.

"How does the data science team interact with the business functions it supports?"

Green: Regular joint sessions, shared metrics, embedded team members, or frequent direct communication.

Amber: Periodic presentations to business stakeholders.

Red: The data science team works in isolation and delivers outputs without ongoing relationship with the functions they are serving.

## On Learning and Failure

"Can you describe a project that did not go as planned, and what the team learned from it?"

Green: A specific story, a specific failure mode, a specific learning, evidence that the learning was applied to subsequent work.

Amber: A general acknowledgement that projects sometimes face challenges.

Red: The question is deflected, or the answer implies that projects always go as planned, which means either that failure is not acknowledged or that the team is not doing work risky enough to fail.

"How does the team capture and share learnings from projects after they complete?"

Green: A defined retrospective process, documented learnings, evidence of learnings influencing future projects.

Amber: Informal knowledge sharing without structure.

Red: No retrospective process, or the culture makes acknowledging failure uncomfortable enough that learnings are not captured.

## On Maintenance and Long-Term Ownership

"Who is responsible for monitoring and maintaining production ML systems after they are deployed?"

Green: A named function or named person, a defined monitoring process, a clear escalation path.

Amber: Shared responsibility between the ML team and a DevOps or platform team without clear ownership.

Red: No clear owner, or maintenance is treated as someone else's problem once the model is deployed.

"How often are models retrained, and what triggers that decision?"

Green: A defined trigger, performance degradation below a threshold, data distribution shift above a threshold, or a scheduled retraining cycle, with evidence that it is actually followed.

Amber: Retraining happens when someone notices a problem.

Red: Models are not retrained, or the team does not know when the last retraining occurred.

## On Context Density (The GCC Trap Questions)

"Who makes the final call on system design decisions, the Indian team or a remote architecture function?"

Green: The Indian team owns architecture decisions, with remote review rather than remote approval.

Amber: Architecture decisions are made collaboratively with remote teams.

Red: All significant technical decisions require approval from a remote team, with the Indian team implementing rather than designing.

"Where does the product roadmap come from, and has the Indian team contributed to or challenged it?"

Green: The Indian team has shaped the roadmap, with specific examples of local input changing the direction.

Amber: The Indian team is consulted on the roadmap.

Red: The roadmap arrives from headquarters as a fixed document.

"What does success look like at twelve months in this role, in concrete terms?"

Green: Specific, measurable outcomes that reflect genuine strategic contribution.

Amber: Vague references to impact or value creation.

Red: Success metrics are delivery-oriented, on time, on budget, tickets resolved, rather than outcome-oriented.

"Has anyone in the Indian team been promoted into a role with significantly broader scope in the last two years?"

Green: Yes, with a specific example.

Amber: Promotions happen but within the same scope level.

Red: No, or the question is deflected.

"Does the Indian team have the authority to push back on requirements from headquarters?"

Green: Yes, with a specific recent example.

Amber: There is a process for escalation but it is rarely used.

Red: Pushing back is not part of the culture, or the question seems surprising to the interviewer.

## Scoring Your Assessment

After completing interviews across multiple people in the organisation, count your colours.

Mostly green across the core questions, the role is likely what it claims to be. Proceed with confidence.

Mixed green and amber, the role has genuine strengths and real limitations. Make sure you understand which questions came back amber and whether those limitations are acceptable given what you are optimising for at your current phase.

Multiple reds in any single category, take this seriously. One red in the data section and one in the maintenance section, for example, suggests a team that has not thought carefully about the full ML lifecycle and will produce the failure modes described in Chapter 7.

Reds in the context density questions, use the analysis from Chapter 8 to think carefully about whether this role will develop you or merely employ you. The compensation may be good. The learning may not be. Over a five-year horizon, that trade compounds in ways that are difficult to reverse.

Any question that the interviewer found surprising or seemed unprepared for, note this. An organisation where experienced ML professionals have never been asked about evaluation datasets or model drift monitoring is an organisation that has not yet built the habits of production ML work. You will be working inside that absence.

# Appendix E: Sources and Further Reading

This appendix attributes the key statistics and claims that appear throughout the book, and lists further reading organised by chapter. The book is trade nonfiction, not an academic monograph, so sources are presented accessibly rather than in citation format. Where data was contested or uncertain, the text notes this explicitly.

**Key Statistics: Sources**

AI job postings doubled from 2.9% to 6.5% of all Indian vacancies (2023–2025): PIB / AI@Work report, India Ministry of Labour data, 2025.

India ranks third in global AI vibrancy index: Stanford HAI AI Index Report 2025.

India GenAI market USD 1.5 billion (2025), projected USD 6.2 billion by 2034: India Generative AI Market Outlook 2026–2034, OpenPR / market research aggregators, 2026.

87% of Indian enterprises using AI in at least one function: EY Work Reimagined Survey 2025, India chapter.

14% average productivity boost from GenAI; 34% for novice workers: Brookings Institution, AI Growth Acceleration versus Distributional Fairness, 2025.

19% increase in completion times for experienced developers on complex tasks when using AI tools: Cited in Brookings Institution analysis of AI productivity research, 2025. The specific finding is from controlled trials on senior developer workflows; the effect varies by task complexity and is not universal.

Geographic AI job posting concentration (Bangalore 11%, Hyderabad 9.57%, Pune 6.95%, Chennai 6.62%): PIB / AI@Work India report, 2025.

28% wage premium for AI roles over general tech roles: PIB / AI@Work India report, 2025. The 12% premium figure for general digital skills is from the same source.

AI talent gap estimated at 50–55% of demand: NASSCOM AI Talent Report 2025; corroborated by TeamLease EdTech Career Outlook Report, Jan–June 2026.

18% of GCCs at transformation hub status; 44% portfolio hubs; 25% satellite units: Zinnov Five-Year GCC Landscape Report, 2024.

58% of GCCs investing in agentic AI; 83% scaling GenAI projects: EY GCC Pulse Report, 2025.

GCC sector: 1.9 million professionals, USD 64.6 billion revenue (FY2024): NASSCOM GCC Annual Report 2024.

GCC average increment 10.4% annually: EY GCC Pulse Report 2025.

Indian IT firms reduced more positions in Q1 2026 than all of 2025: Economic Times, April 2026; Business Today, April 2026; CNBC India, August 2025. Note: aggregate figures are based on news reporting and industry estimates, not a single authoritative dataset.

India PIP termination rate 80–90% vs 30–50% in US/Europe: India Today, "When PIP turns into layoff: A corporate India reality check," 26 February 2026; Economic Times, "Got a PIP at work? Here's what it really means," 2026; HR Acuity / LeadDev, "The Relentless Rise of the PIP," 2024. Confidence rating: low-medium; no large-scale independent dataset exists. The figure is drawn from HR industry commentary and is presented as indicative.

50,000 Indian IT jobs at risk through silent layoff mechanisms (2024–25): Times of India, "Indian IT sector hit by silent layoffs: 50,000 people may lose jobs this year," 2025; Economic

Times/Medial, "Silent layoffs tighten grip in 2025: 50k tech jobs on the line," 2025; Business Standard/Xpheno, "Costly middle layer faces the axe amid IT sector layoff drill," August 2025.

7,700 senior professionals (15+ years) exited top 7 Indian IT firms in 12 months: Business Standard / Xpheno staffing firm data, 2024–25.

90% of caste-linked hiring disparities originate in subjective fit assessments: Shukla, "Making the Elite: Caste Discrimination in Elite Recruitment," Working Paper, 2024; corroborated by Deshmukh et al., "Caste affiliation and access to high-authority jobs in the Indian service sector," Journal of the Asia Pacific Economy, Vol.30 No.4, September 2024.

Women earn ₹74–81 per ₹100 earned by men in equivalent Data Science roles: 6figr salary database 2026; corroborated by TeamLease / Business Standard gender pay gap reporting.

Salary benchmarks (Appendix C): Michael Page India Salary Guide 2026; TeamLease EdTech Career Outlook Report, Jan–June 2026; upGrad salary surveys 2026; IIT Kharagpur industry compensation data; Intellipaat; 6figr (user-submitted, skews high, treated as upper-bound indicator). AI engineer salary, Intellipaat 2026; LLM engineer salary, upGrad 2026; MLOps salary, upGrad / Brolly AI 2026; Data Scientist salary, upGrad / 6figr 2026.

Technical skills obsolete within 18–24 months: TeamLease EdTech Career Outlook; corroborated by multiple industry survey sources. Presented as industry estimate rather than empirically validated finding.

50% of Indian tech professionals receiving AI training at work: Naukri.com blog, 2026.

## Further Reading by Chapter

### Chapters 1–3: The Landscape and the Indian IT Sector

NASSCOM GCC Annual Report 2024. The sector's own account of itself, useful for the official narrative, and for calibrating where the narrative diverges from the data.

Zinnov Five-Year GCC Landscape Report, 2024. The most rigorous public data on GCC configuration and innovation status.

EY GCC Pulse Report 2025. EY's annual survey of GCC investment priorities and capability.

Stanford HAI AI Index Report 2025. The most comprehensive annual survey of AI development globally, with India-specific data.

World Economic Forum Future of Jobs Report 2025. The global context for AI-era employment shifts.

The Ken (the-ken.com). The best independent journalism on the Indian technology sector. Paywalled; worth it.

### Chapters 4–5: The Career Loop and Skills

Huyen, Chip. Designing Machine Learning Systems. O'Reilly, 2022. The essential book for Phase 2 ML engineers. Teaches system thinking, not model thinking.

Géron, Aurélien. Hands-On Machine Learning with Scikit-Learn, Keras, and TensorFlow. O'Reilly, 2022/2025. The clearest practical guide from ML concepts to working code.

fast.ai courses (fast.ai). Top-down practical ML learning. Free. Still the gold standard for getting to working code quickly.

Roadmap.sh/ai-data-scientist. A visual, living map of the AI/ML skill ecosystem.

### Chapter 6: Psychological Pressures

Newport, Cal. So Good They Can't Ignore You. Grand Central Publishing, 2012. The best counter-argument to "follow your passion" career advice; relevant to the skill-building-over-credentialing argument.

Kahneman, Daniel. Thinking, Fast and Slow. Farrar, Straus and Giroux, 2011. The research foundation for understanding decision-making under uncertainty and cognitive bias.

## Chapters 7–8: Why Projects Fail and the GCC Trap

The following academic sources provide the theoretical foundation for Chapter 8's analysis of GCC structural dynamics: Birkinshaw, J., "Entrepreneurship in multinational corporations: The characteristics of subsidiary initiatives," Strategic Management Journal, Vol.18 No.3, 1997. Mudambi, R., "Hierarchy, coordination, and innovation in the multinational enterprise," Global Strategy Journal, Vol.1 No.3–4, 2011. Oliver Wyman and NASSCOM, "The Next Evolution of India's Global Capability Centers," 2025. IIM Bangalore Management Review / ScienceDirect, "Global Capability Centres: Emerging opportunities and challenges," 2025. Zinnov, "India GCC Landscape: The Five-Year Report," 2024.

Birkinshaw, Julian. Entrepreneurship in multinational corporations: The characteristics of subsidiary initiatives. Strategic Management Journal, 1997. One of the foundational papers on how subsidiaries can and cannot build strategic capacity.

Mudambi, Ram. Hierarchy, coordination, and innovation in the multinational enterprise. Global Strategy Journal, 2011. The fine-slicing framework that explains why GCCs tend toward execution.

Oliver Wyman and NASSCOM. The Next Evolution of India's Global Capability Centers, 2025. The most recent strategic analysis of GCC positioning.

## Chapter 11: If You Just Got Let Go

The following sources from published research and investigative journalism underpin Chapter 11's analysis of Indian tech exit practices: PeopleManager.co.in, "Forced Resignations in India's IT Sector: A Legal Blind Spot Demanding Urgent Reform," 2026. HR Acuity / LeadDev, "The Relentless Rise of the PIP," 2024. Primary data source for the 30% rise in US formal performance procedures (2020–2023). Sharma, V. et al., "Psychological impacts of AI-induced job displacement among Indian IT professionals: a Delphi-validated thematic analysis," International Journal of Qualitative Studies on Health and Well-being, Taylor & Francis / PMC, September 2025. Business Standard / Xpheno, "Costly middle layer faces the axe amid IT sector layoff drill," August 2025. Source for the 7,700 senior professionals statistic. Business Today, "Lock a job by 46 or risk forced retirement: HR insider reveals brutal hiring reality," 31 July 2025. Times of India, "Silent layoffs on the rise in Indian tech sector," 2026. ICLG, "Employment & Labour Laws and Regulations Report 2026: India," International Comparative Legal Guides, 2026. Source for the IDA wage ceiling and IRC 2020 analysis.

HR Acuity US Formal Performance Procedure Data, 2023. The primary source for the 30% rise in US performance procedures (2020–2023).

**Chapter 12: Playing the Long Game**

Meadows, Donella. Thinking in Systems. Chelsea Green, 2008. The clearest introduction to systems thinking available. Phase 3 work is fundamentally systems work.

Christensen, Clayton. The Innovator's Dilemma. Harvard Business Review Press, 1997. Still the clearest framework for understanding why established organisations struggle to respond to disruptive technology.

Agrawal, Ajay, Gans, Joshua, and Goldfarb, Avi. Prediction Machines. Harvard Business Review Press, 2018. The clearest economic framework for thinking about what AI actually does and where it creates value.

Larson, Camille. The Manager's Path. O'Reilly, 2017. The clearest guide to the IC-to-management transition and managing technical teams.

AI Now Institute Annual Reports (ainowinstitute.org). The most rigorous academic analysis of AI's social and institutional impacts. Phase 4 professionals making consequential decisions about AI deployment should be reading this.

# Appendix F: Glossary

Terms are grouped into two categories: concepts original to this book, and technical terms that non-specialist readers may encounter. Each definition is kept to two or three sentences.

## Concepts Original to This Book

Builder (Phase 2). The second phase of the AI career loop, covering roughly 2–5 years of experience. Characterised by the transition from individual model development to systems thinking: building pipelines, deploying to production, and handling reliability at scale.

Context density. The degree to which a role provides access to tacit organisational knowledge, decision-making authority, proximity to risk, and consequential outcomes. High context density roles develop judgment. Low context density roles develop execution speed. The distinction determines whether a role compounds your career or merely employs you.

Coordination-Context Gap. The distance between where strategic decisions are made (headquarters) and where the work is done (GCC or subsidiary). When this gap is wide, execution is efficient but innovation is structurally constrained, regardless of individual talent.

Execution layer. The portion of technology work that is well-defined, repetitive, bounded by clear requirements, and measurable against objective criteria. This is the layer most directly affected by AI automation. Contrast with the judgment layer.

Governance Debt. By analogy with technical debt: the accumulated cost of deferred governance reforms in a GCC or subsidiary that would be needed to enable genuine strategic innovation, but have been postponed in favour of near-term execution efficiency. Governance Debt compounds over time, making the gap between a

GCC's stated innovation mandate and its actual innovation output increasingly difficult to close.

Judgment layer. The portion of technology work that requires understanding of context, consequence, and human complexity: problem framing, stakeholder navigation, ethical assessment, domain synthesis, and systems thinking. This layer is not being automated by current AI tools and is becoming more valuable as the execution layer contracts.

Shaper (Phase 4). The fourth phase of the AI career loop, covering 10 or more years of experience. Characterised by strategy, taste, and institutional knowledge: deciding what gets built rather than how to build it.

Tool User (Phase 1). The first phase of the AI career loop, covering 0–2 years of experience. The phase in which the primary learning is not how AI works but how AI fails: messy data, broken assumptions, silent drift, the gap between notebook performance and production behaviour.

Translator (Phase 3). The third phase of the AI career loop, covering 5–10 years of experience. Characterised by problem framing, stakeholder communication, and the ability to decide what not to build. The transition from execution to judgment.

## Technical Terms

Agentic AI. AI systems capable of independent planning, tool usage, memory management, and cross-agent delegation to achieve complex goals. Distinguished from single-call prompt systems by their ability to reason across multiple steps, use external tools, and adapt when initial approaches fail.

Embedding model. A model that converts text, images, or other data into numerical vectors (lists of numbers) that capture semantic meaning. Embedding models are distinct from generative models: they do not produce text, they produce representations used for similarity search and retrieval.

Fine-tuning. The process of taking a pre-trained model and training it further on a specific dataset to adapt its behaviour to a particular task or domain. Contrast with RAG, which provides relevant information at inference time without changing the model's weights. Fine-tuning is more expensive and less flexible; RAG is more maintainable and usually preferred for enterprise applications.

Foundation model. A large AI model trained on broad data that can be adapted to many tasks. GPT-4, Claude, Gemini, and Llama are examples. Foundation models are the base on which most current AI applications are built, either through direct API access, fine-tuning, or RAG.

GCC (Global Capability Centre). The Indian arm of a multinational company, established to provide technology services, analytics, or engineering support. Originally created for cost arbitrage; increasingly positioned as innovation hubs, though the evidence for this transition is more limited than official communications suggest.

Hallucination. When an AI model produces confident-sounding output that is factually incorrect or fabricated. Hallucination is an inherent feature of current generative models, not a bug that will be fully eliminated. Managing hallucination, through RAG, evaluation frameworks, and human review, is a core skill of production AI work.

Inference. Running a trained model to produce predictions or outputs. Inference optimisation, making models run faster and cheaper in production, is a distinct engineering discipline from model training. Senior AI engineers are expected to understand inference costs and how to manage them.

LLM (Large Language Model). A neural network trained on large amounts of text data that can generate, summarise, translate, and reason about text. The technology underlying ChatGPT, Claude, Gemini, and most current AI applications.

LLM-as-a-Judge. An evaluation approach in which a language model is used to assess the quality of another model's outputs, scoring them for accuracy, relevance, and coherence. Used to automate evaluation at scale where human review of every output is impractical.

LLMOps. The operational discipline of managing large language model applications in production: prompt versioning, output monitoring, cost management, evaluation pipelines, and model updates. The LLM-specific extension of MLOps.

LoRA / QLoRA (Low-Rank Adaptation / Quantised Low-Rank Adaptation). Parameter-efficient fine-tuning techniques that adapt a model to a specific task without retraining all its weights, dramatically reducing the compute and memory required. The standard approach to fine-tuning when full retraining is impractical.

MCP (Model Context Protocol). An emerging standard for how AI agents securely access local data and tools. Enables agents to maintain memory and share information across multi-step workflows. Increasingly appearing in senior AI engineering job descriptions as a required familiarity.

MLOps (Machine Learning Operations). The engineering discipline of deploying, monitoring, and maintaining machine learning models in production. Covers experiment tracking, CI/CD pipelines for ML, model drift detection, retraining triggers, and infrastructure reliability. No longer a specialisation; a baseline expectation for production ML engineers in 2026.

Model drift. The degradation of a model's performance over time as the data it encounters in production diverges from the data it was trained on. A production ML system that is not monitored for drift will silently become less reliable. Detecting and responding to drift is a core MLOps responsibility.

Multimodal AI. AI systems that process and generate multiple types of input and output, text, images, audio, video, within a single model or pipeline. Increasingly standard for live-interaction products and a premium skill in the 2026 market.

Quantisation. A technique for reducing the precision of a model's numerical representations (from 32-bit to 16-bit or 8-bit floating point) to make it run faster and use less memory with minimal loss of accuracy. A key tool for making large models deployable on modest hardware or at lower cost.

RAG (Retrieval-Augmented Generation). A technique that improves LLM outputs by retrieving relevant information from an external knowledge base and providing it to the model at inference time, rather than relying solely on the model's training data. Reduces hallucination, keeps information current, and is usually preferable to fine-tuning for enterprise applications.

ReAct framework. A prompting and agent design pattern that combines reasoning (thinking through a problem step by step) with acting (taking actions using tools). Used in agentic AI systems to guide agents through multi-step tasks with explicit reasoning traces.

RLHF (Reinforcement Learning from Human Feedback). A training technique used to align language models with human preferences. Human raters score model outputs; these scores are used to train the model to produce outputs that humans find more helpful, accurate, and safe. The primary alignment technique used for most current frontier models.

Transformer. The neural network architecture underlying most current large language models. Introduced in the 2017 paper "Attention Is All You Need" by Vaswani et al. The key innovation is the attention mechanism, which allows the model to weigh the relevance of different parts of the input when producing each part of the output.

Vector database. A database designed to store and search vector embeddings efficiently. Used in RAG systems to retrieve the most semantically relevant documents for a given query. Common examples include Pinecone, Weaviate, ChromaDB, and FAISS.

# Appendix G: Interview Practice Questions

This appendix gives you concrete questions to practise across the seven main interview domains, along with sample answers and preparation hints. The answers are intentionally conversational rather than exhaustive: they show the kind of thinking and communication that impresses interviewers, not the kind of comprehensive coverage that belongs in a textbook.

Work through each section out loud. The difference between knowing an answer and being able to deliver it clearly under interview pressure is larger than most people expect.

## 1. Transformer Architecture

These questions appear in virtually every senior ML interview. You should be able to answer all of them without notes, including the mathematical intuition.

### Q1. Explain how attention works in a transformer. What are keys, queries, and values?

Sample answer: Attention is a mechanism for a model to decide which parts of the input to focus on when producing each part of the output. You have three learned projections of the input: queries represent what you are looking for, keys represent what each token offers, and values represent the actual content. You compute a dot product between a query and all keys, scale it by the square root of the key dimension to prevent vanishing gradients, apply softmax to get a probability distribution, then take a weighted sum of the values. The result is a context-aware representation of each token relative to every other token.

Hint: Practice drawing the attention mechanism from scratch on paper. If you cannot draw it, you do not know it well enough.

### Q2. Why do transformers need positional encodings?

Sample answer: The attention mechanism itself is permutation-invariant: if you shuffle the input tokens, the output is the same shuffle of the same vectors. This means the model has no inherent sense of order. Positional encodings inject sequence position information, either as fixed sinusoidal functions (the original paper) or as learned embeddings. Without them, the model cannot distinguish between the same words in different positions, which matters enormously for language.

Hint: Follow-up often asked: what are RoPE (rotary positional embeddings) and why do modern LLMs prefer them? Read the LLaMA or Mistral technical reports.

## Q3. What is multi-head attention and why is it useful?

Sample answer: Instead of computing attention once with the full key-query-value dimensions, multi-head attention projects into several smaller subspaces and runs attention in each independently, then concatenates the results. Each head can learn to attend to different kinds of relationships: one head might capture syntactic dependencies, another semantic similarity, another coreference. The parallel computation is efficient and the ensemble of perspectives gives richer representations than a single attention head.

Hint: Be ready to state the complexity: O(n squared d) where n is sequence length and d is model dimension. This is why long contexts are expensive, and why flash attention and sliding window attention exist.

## Q4. What happens in the feedforward sublayer of a transformer block?

Sample answer: After the attention sublayer (with residual connection and layer normalisation), each token passes through a two-layer feedforward network independently. The first layer expands the dimension, typically by a factor of four, applies a nonlinearity, and the second layer projects back. The feedforward layer is where the model stores factual knowledge and applies nonlinear transformations that attention alone cannot represent. It operates position-wise, meaning each token is processed identically and independently, unlike attention which mixes information across positions.

Hint: Know what SwiGLU and GeLU activations are: they appear in modern LLMs and interviewers at AI-product companies will ask about them.

### Q5. How does BERT differ from GPT architecturally, and why does it matter?

Sample answer: BERT is a bidirectional encoder: each token attends to all other tokens in both directions. It is trained with masked language modelling, predicting randomly masked tokens using the full context. GPT is an autoregressive decoder: each token can only attend to previous tokens (causal masking), and it is trained to predict the next token. BERT learns better representations for understanding tasks because it has access to full context. GPT learns to generate text because the causal constraint forces it to model distributions over sequences. Fine-tuned BERT dominated classification and NER tasks for years; GPT-family models dominate generation and few-shot prompting.

Hint: Interviewer follow-up: why can GPT do few-shot learning without fine-tuning? The answer is in-context learning, and it connects to how transformers store and retrieve patterns.

## 1a. Transformer Architecture: Deeper Questions

The following questions go beyond the basics covered above. They appear at Phase 3 and Phase 4 interviews at product companies and AI-first startups.

### Q6. Derive why the 1/sqrt(d_k) scaling factor is necessary. What happens to gradients if it is omitted?

Sample answer: When you compute the dot product Q times K-transpose, the expected magnitude of each element grows with the key dimension d_k. Specifically, if Q and K have zero-mean unit-variance entries, the dot product has variance d_k. For large d_k (say 512 or 1024), these values become very large before the softmax. The softmax function applied to large values saturates: it produces near-zero gradients for all but the single highest-scoring token, collapsing the attention distribution to a one-hot vector. This is the vanishing gradient problem in the attention layer specifically. Scaling by

1/sqrt(d_k) brings the variance of the dot products back to approximately 1, keeping the softmax in a region with useful gradient flow during backpropagation.

Hint: Interviewers who ask this are testing whether you know the mechanics rather than just the formula. Draw the softmax curve and show where saturation happens.

## Q7. Explain LoRA. What are the matrix dimensions involved and why does it save memory during training?

Sample answer: LoRA (Low-Rank Adaptation) is a parameter-efficient fine-tuning method. Instead of updating a weight matrix W of shape d by d during fine-tuning, you freeze W and add a low-rank update: delta-W equals A times B, where A is d by r and B is r by d, and r is much smaller than d (typically 4, 8, or 16). During the forward pass, the effective weight is W plus A times B. Only A and B are trained, reducing the number of trainable parameters from d-squared to 2 times d times r. Memory savings during training come from two sources: fewer parameters to store optimizer states for (Adam stores first and second moment estimates for each parameter, so this is a 2x multiplier on the parameter count savings), and not needing gradients for the frozen W. QLoRA extends this by also quantising W to 4-bit during training, further reducing the GPU memory required for the base model weights.

Hint: Follow-up: why is the update guaranteed to be low-rank? Because any rank-r matrix can be expressed as a product of two lower-dimensional matrices. The assumption is that the task-specific weight update lives in a low-dimensional subspace of the full parameter space.

## Q8. Explain greedy search, beam search, and top-p sampling. When would you use each?

Sample answer: Greedy search picks the highest-probability token at each step. It is fast and deterministic but tends toward repetitive, generic text because it never considers paths that start with a lower-probability token but lead to higher-probability sequences overall. Beam search maintains the k most likely partial sequences in parallel (k is the beam width), expanding each at every step and pruning to keep the top k. It produces better outputs than greedy for tasks with a clear correct answer (translation, summarisation) because it explores multiple paths. Top-p (nucleus) sampling is used for creative or diverse generation. At each step, you find the smallest set of tokens whose cumulative probability exceeds p (say 0.9), and sample uniformly from that set. This adapts the effective vocabulary size dynamically: at uncertain positions the set is large, at confident positions it is small. Temperature modulates the distribution before sampling: high temperature flattens it (more randomness), low temperature sharpens it (more determinism). For a factual QA system or structured output, use beam search or greedy. For a creative writing or dialogue system, use top-p with a moderate temperature.

Hint: Know that most production LLM APIs give you temperature and top_p as parameters. Understanding what they control is expected in any LLM engineering interview.

## Q9. How does BART differ from BERT and from GPT, and when would you choose an encoder-decoder model like BART or T5 over a decoder-only LLM?

Sample answer: BART is a denoising autoencoder combining a bidirectional encoder (like BERT) with an autoregressive decoder (like GPT), pretrained by corrupting text and learning to reconstruct it. BERT is encoder-only, suited to understanding tasks like classification, since it never learns to generate text autoregressively. GPT is decoder-only, suited to open-ended generation. Because BART's encoder processes the full input bidirectionally before generation starts, encoder-decoder models like BART or T5 tend to be more parameter-efficient than decoder-only LLMs for well-defined transformation tasks with a fixed input-output shape, summarisation, translation, structured extraction, and are often cheaper to serve in production once fine-tuned for one job. Decoder-only LLMs win when the task is open-ended, requires broad world knowledge and reasoning, or needs to handle varied instructions without task-specific fine-tuning.

Hint: The interviewer is testing whether you think in terms of encoder-only, decoder-only, and encoder-decoder as three points on a spectrum, each suited to a different task shape, rather than treating every model as a variant of GPT.

## Q10. Implement scaled dot-product attention and multi-head attention from scratch in PyTorch.

Sample answer: Build it in two pieces. Scaled dot-product attention computes attention weights from queries and keys, applies an optional mask, and produces a weighted sum of values. Multi-head attention projects the input into multiple lower-dimensional query, key, and value subspaces, runs scaled dot-product attention independently in each, then concatenates and projects the result back:

```
import torch
import torch.nn as nn
import math


def scaled_dot_product_attention(q, k, v, mask=None):
    d_k = q.size(-1)
    scores = torch.matmul(q, k.transpose(-2, -1)) / math.sqrt(d_k)
    if mask is not None:
        scores = scores.masked_fill(mask == 0, float('-inf'))
    weights = torch.softmax(scores, dim=-1)
    return torch.matmul(weights, v), weights


class MultiHeadAttention(nn.Module):
    def __init__(self, d_model, num_heads):
        super().__init__()
        assert d_model % num_heads == 0
        self.d_k = d_model // num_heads
        self.num_heads = num_heads
        self.w_q = nn.Linear(d_model, d_model)
        self.w_k = nn.Linear(d_model, d_model)
        self.w_v = nn.Linear(d_model, d_model)
        self.w_o = nn.Linear(d_model, d_model)

    def split_heads(self, x, batch_size):
        x = x.view(batch_size, -1, self.num_heads, self.d_k)
        return x.transpose(1, 2)  # (batch, heads, seq, d_k)

    def forward(self, x, mask=None):
        batch_size = x.size(0)
        q = self.split_heads(self.w_q(x), batch_size)
        k = self.split_heads(self.w_k(x), batch_size)
```

```
        v = self.split_heads(self.w_v(x), batch_size)
        attn_out, _ = scaled_dot_product_attention(q, k, v,
mask)
        attn_out = attn_out.transpose(1, 2).contiguous()
        attn_out = attn_out.view(batch_size, -1,
self.num_heads * self.d_k)
        return self.w_o(attn_out)
```

Hint: Narrate the tensor shapes out loud as you write, batch, sequence length, num_heads, d_k, since the reshape and transpose steps around split_heads are exactly where candidates make silent errors under pressure. Also restate the complexity, O(n squared times d) in sequence length, which is why long-context serving needs flash attention or sparse attention variants in practice.

## 8. Agentic AI and Multi-Agent Systems

This is the fastest-growing interview topic for 2026 senior roles. Questions here separate candidates who have read about agents from candidates who have built them and debugged their failure modes.

### Q1. Explain the ReAct framework. How does it differ from a simple chain-of-thought prompt?

Sample answer: ReAct (Reasoning and Acting) is a prompting pattern that interleaves reasoning steps with tool-calling actions. In a standard chain-of-thought prompt, the model reasons through a problem in text and produces a final answer. ReAct adds an action step: after reasoning, the model emits a structured tool call (search, calculator, database query), receives the tool output, incorporates it into its next reasoning step, and continues until it can produce a grounded answer. The loop is: Thought -> Action -> Observation -> Thought. This matters because it grounds LLM reasoning in external reality, reducing hallucination on tasks that require factual lookup or computation. The failure mode is that the reasoning and the tool call can diverge: the model may reason correctly but emit a malformed action, or receive a valid observation and misinterpret it.

Hint: Know the frameworks that implement ReAct: LangGraph, LangChain agents, and the native tool-use APIs from Anthropic and

OpenAI. Be able to describe the message loop at the API level, not just at the abstraction level.

### Q2. Design a multi-agent system where Agent A queries a SQL database and Agent B sanitises the output. How do you prevent infinite loops if Agent A keeps receiving malformed tool-call exceptions?

Sample answer: Define a maximum retry count at the orchestrator level, not within each agent. When Agent A fails a tool call, the orchestrator increments a failure counter for that task. After exceeding a threshold (say three retries), the orchestrator routes to a fallback path: either a human-in-the-loop escalation, a cached response if one exists, or a graceful degradation that returns an explicit failure signal to the caller. Never let the retry logic live inside the agent itself, because agents do not have reliable access to their own execution history across turns. Also: Agent B should validate inputs before processing them and return a structured error type (not a plain string) so the orchestrator can distinguish between sanitisation failures (Agent B problem) and query failures (Agent A problem) and route accordingly. Use typed message schemas between agents.

Hint: Interviewers asking this want to see that you think about failure states as primary design constraints, not afterthoughts. Mention idempotency: if Agent A retries, the tool call should not cause side effects on the database.

### Q3. How would you use the Model Context Protocol (MCP) to give an autonomous agent context-aware access to a database without exposing the full enterprise schema?

Sample answer: MCP defines a standard interface between an LLM host and external tools or resources. Instead of giving the agent a raw database connection with full schema access, you implement an MCP server that exposes only the specific resources and tools the agent needs: a read-only query tool scoped to permitted tables, schema descriptions that expose only the relevant columns, and a resource endpoint that returns data in a format the model can reason over. The MCP server handles authentication and authorisation, enforcing row-level security before returning data. The agent never sees the full schema: it only knows about the tools the MCP server exposes. This applies the principle of least privilege at the agent-tool boundary. You can also implement query validation in the MCP server: if the agent constructs a query that accesses unpermitted tables, the server rejects it before execution.

Hint: MCP is increasingly appearing in senior GenAI role interviews. Know that it is a protocol, not a library: it standardises how context is provided to models via hosts, clients, and servers.

### Q4. What are the main failure modes of agentic systems, and how do you design against them?

Sample answer: The main failure modes are: hallucinated tool calls (the model invokes a tool that does not exist or with parameters it invents); loop states (the agent cannot make progress and keeps calling the same tool or asking the same sub-question); context window exhaustion (in a long-running agent loop, the accumulated history exceeds the model context, causing the model to lose early reasoning); cascading errors (a wrong tool result in step two corrupts all subsequent reasoning); and goal drift (in multi-step tasks, the model loses track of the original objective and pursues a local sub-goal). Design against these by: validating tool calls before execution against a schema; setting hard iteration limits at the orchestrator level; summarising or compressing context when it approaches the window limit; checkpointing state so that individual step failures can be retried without restarting the full loop; and injecting the original objective into every prompt to prevent drift.

Hint: Production agentic systems require observability as much as any other distributed system. Structured logging of each thought-action-observation triple is the minimum; distributed tracing across agent boundaries is the standard for multi-agent systems.

### Q5. What is an agent harness, and what does LangChain actually provide versus what you write yourself?

Sample answer: An agent harness is the surrounding scaffolding that turns a raw LLM call into a system that can plan, use tools, maintain state, and take multiple steps toward a goal, the loop that decides what the model sees at each step, executes tool calls, feeds results back, and decides when to stop. LangChain provides reusable building blocks: standardised tool interfaces, prompt templates, memory objects, and pre-built agent loop implementations like ReAct-style reasoning-and-acting loops. What it does not provide is judgment specific to your application, handling a failed tool call, preventing infinite loops, deciding when the agent has genuinely finished versus stalling, and evaluating whether the agent's trajectory was actually correct; those are usually hand-built on top of the framework's primitives.

Hint: A senior answer distinguishes the framework (LangChain, LangGraph) from the actual agentic behaviour (planning, tool selection, self-correction), since interviewers want to know you understand the difference between using a library and designing a system.

## Q6. How do you tell whether an application is genuinely agentic, or is just an LLM call wrapped in Python control flow?

Sample answer: The distinguishing feature is whether control flow is determined by the model at runtime or fixed in advance by the developer. A Python script with an if/else chain that calls an LLM at fixed points and decides what happens next with your own logic is a pipeline with LLM steps, not an agent. A system is genuinely agentic when the model itself decides, at runtime, which tool to call next and when to stop, based on results of previous steps, with the sequence not fixed in advance. A practical test: if you can draw the full flowchart of every possible path before running it, it is a pipeline; if the model's own output determines which branch is taken, it is agentic.

Hint: This distinction matters commercially too, a lot of what is marketed as 'agentic AI' in 2026 is closer to a well-designed pipeline, and interviewers who have built real agent systems appreciate a candidate who does not overclaim what qualifies.

## Q7. Walk through what actually happens internally when one agent hands off to another in LangGraph versus CrewAI.

Sample answer: The two frameworks model the handoff differently, and knowing the difference is what separates having used a framework from understanding what it is doing underneath. LangGraph represents the whole system as an explicit graph: nodes are functions (an LLM call, a tool call, a routing function) and edges define allowed transitions, with a shared, typed state object passed along every edge and updated by each node as it runs. A handoff from one agent to another is a normal edge transition: node A returns an update to the shared state, a conditional edge function inspects that state and decides which node runs next, and node B receives the same shared state, not a fresh message. Because the graph and its transitions are explicit, you can inspect, checkpoint, or resume execution at any node boundary, which is why LangGraph is the better choice when you need fine-grained control over exactly what happens at each step.

CrewAI models the handoff more like a team than a graph. Agents are defined with roles, goals, and backstories, and a process, sequential or hierarchical, determines execution order. In sequential mode, each agent's task output is passed as context into the next agent's prompt; internally this is still just an LLM call with the previous agent's output concatenated into the new prompt's context, not a special inter-process message format. In hierarchical mode, a manager agent (itself an LLM call) delegates tasks to worker agents and synthesises their outputs, so the 'delegation' an interviewer asks about is, mechanically, one more LLM call deciding which other prompt to trigger next. The abstraction reads as agents talking to each other, but underneath both frameworks it is still a sequence of LLM calls with state or context threaded between them by the orchestration code, not agents communicating over some agent-native protocol.

Hint: The trap in this question is answering only at the marketing-abstraction level, 'agents collaborate.' The senior answer names the actual mechanism, shared state object plus conditional edges for LangGraph, prompt-context concatenation plus a delegating LLM call for CrewAI, since that is what distinguishes someone who has read the docs from someone who has debugged a broken handoff at 2am.

## 9. MLOps and LLMOps

MLOps questions are consistently underestimated by candidates. They appear in every ML engineering interview and in many senior data science interviews. LLMOps questions have become standard for any GenAI role. The underlying theme in all of them is: how do you manage an ML system over time, not just at launch?

### Q1. What is model drift and how do you detect it?

Sample answer: Model drift is the degradation of model performance over time due to changes in the real-world distribution that the model has not seen. Two types matter in practice. Data drift (also called covariate shift) means the distribution of input features has changed: the population of users has shifted, the kinds of transactions being processed have changed, or the language being used has evolved. Concept drift means the relationship between inputs and outputs has changed: what constitutes fraud in 2024 is different from 2026 because fraudsters have adapted. Detection methods: statistical tests (KS test, population stability index) on feature distributions over time, monitoring prediction confidence distributions (if the model is suddenly less confident, the inputs have moved out of distribution), and tracking the distribution of predictions themselves. The most reliable signal is business metrics: if downstream KPIs degrade when the model performance metrics appear stable, investigate concept drift first.

Hint: Know the difference between detecting drift and responding to it. Detection is monitoring. Response is retraining, which requires a trigger (drift threshold exceeded), a validated new dataset, and a deployment process that includes a comparison against the current production model before cutover.

### Q2. Explain CI/CD for ML. How does it differ from software CI/CD?

Sample answer: Software CI/CD validates that code changes are correct (unit tests, integration tests) and deploys them automatically if they pass. ML CI/CD has to validate three things, not one: that the code is correct, that the data is correct, and that the trained model is correct. The data validation step checks for schema changes, missing values, distribution shifts in the training data, and label quality issues before training begins. The model validation step runs the newly trained model against a held-out evaluation set and compares its performance metrics against the current production model: if the new model is not at least as good on key metrics, deployment is blocked. Tools like MLflow, DVC, and Weights and Biases handle experiment tracking; platforms like Kubeflow or SageMaker Pipelines orchestrate the training and validation steps; deployment happens through a model registry with version control.

Hint: A candidate who knows what a shadow mode deployment is (running the new model in parallel with the existing one, logging its predictions but not acting on them) is demonstrating production awareness that most candidates lack.

## Q3. How would you roll back a bad model deployment?

Sample answer: The ability to roll back depends entirely on what you built before deployment. If you used a model registry with immutable versioned artifacts, rollback is a matter of pointing your serving infrastructure back at the previous version and waiting for the new instances to start. If you deployed via blue-green deployment (two production environments, with traffic switched between them), rollback is a traffic switch that takes seconds. If you deployed via canary (gradually routing traffic to the new model), you roll back by stopping the canary and returning all traffic to the current production model. The most dangerous scenario is when there is no versioning: the new model weights overwrite the old ones, and rollback requires retraining from a checkpoint, which takes hours. The design principle is: never overwrite production artifacts. Store every version, tag it with the evaluation results it achieved, and make rollback a one-command operation before any deployment happens.

Hint: Know the difference between a model rollback and a feature rollback. If the new model was trained on new features that the old model did not use, you may also need to roll back the feature pipeline, not just the model weights.

## Q4. What specific metrics would you track for a production LLM application?

Sample answer: Track at three levels. Infrastructure metrics: latency (p50, p95, p99 separately, because p99 tells you about tail latency that users experience), throughput (tokens per second), error rates (API failures, timeout rates, malformed output rates), and cost per query. Model quality metrics: for a RAG system, faithfulness score and context recall on a rolling sample evaluated by an LLM-as-a-Judge; for a classification system, standard metrics on a labelled holdout updated weekly. User experience metrics: thumbs up/down rates if surfaced, task completion rates, session abandonment, and re-query rate (if users immediately re-query after a response, the first response was likely unsatisfactory). Tie model quality metrics to business outcomes:

if faithfulness goes up but task completion goes down, you are optimising the wrong thing.

Hint: Know what LLM-as-a-Judge is and its limitations: it is using a strong model (GPT-4, Claude Opus) to evaluate the outputs of a weaker or task-specific model. Limitations include judge bias toward verbose outputs, judge agreement with its own style, and inability to evaluate factual accuracy without external grounding.

### Q5. How would you detect whether a model is biased against a protected group?

Sample answer: Start by defining which fairness criterion matters for the use case, since different fairness definitions can be mathematically incompatible with each other. Demographic parity checks whether the positive prediction rate is similar across groups. Equalised odds checks whether true and false positive rates are similar across groups, generally the more appropriate criterion when the outcome has real consequences. Calibration checks whether, among people given the same predicted probability, the actual outcome rate is the same across groups. In practice, compute the confusion matrix separately per protected group and compare error rates, using disaggregated evaluation throughout rather than one aggregate accuracy number that can mask large group-level disparities.

Hint: Be ready to explain the impossibility result, you generally cannot satisfy demographic parity, equalised odds, and calibration simultaneously unless base rates are equal across groups, so fairness requires a deliberate tradeoff, not a single metric that solves everything.

### Q6. Once you have detected bias, what are the main mitigation strategies, and at what stage of the pipeline does each apply?

Sample answer: Pre-processing mitigations act on training data before the model sees it, reweighting samples so protected groups are represented proportionally, or removing features that proxy for the protected attribute, keeping in mind proxies like zip code are often hard to fully eliminate. In-processing mitigations modify the training objective itself, adding a fairness constraint or penalty term so the model optimises jointly for accuracy and fairness. Post-processing mitigations adjust outputs after training, for example different decision thresholds per group to equalise a chosen fairness metric, the fastest to deploy but least principled, since it treats the symptom rather than the cause.

Hint: Close with monitoring, a model fair on the training distribution can drift into unfairness as the deployed population's demographics or behaviour shift over time, so fairness work needs ongoing production monitoring, not a one-time audit.

## Q7. What are the concrete, end-to-end steps to deploy an LLM or ML system on AWS, and which AWS pieces does each step actually use?

Sample answer: Treat it as a checklist rather than a service list, since interviewers are usually checking whether you understand the order of operations, not just the names. First, artifact storage: the trained model weights or fine-tuned adapter go into S3, versioned by path or with S3 versioning enabled, so every deployment references an immutable artifact. Second, packaging: containerise the serving code (FastAPI or a Triton/vLLM server) into a Docker image and push it to ECR. Third, compute and orchestration: choose the serving target based on how much control you need, SageMaker endpoints if you want managed autoscaling, health checks, and blue-green deployment with minimal setup, or ECS/EKS if you need custom batching logic, a specific inference engine, or multi-model routing that SageMaker's abstractions do not fit cleanly. Fourth, networking and access: the service sits behind an Application Load Balancer or API Gateway, inside a VPC with private subnets for the compute and a NAT gateway for any outbound calls, with IAM roles scoped per service, the serving containers should not hold broad account permissions. Fifth, secrets and configuration: API keys and database credentials go into Secrets Manager or Parameter Store, never into the container image or environment variables committed to source. Sixth, autoscaling: configure scaling policies on request queue depth or GPU utilisation rather than plain CPU, since GPU-bound inference workloads saturate memory bandwidth long before CPU. Seventh, observability: CloudWatch metrics and logs, plus structured application-level tracing (LangSmith or an OpenTelemetry-based tracer) for anything LLM-specific, since CloudWatch alone will not show you a prompt, a retrieved chunk, or a token count. Eighth, asynchronous paths: anything that does not need a synchronous response goes through SQS so a queue absorbs bursts without the serving layer falling over.

Hint: If the interviewer only wants the surface answer, name the core five: S3 for artifacts, ECR for images, SageMaker or EKS/ECS for serving, IAM for access, CloudWatch for observability. If they push for depth, walk the order above and be ready to justify SageMaker versus EKS specifically, since that choice is the one senior interviewers probe hardest.

## Q8. How does Kafka consumer threading actually work, and what is the most common mistake candidates make describing it?

Sample answer: A Kafka topic is split into partitions, and Kafka's parallelism model is built entirely around that split: within one consumer group, each partition is consumed by exactly one consumer instance at a time, so the natural unit of parallelism is the partition, not an arbitrary thread pool. The common mistake is describing throughput scaling as 'add more threads to the consumer,' which misses the actual constraint: a single KafkaConsumer client instance is not thread-safe and must not be shared across threads, calling it concurrently from multiple threads corrupts its internal state. The correct patterns are one of two shapes. Either run one consumer instance per thread (or per process), each assigned its own subset of partitions by the consumer group protocol, so parallelism comes from multiple single-threaded consumer loops rather than one consumer being called concurrently; or run a single-threaded consumer that only polls and immediately hands each record off to a separate worker thread pool for processing, keeping all Kafka client calls, poll and commit, on the one owning thread while the actual work happens elsewhere. The number of partitions is therefore the hard ceiling on consumption parallelism for a topic, adding a fourth consumer to a group already consuming a three-partition topic leaves that fourth consumer idle.

Hint: If the question is really about scaling a streaming feature pipeline rather than Kafka internals specifically, land on the practical consequence: partition count is a capacity-planning decision made at topic-creation time, under-provisioning it is a common production bottleneck that is expensive to fix later because repartitioning an existing topic is disruptive.

### Q9. How do you upgrade a live production ML or LLM system, model, code, or schema, without downtime?

Sample answer: The mechanism depends on what is changing, and a senior answer names the right one rather than defaulting to one pattern for everything. For a model version upgrade with no API contract change, blue-green deployment (a full second environment running the new version, traffic switched over at the load balancer once health checks pass) gives an instant, low-risk cutover and an equally instant rollback. For a riskier change you want to validate against real traffic before committing, canary deployment routes a small percentage of traffic to the new version, watches the quality and latency metrics, and ramps up gradually, or aborts and rolls back automatically if a metric regresses past a threshold. For a change to the request or response contract, an API version change, a new required field, run both versions of the API concurrently behind versioned routes for a deprecation window, so existing callers are not broken the moment the new version ships. For a database or feature-store schema change, use expand-contract: first deploy a schema change that is additive only (expand), deploy the code that writes to both old and new shapes, backfill, cut reads over to the new shape, and only then remove the old columns (contract), so there is never a moment where old and new code cannot both run against the live schema. Kubernetes rolling updates handle the mechanics of swapping pod versions without downtime underneath any of these, replacing old pods with new ones a few at a time behind a readiness check, but rolling updates alone do not solve a breaking contract change, that needs the versioning or expand-contract discipline above regardless of what is orchestrating the pods.

Hint: The trap is answering only 'Kubernetes does rolling updates' and stopping there. That is the deployment mechanic, not the compatibility strategy; an interviewer who asks this is usually checking whether you understand that a schema or contract change needs a compatibility plan that exists independently of whatever infrastructure is doing the rollout.

## 10. Behavioural Questions

Almost every AI candidate under-prepares for behavioural questions. This is a strategic error: behavioural rounds are where Phase 3 and Phase 4 candidates get eliminated, because technically strong candidates often give answers that are either too vague (performed humility) or too specific without a clear point (chronological story with no takeaway).

Use the Context-Challenge-Action-Result-Learning structure for each question. The Learning is the element most candidates omit and most interviewers weigh most heavily.

## Q1. Tell me about yourself.

What it is actually asking: Can you give me a coherent narrative of your career that connects to why you are sitting in this interview today?

Structure: Three parts, about two minutes total. Where you started and what thread has connected your work (the through-line). The specific experience that is most relevant to this role. Why you are here now and what you are looking for next.

Common mistake: Reciting your resume chronologically. The interviewer has already read your resume. They want the narrative that makes sense of it, not the facts themselves.

Hint: End with a bridge: your last sentence should be something like: which is why this role caught my attention, because it combines X with Y, which maps directly to where I want to take my work next. This signals that you have thought about the specific role, not just practised a generic answer.

## Q2. Tell me about a time a production ML system failed and how you handled it.

What it is actually asking: Do you have real production experience? Can you be honest about failure? Do you learn from it systematically?

Strong answer elements: A specific system and failure mode (not a vague reference to things going wrong). What you thought the cause was and why you were wrong initially (shows genuine diagnosis rather than retrofitted clarity). What the actual fix was and how you validated it. What you changed about the system or your process so the failure mode could not recur.

Common mistake: Describing a failure that was entirely someone else's fault, or one where the cause was immediately obvious. Interviewers are testing whether you can sit with uncertainty and diagnose under pressure.

Hint: If you have not had a production failure, think carefully: any model whose performance degraded in production, any pipeline that produced incorrect outputs that were caught downstream, any feature engineering error that introduced data leakage. These all qualify.

## Q3. Tell me about a disagreement with a stakeholder or manager and how you resolved it.

What it is actually asking: Can you hold a position under social pressure? Do you know when to update your view versus when to hold it? Can you disagree without damaging the relationship?

Strong answer elements: A substantive technical or strategic disagreement (not a scheduling or resource conflict). What position you held and why (the reasoning matters). How you presented your position and what happened. What the outcome was and how you felt about it in retrospect.

Common mistake: Describing a conflict where you immediately deferred, then saying the outcome was fine. This tells the interviewer you will defer under pressure, which is a liability in a senior technical role.

Hint: It is acceptable for your answer to end with: I held my position, we went with the other approach, and it turned out I was right. The interviewer is checking whether you can be honest about outcomes. Manufactured stories where everyone learned and everything worked out often read as performed.

## Q4. What is your biggest weakness?

What it is actually asking: Do you have genuine self-awareness? Are you actively working on your development edges?

Strong answer: A specific, real limitation that is relevant to the role but not disqualifying. What you understand about why it happens. What you are specifically doing to address it, with concrete examples.

Example of a strong answer: I tend to go deep on technical details before confirming that the problem I am solving is the right problem to be solving. I have missed the forest for the trees on a couple of projects. What I do now is force myself to write a one-paragraph problem statement that a non-technical stakeholder can validate before I start any significant technical work. It slows down the first day and saves weeks later.

Common mistake: Giving a strength disguised as a weakness (I work too hard, I care too much about quality). Experienced interviewers find this condescending. Give something real.

Hint: The weakness you choose should be something you have genuinely worked on and have a credible improvement story for. Not something you are still fully stuck on (signals poor self-management) and not something trivial (signals low self-awareness).

### Q5. Why are you leaving your current role?

What it is actually asking: Are there red flags about you that your current employer knows? Can you speak about a difficult situation professionally?

Strong answer: Honest but forward-looking. What you have learned, what you are looking for next, and why this role specifically offers that. If the reason involves organisational dysfunction, acknowledge it briefly and without bitterness, then pivot quickly to what you want next.

Common mistake: Speaking critically about your current employer at length. Even if everything you say is accurate, it signals to the interviewer that you will speak similarly about them if you leave.

Hint: The Indian job market has specific expectations here. If you were part of a layoff, say so directly. It is not a stigma in 2026 and attempting to obscure it looks worse than naming it.

## 11. The Interview Red Flag Checklist: Questions to Ask the Interviewer

The questions you ask at the end of an interview reveal your judgment as much as your answers do. This section gives you questions that serve a dual purpose: they demonstrate strategic thinking to the interviewer, and they give you genuine signal about whether the role is worth taking.

The red flags below are signals that a company is chasing AI capability without the organisational infrastructure to use it well. You are likely to spend your time on work that is cancelled, de-prioritised, or never reaches production.

**Questions to ask, and what the answers reveal:**

**"Can you describe a specific AI project that reached production in the last 12 months and what its measured impact was?"**

What you are listening for: A specific system, a concrete metric, a number. Red flag: a vague answer about things being in progress, pilots underway, or a single demo that leadership loved. A company with genuine production AI can name it.

**"How does the ML team interact with the product and engineering teams? Who owns the success metric for an ML system?"**

What you are listening for: A clear ownership model and a described feedback loop. Red flag: the ML team reports to data, which reports to IT, which advises the product team. If ML is two or more reporting layers away from the product decisions, your work will struggle to reach production.

**"What does the data infrastructure look like? How long does it typically take to get access to a new dataset?"**

What you are listening for: A described stack, a realistic timeframe (days to weeks for a mature organisation). Red flag: the interviewer looks uncertain, mentions multiple ticketing systems, or describes a process that takes months. Data access is the primary constraint on ML productivity and it reflects organisational maturity more than almost any other signal.

**"What was the last ML model that was deprecated or shut down, and why?"**

What you are listening for: A specific example and a clear reason. Red flag: the interviewer cannot think of one, or says models are never deprecated. Organisations with mature AI practices retire models when they are no longer the best solution. Organisations without that maturity keep everything running because deprecation requires ownership and accountability they have not established.

**"How is this role funded: is it under a specific product budget, a central AI team budget, or a research allocation?"**

What you are listening for: A clear answer. Red flag: the funding is described as a special initiative, a centre of excellence, or a strategic priority without a specific budget line. Initiatives with unclear funding are the first to be cut. If the role is funded by a product team with a specific revenue objective, it is more likely to survive a downturn.

**"What does this team need that it does not currently have?"**

What you are listening for: An honest answer about a specific gap (we do not have anyone who can own the evaluation framework end-to-end; we need someone who has done production RAG at scale). Red flag: the answer is some variation of we just need more capacity or we need someone to lead AI strategy. Vague hiring signals vague expectations, which means your performance will be judged against criteria that shift.

Company-level red flags that indicate you are interviewing for a role that will not deliver what it promises:

One person expected to do everything: the job description lists data engineering, model training, deployment, monitoring, and stakeholder communication as equal expectations for a single hire. This is a signal that the company does not understand what these roles actually require.

No described evaluation process: the company cannot tell you how they will measure whether the AI system is working. If there is no evaluation framework before you join, you will spend your time building one while being asked why the model is not in production yet.

AI as a feature addition to an existing product: the company wants to add AI to a product that was not designed for it, without rethinking the product architecture. This produces integrations that are fragile, expensive to maintain, and often cancelled after the initial demo.

The hiring manager cannot describe a specific problem: if the interviewer describes the role in terms of AI and LLMs and GenAI without being able to name a specific business problem the role will solve, the company is hiring into a capability gap rather than into a defined need. These roles often end badly.

## Final note on this appendix

The three-tier answer structure used for the LLM cost migration question (trap answer, strategic hint, production answer) is worth internalising as a self-evaluation tool. For any question in this appendix, after you have practised your own answer, ask yourself: am I giving the Phase 1 answer (reciting a definition), the Phase 2 answer (describing implementation), or the Phase 3 answer (reasoning about trade-offs and failure modes)? The phase of your answer often determines the phase of role you will be offered.

# 2. LLM Concepts and Production

These questions test whether you understand LLMs as engineering systems, not just as interfaces. Senior roles require both.

### Q1. What is hallucination in LLMs and what causes it?

Sample answer: Hallucination is when an LLM produces output that is fluent and confident but factually wrong or fabricated. The root cause is that LLMs are trained to produce probable next tokens, not true statements. When the training distribution does not contain a fact, or when the model is prompted in a way that conflicts with its training, it confabulates a plausible-sounding answer rather than saying it does not know. Contributing factors include: memorisation gaps, over-reliance on surface patterns, the mismatch between RLHF training (which rewards confident, helpful-sounding outputs) and epistemic honesty, and distributional shift at inference time.

Hint: Mitigation strategies to know: retrieval augmentation, self-consistency sampling, chain-of-thought prompting, output verification, factuality-aware RLHF.

## Q2. Explain RLHF. What problem does it solve and what are its limitations?

Sample answer: RLHF (Reinforcement Learning from Human Feedback) fine-tunes a language model to produce outputs that human raters prefer. A reward model is trained on human comparisons of model outputs, then the base LLM is optimised to maximise this reward using PPO or similar RL algorithms. It solves the alignment problem between raw next-token prediction and human-valued helpfulness and harmlessness. Limitations: reward model hacking (the model finds outputs that score well but are not actually useful), mode collapse (diversity of outputs decreases), expensive human annotation, rater disagreement, and difficulty specifying what humans actually want versus what they rate highly.

Hint: Know DPO (Direct Preference Optimisation) as a simpler RLHF alternative: it skips the reward model and directly optimises the policy using preference data.

## Q3. What is the difference between fine-tuning and RAG? When would you choose each?

Sample answer: Fine-tuning updates the model weights on domain-specific data, baking knowledge into the parameters. RAG retrieves relevant documents at inference time and provides them as context, keeping the base model frozen. Choose fine-tuning when: the domain has distinct style, format, or vocabulary requirements, you need reliable recall of specific facts without retrieval latency, or you are customising behaviour rather than adding knowledge. Choose RAG when: the knowledge base changes frequently and retraining is expensive, you need citations and traceable sources, the knowledge corpus is too large to fit in context but documents can be retrieved selectively, or you need to avoid hallucinating from parametric memory. Hybrid approaches use fine-tuning for style and RAG for factual grounding.

Hint: A common follow-up: what is LoRA and when do you use it instead of full fine-tuning? LoRA adds low-rank weight updates, reducing trainable parameters by 90 percent or more, making fine-tuning feasible on smaller hardware.

## Q4. How would you evaluate the output quality of an LLM application?

Sample answer: Evaluation depends on the task. For factual QA: exact match, F1 against reference answers, or retrieval recall if using RAG. For generation tasks: human evaluation is gold standard but expensive; automated proxies include ROUGE, BERTScore, and LLM-as-a-Judge (using a strong model to score outputs). For production systems: user satisfaction signals (thumbs up, task completion, session length), A/B comparisons, and failure analysis on a labelled error set. For safety: red-teaming, adversarial probing, and refusal rate on known harmful inputs. The key principle: never use a single metric. Different metrics catch different failure modes.

Hint: Know what Ragas is: it is an open-source framework specifically for RAG pipeline evaluation covering faithfulness, answer relevancy, and context precision.

## Q5. What are quantisation and distillation? Why do they matter for deployment?

Sample answer: Quantisation reduces the numerical precision of model weights, from 32-bit floats to 8-bit or 4-bit integers, reducing memory footprint and often accelerating inference with minimal quality loss. Methods like GPTQ and AWQ apply quantisation post-training. Distillation trains a smaller student model to replicate the outputs of a larger teacher, transferring capability into a more deployable size. They matter for deployment because large LLMs are expensive to serve: a 70B parameter model requires multiple high-memory GPUs. Quantisation and distillation make capable models accessible on smaller hardware, reducing inference cost by 2-4x or more.

Hint: Know llama.cpp and Ollama: both enable local LLM deployment using quantised models. Being familiar with these tools signals practical deployment awareness.

## Q6. How would you design a multimodal model that takes both text and another signal type, e.g. audio or sensor data, rather than text alone?

Sample answer: Encode each modality separately into a shared embedding space, then fuse. For audio, a pretrained audio encoder (Whisper's encoder, wav2vec2) converts raw waveform into a sequence of embeddings analogous to token embeddings; for continuous sensor data, a small transformer or 1D CNN plays the same role. Fusion can be early (concatenate embeddings before a shared transformer, richer cross-modal learning but more data-hungry), late (separate towers combined only at the output, cheaper but misses fine-grained interaction), or cross-attention (text tokens attend to image or audio embeddings via added cross-attention layers, as in Flamingo or LLaVA-style architectures), which is the current standard for strong performance while keeping the language backbone mostly intact.

Hint: Mention alignment, whichever fusion strategy you pick, you need paired training data to teach the model the correspondence between modalities; without paired data, contrastive pretraining (CLIP-style) is the fallback.

## Q7. What is a small language model (SLM), and what does 'training' typically mean in that context?

Sample answer: An SLM is a language model in roughly the 1 to 10 billion parameter range, small enough to run on a single GPU or on-device, as opposed to frontier models with hundreds of billions of parameters. 'Training' rarely means pretraining from scratch, that needs trillions of tokens and compute most companies do not have. In practice it means starting from an open-weight base model (Llama, Mistral, Phi, Gemma) and doing continued pretraining on domain text to adapt what the model knows, supervised fine-tuning (SFT) on instruction-response pairs to adapt how it behaves, or parameter-efficient fine-tuning (LoRA or QLoRA), which freezes the base weights and trains small low-rank adapter matrices, cutting compute and memory cost by orders of magnitude.

Hint: Be ready to explain LoRA mechanically, it decomposes a weight update into two low-rank matrices whose product approximates the full update, while keeping the frozen base model's general capability intact.

## Q8. What input guardrails would you put in front of an LLM application, and what does each protect against?

Sample answer: Prompt injection detection screens incoming text, including retrieved documents in a RAG system, for attempts to override the system prompt, typically via a classifier or a secondary LLM check rather than keyword matching, since injection attempts vary adversarially. PII detection and redaction scans input before it reaches the model or gets logged. Topic and scope filtering rejects queries outside the application's intended domain, limiting misuse and liability. Rate limiting and anomaly detection catch abuse patterns, such as one user issuing thousands of jailbreak variants.

Hint: Mention layering, cheap regex checks first, expensive classifier or LLM-based checks only when the cheap check is ambiguous, to keep added latency low on the common case.

### Q9. What output guardrails matter most for a production LLM application?

Sample answer: Groundedness checking verifies the output does not make claims unsupported by the retrieved context, typically via an LLM-as-a-judge call or a natural language inference model. Toxicity and safety filtering screens generated output with a dedicated classifier, independent of the generating model's own alignment. Format and schema validation checks that structured output actually parses correctly before it feeds a downstream system, with a retry or fallback if not. PII leakage checking mirrors the input check, in case the model echoes back sensitive context. For high-stakes applications, human-in-the-loop review for outputs below a confidence threshold is the most reliable guardrail, even though it does not scale to full automation.

Hint: Distinguish guardrails that block a response outright from ones that just flag it for review, since the right response depends on the cost of a false positive versus a false negative.

## 3. Coding: LeetCodc Patterns

Most ML engineer roles test at medium difficulty. The goal is not memorising solutions but recognising patterns and communicating reasoning clearly while coding. These are the ten most important patterns, with a representative question for each.

### Before the patterns: do not code until you can name the search space

Most coding-round eliminations happen before the first line of syntax, at the moment a candidate starts typing without having identified the computational structure of the problem. The discipline that prevents it is a sixty-second checklist run in your head or out loud: what are the choices available at each step, what state must be carried between steps, what is the base case, does the structure require recursion or backtracking, and can anything be pruned. Only after those five answers exist should Python begin. A problem asking for all expressions over a digit string that reach a target is not a string problem or a zip-two-lists problem; naming it as partition plus operator choice plus recursive search identifies it as backtracking before any code exists, and the code then largely writes itself. The consulting-firm interview log later in this appendix contains a worked example of exactly this failure and its repair.

The combinatorial families worth recognising on sight, because coding rounds draw from them constantly, are subsets, permutations, combinations, partitions of a string or array, operator or choice insertion between elements, and general DFS backtracking with pruning. If a problem statement contains the words all possible, the answer is almost always one of these.

### Pattern 1: Two Pointers

## Q: Given a sorted array and a target sum, find two indices whose values sum to the target.

Approach: Start with one pointer at the left and one at the right. If the sum is too small, move left right. If too large, move right left. O(n) time, O(1) space. Recognition signal: sorted array, pair search, avoid O(n squared) naive approach.

Hint: Related problems: 3Sum, container with most water, trapping rain water.

### Pattern 2: Sliding Window

## Q: Find the maximum sum subarray of length k.

Approach: Compute sum of first k elements. Slide the window forward: add the new element, subtract the element leaving the window, track the maximum. O(n) time. Recognition signal: contiguous subarray or substring with a fixed or variable constraint.

Hint: Variable window variant: longest substring without repeating characters uses a hashmap to track character positions.

### Pattern 3: Binary Search

### Q: Find the leftmost position where a sorted array value equals the target.

Approach: Standard binary search with the modification that on finding target, record the position and continue searching left (move right = mid - 1). Know three variants: find exact, find leftmost, find rightmost. O(log n). Recognition signal: sorted array, minimise/maximise with a monotonic property.

Hint: Many non-obvious problems use binary search on the answer space, not the array itself: minimum capacity to ship packages in d days, minimum eating speed for Koko.

### Pattern 4: Linked List Manipulation

### Q: Detect a cycle in a linked list.

Approach: Floyd's cycle detection (fast and slow pointers). Slow moves one step, fast moves two. If they meet, there is a cycle. If fast reaches null, there is no cycle. O(n) time, O(1) space. Know also: reverse a linked list iteratively (three pointers: prev, curr, next), merge two sorted lists, find middle of a list (fast and slow again).

Hint: Reversing a linked list is a building block for many harder problems. Practise until it is automatic.

### Pattern 5: Trees and DFS/BFS

### Q: Find the maximum depth of a binary tree.

Approach: Recursive DFS returns max(left depth, right depth) + 1. Iterative BFS uses a queue and counts levels. Know both. Core tree operations to have automatic: inorder/preorder/postorder traversal, lowest common ancestor, path sum problems, level-order traversal, validate BST.

Hint: Most tree problems are solved by asking: what should this function return for a leaf node? Then build up from there.

### Pattern 6: Graphs (BFS/DFS)

**Q: Number of islands: count connected components of 1s in a 2D grid.**

Approach: Iterate over the grid. When you hit a 1, run DFS or BFS from that cell, marking all connected 1s as visited (set to 0 or use a visited set). Increment a counter for each new component found. O(m x n) time. Recognition signal: connected components, shortest path in unweighted graph (BFS), explore all possibilities (DFS).

Hint: Dijkstra for weighted shortest path, BFS for unweighted. Be comfortable implementing both with an adjacency list representation.

## Pattern 7: Dynamic Programming

**Q: Longest common subsequence of two strings.**

Approach: Build a 2D DP table. dp[i][j] is the LCS length for the first i characters of string 1 and first j characters of string 2. If characters match, dp[i][j] = dp[i-1][j-1] + 1. Otherwise, dp[i][j] = max(dp[i-1][j], dp[i][j-1]). O(m x n) time and space. DP recognition signal: optimal substructure (optimal solution built from optimal sub-solutions), overlapping subproblems.

Hint: Core DP problems to know: 0/1 knapsack, coin change, climbing stairs, house robber, edit distance, word break.

## Pattern 8: Stack and Monotonic Stack

**Q: Next greater element: for each element in an array, find the next element to its right that is greater.**

Approach: Process right to left using a stack that maintains a decreasing sequence. For each element, pop everything smaller from the stack (they cannot be the answer for any future element to the left). The top of the stack is the answer. Push current element. O(n) time. Recognition signal: next/previous greater or smaller element, spans, histogram problems.

Hint: Largest rectangle in histogram is the classic hard monotonic stack problem. Understanding it deeply covers many related questions.

## Pattern 9: Heaps

**Q: Find the k-th largest element in an array.**

Approach: Maintain a min-heap of size k. For each element, add it to the heap. If heap size exceeds k, pop the minimum. After processing all elements, the heap top is the k-th largest. O(n log k) time. Alternative: Quickselect algorithm gives O(n) average. In Python use heapq (min-heap by default; negate values for max-heap behaviour).

Hint: Heaps also solve: merge k sorted lists, task scheduler, find median from a data stream (two heaps).

### Pattern 10: Backtracking

### Q: Generate all subsets of a set.

Approach: At each position, make two choices: include the current element or not. Recurse for both choices, tracking the current subset. Add to results when you have made a decision for every element. O(2^n) time (unavoidable for subset enumeration). Recognition signal: generate all valid configurations, permutations, combinations, solve a constraint satisfaction problem by exploring and pruning.

Hint: The key to backtracking: define what a valid state looks like, what the base case is (add to results), and what choices are available at each step. Prune early when a partial state cannot lead to a valid solution.

## 4. ML System Design

ML system design interviews are open-ended by design. The evaluator is watching how you structure an ambiguous problem, what questions you ask, and how you reason about trade-offs. Use the six-step framework from Chapter 9.

### Q1. Design a content recommendation system for a streaming platform.

Clarify: Optimising for what? (Watch time, completion rate, discovery of new content, engagement.) What is the latency requirement for serving recommendations? Is personalisation required from session start or after some watch history?

ML framing: Ranking problem. Given a user and a candidate pool of items, rank by predicted engagement. Inputs: user history, item metadata, time of day, session context. Output: ranked list of items.

Model choice: Start with collaborative filtering (matrix factorisation or two-tower neural embedding). Add content-based features for cold-start. Move to a sequential model (LSTM or transformer over watch history) for context-aware ranking.

Deployment: Two-stage retrieval and ranking. First stage: approximate nearest neighbour search over user and item embeddings, retrieving candidate set of 100-500 items. Second stage: a heavier ranking model scores candidates. Serving latency target is typically under 100ms.

Monitoring: Track CTR, completion rate, coverage (diversity of recommendations), and filter bubble metrics. Detect distribution shift between training data and live traffic.

Hint: Common follow-up: how do you handle the cold-start problem for new users and new content? For users: use demographic defaults or onboarding signals. For content: use content embeddings from metadata until engagement data accumulates.

### Q2. Design a fraud detection system for a UPI payment provider.

Clarify: What is the acceptable false positive rate (flagging legitimate transactions)? What is the cost of false negatives (missed fraud)? Real-time decision or batch? What regulatory reporting requirements exist?

ML framing: Binary classification with severe class imbalance (fraud is typically under 1 percent of transactions). Need high recall (catching fraud) with precision high enough that legitimate users are not excessively disrupted.

Features: Transaction amount and deviation from user average, recipient identity and history, velocity features (transactions in last hour/day), device fingerprint, location, time of day, social graph features (has this payee been used by this user before?).

Model: Ensemble of gradient boosting (XGBoost, LightGBM) for tabular features plus a sequence model for transaction history. Use SMOTE or cost-sensitive learning for class imbalance. Rule-based hard blocks for known fraud patterns.

Latency: Real-time decisions require inference under 50ms. Use a streaming pipeline (Kafka) and pre-computed features where possible.

Monitoring: Track precision, recall, and AUC on a rolling labelled window. Fraud patterns shift: model needs regular retraining on recent data. Human review queue for borderline cases.

Hint: Know the difference between online and offline evaluation for fraud detection: offline AUC looks great; online metrics matter because the fraud population shifts as fraudsters adapt to your model.

## Q3. Design a document Q&A system for an enterprise knowledge base.

Clarify: What types of documents? (PDFs, Word, markdown, wikis.) What is the scale of the corpus? Does the system need to cite sources? What is the latency requirement? Is it an internal tool or customer-facing?

Architecture: RAG pipeline. Offline: ingest documents, chunk with overlap (512 tokens, 50-token overlap), embed with a sentence transformer (e.g. BGE-large or a hosted model), store in a vector database (Pinecone, Weaviate, or FAISS for smaller scale). Online: embed the user query, retrieve top-k chunks by cosine similarity, optionally rerank with a cross-encoder, pass retrieved context plus query to an LLM for generation.

Retrieval quality: Hybrid retrieval (dense vector + sparse BM25) typically outperforms either alone. Reranking with a cross-encoder improves precision of the final context. Query expansion and HyDE (hypothetical document embeddings) improve recall on difficult queries.

Evaluation: Faithfulness (does the answer stay within the retrieved context?), answer relevancy, context precision, and context recall. Ragas framework covers all of these.

Production concerns: Document versioning (how do you handle updated documents?), access control (users should only retrieve documents they are authorised to see), cost management for embedding and generation calls.

Hint: Know chunking strategies: fixed size, sentence boundary, recursive character splitting, document-structure-aware (split on headers). Chunking is often the highest-leverage improvement in a RAG pipeline.

*The two questions that follow are not constructed for this book. They are close versions of system design assignments given in real 2026 interview processes, included here because a live assignment is almost always more demanding, and more useful to rehearse against, than an invented one.*

## Q4. Design an MLOps platform to train ten thousand models and run batch inference on 750 million records per model inside a day.

Clarify: Do the arithmetic before anything else. 750 million records scored against 10,000 models is 7.5 trillion scoring operations a day, which is not a workload any sane platform actually runs in full. The real question is why all 10,000 models would ever need to see all 750 million records. In production, they almost never do: geography and access restrictions typically apply (a model trained on US data is often legally barred from scoring a record belonging to an Indian user), and most records only qualify for a small subset of models in the first place.

Architecture: A routing layer that narrows the applicable model set per record from 10,000 down to roughly 10–50, based on geography, role, and product line, drops the real workload from 7.5 trillion to somewhere between 7.5 and 37.5 billion operations, two to three orders of magnitude smaller. Decouple the platform into four layers, data, feature, training, and inference, so a change to inference cluster size never touches feature logic or training code. Kubernetes sits underneath all four: elastic compute, namespace-level multi-tenancy across business units, and one deployment model whether the workload is a Spark job, a Kubeflow pipeline, or something else entirely.

Data and features: Raw data lands in a lake (S3 or Iceberg). Most of the 25,000–30,000 transformed features are shared across many of the 10,000 models, demographic, behavioural, and product features recur constantly, so compute them once and store them in a feature store rather than per model: Parquet for stable features, Redis for ones that change fast. Each model declares the features it needs in a config file; at inference time, the model's metadata determines which feature-store columns get pulled, rather than recomputing feature logic per model.

Training and inference: Each model is a YAML or JSON spec, objective, type, geography, hyperparameters, orchestrated through Kubeflow pipelines on Kubernetes. Shallow models (XGBoost,

LightGBM) handle most tabular cases on CPU; deep learning models run on GPU where justified. MLflow tracks every run's version, hyperparameters, and metadata. For batch inference, the same routing table applies: partition data and models on the same keys, so a Spark job processing one partition only ever loads the models registered against it, and broadcast each model to compute nodes once per partition rather than once per batch.

Governance: Log everything a run depends on, code commit hash, training data version, feature view version, hyperparameters, random seed, directly into the MLflow run record; this is the reproducibility backbone, supplemented by OpenLineage for lineage tracking. Features carry an explicit lifecycle state (active, deprecated, retired) in the feature registry, and retraining pipelines block or warn when a model config references a retired feature, which is how feature-space changes get handled without silently breaking downstream models. Kubernetes RBAC plus an audit log covering who touched which data, under what permission, handles access control.

Limitations worth naming unprompted: this design does not yet address cross-model feature-drift coordination, cold-start serving latency for the long tail of low-traffic models, or what happens when two models in an ensemble are retrained on different schedules and briefly disagree. Naming the gaps in your own design, before the interviewer finds them, reads as more senior than pretending the design is complete.

Hint: This is a cost-and-routing problem dressed up as a scale problem. Most candidates spend their time on parallel training frameworks and never ask the one question that collapses the workload by two orders of magnitude. Do the arithmetic out loud in the first two minutes, and ask what is actually allowed to see what, before designing anything else.

## Q5. Design a RAG and knowledge-graph system that translates a user-defined clinical quality measure into a live computation over hospital data, and a companion system for anomaly detection and root cause analysis.

Clarify: A clinical data element, a lab result, a diagnosis flag, a procedure record, is captured in an electronic health record following a coding standard such as LOINC, ICD, or CPT, but the same underlying concept, HbA1c control, for instance, is often recorded under different local codes by different facilities within the same health system, especially after a merger or an EHR migration. A user-defined quality measure is usually a formula over one or more of these coded elements, sometimes a standard measure, sometimes a custom combination a quality officer defines on the fly: a 30-day readmission rate for diabetic patients over 65, excluding transfers to hospice care.

The failure mode that should shape the whole design: an LLM asked to map a measure description directly to clinical codes will sometimes produce a plausible code that does not exist in this facility's local code set, or exists but means something subtly different in this system's specific EHR configuration. That failure is invisible to the quality officer, who sees a confident, wrong percentage rather than an error, on a number that may feed directly into a public quality report or a reimbursement calculation. The LLM should never be the thing resolving which code is which. A knowledge graph should be.

Architecture, measure translation: Build a property graph (FalkorDB or equivalent) where nodes are abstract clinical concepts and the facility-specific codes that implement each one, with edges encoding which code, in which facility's EHR, satisfies which concept. Layer the formula structure into the graph too, numerator, denominator, cohort filters, exclusions. An LLM parser's only job is to extract structure from the user's free-text definition, the concepts referenced, the arithmetic relationship, the cohort and exclusions. That structured intent is then resolved against the graph, each concept mapped to the real codes available for the facilities in scope, rather than letting the model recall a code from memory. The resolved formula, now expressed in real code identifiers, is what actually runs as a query against the clinical data warehouse.

Before computing anything, show the user the resolved formula in plain language, this computes X divided by Y, for the cohort specified, excluding Z, and ask for confirmation on first use. A wrong interpretation caught before it runs costs five seconds. A wrong interpretation that runs silently costs a quality report submitted on a number that was never actually correct. For the near-real-time requirement, push most of the cost into pre-aggregation: a streaming layer maintains rolling aggregates for measure combinations that recur often, standard quality measures reported monthly or quarterly, so a known measure is mostly a cache lookup, and only genuinely novel custom measures trigger a fresh pass over raw clinical data.

Architecture, anomaly detection and RCA: The same topology graph built for measure resolution is reusable here, care units belong to departments, departments belong to facilities, facilities share a clinical service line or a common EHR instance. Run anomaly detection on the relevant streaming signals per node, combining a statistical baseline (seasonal decomposition fits clinical volume well, given seasonal effects like flu season) with a multivariate detector that catches correlated shifts a single-measure threshold misses.

The graph earns its place at the root cause step. When a measure trips an anomaly threshold in one care unit, walk the topology graph outward to the parent department, sibling units in the same facility, and the shared EHR instance or service line, and check the data for each in the same time window. A spike isolated to one unit with clean neighbours points to a local staffing or workflow issue. The same spike across every unit under one department points upstream, to a department-wide protocol change or an EHR order-set rollout. This is structural reasoning the time-series data alone cannot give, paired with temporal reasoning the graph alone cannot give, queried together rather than left as two dashboards a quality officer has to merge by hand. An agentic layer fits naturally on top: on detecting an anomaly, an agent queries the graph for organisational context, queries the data warehouse for correlated signals in the implicated neighbourhood, and produces a short root-cause summary for a quality and safety officer, citing the specific measures and units that drove the conclusion so the officer can verify rather than just trust it.

Evaluation: Precision and recall against a labelled set of historical quality events, time from anomaly onset to detection, and, most importantly, whether the proposed root cause matched what the post-incident review actually found. That third metric is the one most system designs skip, and the one that matters most.

Hint: Interviewers asking this kind of question are usually checking whether you reach for an LLM to do work a graph should be doing instead. Naming the exact point where the LLM's role stops and a structured lookup takes over is what separates a working design from a demo.

The same pattern applies wherever locally-varying identifiers stand in for standardised concepts, telecom network counters that differ by vendor, banking ledger codes that differ by institution, retail SKU mappings that differ by supplier: an LLM extracts structure from a free-text request, and a knowledge graph resolves that structure to the specific environment's real identifiers, rather than letting the model guess.

## Q6. How would you estimate the size of a ball that is moving across frames in a video?

Sample answer: Split the problem into detection and geometric estimation. Run an object detector (YOLO for real-time use, or a two-stage detector like Faster R-CNN if latency is not critical) to get a bounding box per frame, then track the object across frames with SORT or DeepSORT, which associates detections using motion prediction (typically a Kalman filter) plus appearance matching, so the same ball is not re-detected as a new object each frame. Converting a consistent pixel bounding box to true physical size needs either a calibrated camera (known focal length and distance, via stereo vision or a depth sensor) or a known reference object in the scene. Motion blur on fast-moving objects elongates the bounding box in the direction of motion; using the minor axis as the size estimate mitigates this.

Hint: The interviewer usually wants to see the problem decomposed, detection, tracking, and calibration are separate concerns, rather than reaching straight for one end-to-end model.

## Q7. How does a Kalman filter help with object tracking, and what does it assume?

Sample answer: A Kalman filter maintains a probabilistic estimate of an object's state, typically position and velocity, updated each frame in two steps: prediction, which projects the state forward using a motion model, and update, which corrects the prediction using the new detection, weighted by relative uncertainty. It assumes the process is linear (or linearised, as in an Extended Kalman Filter) with Gaussian noise. This lets a tracker survive brief occlusions or missed detections by trusting its own motion prediction for a few frames, and smooths jittery raw detections into a coherent trajectory.

Hint: If motion is highly non-linear (a bouncing ball changing direction abruptly), mention that a particle filter handles multi-modal uncertainty better, at higher compute cost.

## Q8. Walk through how you would deploy a trained model on AWS, from artifact to serving endpoint.

Sample answer: Store the artifact in S3. For managed serving, SageMaker hosts it directly with autoscaling, health checks, and blue-green deployment built in. For more control, containerise the model behind FastAPI or a Triton inference server, push to ECR, and deploy on ECS or EKS behind a load balancer, autoscaling on request queue depth or GPU utilisation. For asynchronous or batch workloads, decouple the request path with SQS so a queue absorbs bursts while worker instances pull jobs, protecting the serving layer from spikes. Version the model artifact and any preprocessing logic together so a rollback restores both consistently.

Hint: On cost, GPU instances bill whether idle or busy, so for spiky traffic use SageMaker's serverless inference option or autoscale aggressively to zero during idle periods, accepting the cold-start tradeoff.

## Q9. Why does an ML serving workload need Kubernetes, and what does it actually manage for you?

Sample answer: Kubernetes manages scheduling containers onto available nodes, restarting failed pods automatically, horizontal autoscaling on CPU, memory, or custom metrics like GPU utilisation or latency, rolling updates that swap model versions without downtime, and service discovery so other services reach the endpoint through a stable name regardless of which pod is serving. For ML specifically, GPU scheduling needs the NVIDIA device plugin to expose GPUs as a schedulable resource, typically with a dedicated GPU node pool to avoid wasting expensive nodes on CPU-only jobs.

Hint: Distinguish Kubernetes' job, orchestration, scaling, resilience, from the inference server's job, batching requests and optimising the forward pass (Triton, vLLM); they are complementary layers, not substitutes.

### Q10. How would you design an ML system to scale from thousands to millions or billions of users, and what role does Kafka play in that pipeline?

Sample answer: The key shift at scale is moving from synchronous per-request compute to a layered system with caching, batching, and asynchronous processing. A CDN and edge caching absorb repeated requests; a stateless serving layer autoscales behind an API gateway; dynamic request batching (vLLM or Triton for LLMs) improves GPU throughput versus one forward pass per request. For workloads that do not need a synchronous response, push onto Kafka, a distributed append-only log that decouples producers from consumers, and have a pool of consumers process asynchronously, which decouples arrival rate from processing rate. Kafka is the standard backbone for streaming feature computation too, continuously aggregating user events into features a model needs, because it handles very high throughput, retains events so multiple independent consumers can replay the stream, and scales horizontally by adding partitions in a way a database-backed queue does not.

Hint: Mention consumer groups and partitioning, partitioning by user ID guarantees one user's events arrive in order at the same consumer, which matters for stateful feature computation. Billions of users also implies geographic distribution, with regional model replicas kept synchronised on retraining.

### Q11. A production API needs to serve predictions to millions of users with low latency. What are your main levers to reduce it?

Sample answer: Work the request path in order. Model-level: quantisation, distillation, or pruning, plus an optimised runtime (ONNX Runtime, TensorRT, vLLM) rather than the raw training framework. Batching-level: dynamic batching groups concurrent requests to better utilise the GPU, at the cost of a small added queueing delay, a tunable tradeoff. Infrastructure-level: keep the model warm to avoid cold starts, colocate serving close to users geographically, and cache results for repeated or near-duplicate inputs. Architecture-level: a cascade or routing pattern, a small model answers directly and a large model handles only the subset of requests that genuinely need it, trades a little accuracy on easy cases for a large average latency win.

Hint: Always ask what the actual latency budget and traffic pattern are before answering, the right lever depends on whether the bottleneck is compute, network, or queueing.

### Q12. Design a model to predict which of tens of thousands of transactions per user will generate a support complaint, where positive cases are rare.

Sample answer: Frame it as severe class imbalance: accuracy is meaningless, a model that always predicts 'no complaint' could be over 99 percent accurate and useless. Use precision-recall AUC, not ROC-AUC, as the primary offline metric, since ROC-AUC can look deceptively good under heavy imbalance. Engineer aggregated behavioural features per transaction, deviation from the user's own historical spending pattern, transaction velocity in a recent window, merchant category anomalies, rather than treating each transaction as independent, since the meaningful signal is usually 'unusual for this specific user.' For the imbalance itself, prefer algorithm-level handling, class weighting in the loss, or a model like XGBoost with scale_pos_weight, over naive oversampling, which risks overfitting to duplicated examples; SMOTE-style synthetic oversampling is safer than simple duplication if oversampling is needed. In production this becomes a ranking and thresholding problem, not a fixed 0.5 cutoff: contact the top N percent of transactions by predicted risk each day, where N is set by the capacity of whichever team handles follow-up, with the threshold chosen from the actual cost of a missed complaint versus an unnecessary proactive contact, and validated with a held-out control group to confirm the intervention itself reduces complaint rates, not just that the ranking looks good offline.

Hint: Be explicit that this is a ranking problem in production, not binary classification against a fixed threshold, and that F1 implicitly assumes false positives and false negatives are equally costly, which is essentially never true in a real business context.

## 5. Database and SQL

SQL is tested at almost every data science and ML engineering role. Window functions, CTEs, and query optimisation are the areas most likely to separate candidates.

## Q1. Write a query to find the top 3 users by revenue in each country.

SELECT country, user_id, revenue, rank FROM (SELECT country, user_id, revenue, RANK() OVER (PARTITION BY country ORDER BY revenue DESC) AS rank FROM user_revenue) ranked WHERE rank <= 3;

Key concepts: PARTITION BY divides the result into groups (here, by country). ORDER BY within the window function defines the ranking order. RANK() gives ties the same rank with gaps; DENSE_RANK() gives same rank without gaps; ROW_NUMBER() gives unique sequential numbers regardless of ties.

Hint: Know when to use RANK vs DENSE_RANK vs ROW_NUMBER. Interview questions about them are extremely common.

## Q2. Calculate a 7-day rolling average of daily sales.

SELECT date, daily_sales, AVG(daily_sales) OVER (ORDER BY date ROWS BETWEEN 6 PRECEDING AND CURRENT ROW) AS rolling_7_day_avg FROM daily_sales;

The ROWS BETWEEN clause defines the window frame. ROWS BETWEEN 6 PRECEDING AND CURRENT ROW includes the current row and the 6 rows before it, giving a 7-row window. RANGE BETWEEN is the alternative, which operates on value differences rather than physical row positions.

Hint: Common variations: cumulative sum (ROWS BETWEEN UNBOUNDED PRECEDING AND CURRENT ROW), month-over-month growth rate, running maximum.

## Q3. Find users who made purchases in January 2026 but not in February 2026.

Method 1 (NOT IN): SELECT DISTINCT user_id FROM orders WHERE month = '2026-01' AND user_id NOT IN (SELECT user_id FROM orders WHERE month = '2026-02');

Method 2 (LEFT JOIN): SELECT DISTINCT jan.user_id FROM (SELECT user_id FROM orders WHERE month = '2026-01') jan LEFT JOIN (SELECT user_id FROM orders WHERE month = '2026-02') feb ON jan.user_id = feb.user_id WHERE feb.user_id IS NULL;

Method 2 is generally preferred for large tables because NOT IN with subqueries can be slow and handles NULLs unexpectedly. EXCEPT is a cleaner third option where supported.

Hint: Know the NULL behaviour: NOT IN returns no rows if the subquery contains any NULL values. This is a common interview trap.

## Q4. What is the difference between a CTE and a subquery? When would you use each?

Both produce a temporary result set within a query. CTEs (WITH clause) differ in readability: they are named and defined before the main query, making complex multi-step logic easier to read and debug. CTEs can be recursive (for hierarchical data like org charts or tree structures). Subqueries are inline and can sometimes be more efficient for simple cases because some optimisers treat them differently. Use CTEs when you need to reference the intermediate result more than once or when the logic is complex enough to benefit from naming.

Hint: Practice recursive CTEs: the pattern for a CTE that walks a parent-child hierarchy comes up in org chart, product category, and bill of materials questions.

## Q5. How do you optimise a slow query?

Start with EXPLAIN or EXPLAIN ANALYZE to see the query execution plan. Look for: sequential scans on large tables (suggests missing index), nested loop joins on large sets (suggests index or join order issue), high estimated vs actual row count mismatch (suggests stale statistics, run ANALYZE). Common fixes: add an index on the column being filtered or joined (B-tree for equality and range, covering index to avoid table lookups), rewrite correlated subqueries as joins, avoid SELECT *, push filters as early as possible in the query, partition large tables on the column most commonly used for filtering.

Hint: Know the difference between an index scan and an index-only scan: an index-only scan retrieves data directly from the index without touching the table, and is only possible when all columns needed are in the index.

# 6. RAG Systems

RAG questions appear in nearly every GenAI-related interview. Expect questions at three levels: conceptual understanding, system design, and debugging.

### Q1. Walk me through a RAG pipeline from document ingestion to serving a query.

Offline pipeline: Load documents, extract text (handling PDFs, HTML, Word as needed), clean and normalise, chunk into overlapping segments, embed each chunk using an embedding model (e.g. text-embedding-ada-002 or a local model like BGE), store embeddings with metadata (source document, page number, chunk index) in a vector store.

Online pipeline: Receive user query, optionally expand or rephrase it, embed the query using the same embedding model, retrieve top-k semantically similar chunks from the vector store, optionally rerank using a cross-encoder, format the retrieved chunks as context, pass context and query to a generative LLM with a prompt that instructs it to answer using the provided context, return the answer with citations.

Hint: Interviewers will probe each step. Know one specific failure mode at each stage and how you would detect and fix it.

### Q2. How do you evaluate a RAG pipeline?

Evaluate retrieval and generation separately. Retrieval metrics: precision at k (fraction of retrieved chunks that are relevant), recall at k (fraction of relevant chunks that are retrieved), MRR (mean reciprocal rank). Generation metrics: faithfulness (does the answer stay within the retrieved context or hallucinate beyond it?), answer relevancy (does the answer address the question?), groundedness (can each claim be traced to a retrieved chunk?). End-to-end: human evaluation on a labelled QA set, and production metrics like user satisfaction signals.

Hint: Know the Ragas framework: it operationalises faithfulness, answer relevancy, context precision, and context recall with LLM-as-a-Judge scoring, enabling automated evaluation at scale.

### Q3. Your RAG system is producing answers that are correct but not answering the actual question. What do you investigate?

This is a retrieval problem: the system is retrieving chunks that are topically related but not the specific ones that answer the question. Investigate: query-chunk semantic gap (the query phrasing does not match how the answer is expressed in the document, fix with query expansion or HyDE), chunking granularity (chunks may be too large and dilute the relevant sentence in irrelevant context, or too small and miss surrounding context), embedding model mismatch (a general embedding model may not capture domain-specific semantics well, consider fine-tuning or switching to a domain-specific model), retrieval count (retrieving too few chunks may miss the relevant one, try increasing k and adding a reranker to filter).

Hint: Always separate retrieval failures from generation failures. Log the retrieved chunks alongside the answer during development so you can inspect them directly.

## Q4. What is the difference between semantic search and keyword search, and when would you use each?

Keyword search (BM25) ranks documents by exact term overlap, adjusted for document length and term frequency. It is fast, interpretable, and excellent when queries use the same terminology as the documents. Semantic search embeds both query and documents into a vector space and retrieves by cosine similarity. It handles paraphrase, synonyms, and concept-level matching that keyword search misses, but can miss exact terms and is more expensive. Hybrid search (combining BM25 scores and vector similarity, often with RRF fusion) outperforms either alone on most benchmarks and is the practical default for production RAG systems.

Hint: Know Reciprocal Rank Fusion (RRF): it combines ranked lists from multiple retrievers without requiring score normalisation. It is simple and consistently effective.

## Q5. How do you handle a RAG system that needs to answer questions over a frequently updated knowledge base?

Avoid full re-indexing if the update rate is high. Use an incremental indexing pipeline: new or updated documents trigger embedding and upsert operations into the vector store using document IDs. Deleted documents require a delete operation by ID. For real-time requirements, maintain a change data capture pipeline from the document store to the embedding pipeline. Version document chunks so that outdated chunks can be filtered or ranked lower. For very high update rates, consider a two-tier architecture: a live index covering recent documents plus a bulk index for historical content, merged at query time.

Hint: Ask the interviewer about the update frequency during clarification. It determines whether you need streaming ingestion or nightly batch reprocessing.

## Q6. What are the main evaluation metrics for a RAG system, and what does each one catch?

Sample answer: Split evaluation into retrieval quality and generation quality, since a RAG system can fail at either stage independently. For retrieval: context precision (what fraction of retrieved chunks are relevant) and context recall (what fraction of needed information was retrieved) catch an irrelevant or incomplete retriever. For generation, given good retrieval: faithfulness or groundedness (does the answer only use claims supported by the retrieved context) and answer relevance (does the answer actually address the question asked) are the two most important, tracked separately because a system can be well-grounded while answering a slightly different question than what was asked.

Hint: Frameworks like RAGAS implement these using an LLM-as-a-judge approach, a separate LLM call scores faithfulness by checking whether each claim in the answer is entailed by the retrieved context, worth understanding mechanically rather than treating as a black box.

## Q7. What evaluation is specific to a knowledge-graph-based RAG system, beyond standard RAG evals?

Sample answer: KG-RAG adds a structural dimension flat vector RAG does not have. Path correctness checks whether the reasoning path traversed through the graph for a multi-hop question is valid and relevant, not just whether the final answer happens to be right by coincidence. Entity linking accuracy checks whether query mentions were correctly resolved to graph nodes, since a wrong match early on silently derails everything downstream. Graph coverage measures whether the graph itself contains what is needed to answer a class of questions at all. Hop-level faithfulness checks that each intermediate step in a multi-hop chain is individually grounded, not just the final answer.

Hint: Build a curated set of multi-hop test questions with known correct reasoning paths, not just known correct final answers, since getting the right answer via a wrong path is a failure mode flat accuracy metrics miss entirely.

## Q8. What is NDCG, and why is it a better metric than plain precision for a ranked list of retrieved results?

Sample answer: NDCG, Normalised Discounted Cumulative Gain, rewards relevant results for appearing near the top of a ranked list, not just for appearing somewhere in it. Cumulative Gain sums relevance scores but ignores position; Discounted Cumulative Gain (DCG) divides each score by a logarithmic discount based on position, typically log2(position + 1), so a relevant result ranked first contributes far more than one ranked tenth; Normalised DCG divides your DCG by the DCG of the ideal ranking, giving a 0-to-1 score comparable across queries. Plain precision treats every position equally and cannot express 'same relevant documents, worse order,' which is exactly what NDCG is built to catch.

Hint: Be ready to compute a small example by hand: relevance scores [3, 2, 0, 1] at ranks 1 to 4, DCG equals 3/log2(2) + 2/log2(3) + 0/log2(4) + 1/log2(5), compared against the DCG of [3, 2, 1, 0] sorted ideally.

## Q9. How would you use NDCG specifically to evaluate a RAG retriever?

Sample answer: Build a labelled evaluation set of queries with graded relevance judgments across a pool of candidate documents, not just one correct document per query, since real retrieval quality is about getting the best evidence near the top, not just retrieving one right answer somewhere in the list. Run the retriever, take its top-k ranked results, and compute NDCG@k against the labels. This is more informative than context precision or recall alone because it captures ordering, a retriever that finds the most relevant chunk but ranks it fifth is doing meaningfully worse than one that ranks it first, even though both score identically on a binary hit-or-miss metric.

Hint: Mention Mean Reciprocal Rank as the simpler cousin metric, useful when there is typically only one correct answer per query, versus NDCG which handles multiple graded-relevance results more naturally.

How to get graded relevance without ground truth: one way is to have an LLM judge scoring each query-chunk pair against a rubric (3 = directly answers, 2 = substantially relevant, 1 = tangential, 0 = irrelevant), calibrated against a small human-reviewed subset before you trust it at scale.

## Q10. How do you evaluate a RAG (or graph-RAG) system when you have no golden question-answer dataset?

Sample answer: A missing golden dataset is not an excuse for no evaluation, it is an evaluation-design problem, and the way through it is to decompose the evaluation rather than search for one reference-based metric. Split it into retrieval quality, generation quality, and end-to-end outcome, and notice that generation is actually easier to evaluate without ground truth than retrieval is. Faithfulness, or groundedness, checks whether every claim in the answer is supported by the retrieved context, and an LLM judge or claim-level entailment check can do that without ever seeing a correct answer. Answer relevance checks whether the response addresses the question asked, again with no reference required.

Retrieval is the harder half, but it can be bootstrapped rather than hand-labelled from scratch. Sample representative chunks from the corpus, generate realistic questions each chunk can answer, and retain the source chunk as known evidence; running those questions through the retriever and checking whether it recovers the known chunk gives Recall@K and MRR without a human ever writing a question. This is a synthetic or silver evaluation set, not a gold one, and it comes with a real caveat worth stating out loud: generated questions can be unnaturally easy or biased toward the source chunk's own vocabulary, so a representative subset should be validated by a domain expert, and high-value production queries should be progressively curated into a genuine golden set over time. For a graph-RAG system the same logic extends structurally: path correctness (was the multi-hop traversal actually valid, not just the final answer right by coincidence) and entity-linking accuracy can both be checked without ground-truth answers, by validating the reasoning path itself rather than only the output.

The retrieval-eval toolbox: Recall@K (was the evidence retrieved anywhere in top K), Precision@K (how much of what's retrieved is actually relevant, this catches context pollution), Hit Rate@K (did at least one relevant item show up), MRR (how early did the first relevant result land), NDCG@K (how good is the whole ranking given graded, not binary, relevance), MAP (ranking quality across multiple relevant documents). Close with the point that Recall@10 = 94% can still hide a real problem if the important chunks sit at positions 8–10, which is exactly what NDCG catches and Recall alone doesn't.

Here we must remember while deciding what evals to use in a RAG system: no golden dataset (for generation) and no relevance labels (for retrieval) are separate gaps. You can lack a reference answer entirely while still having, or bootstrapping, graded relevance judgments, which means Recall@K, MRR, and NDCG@K are all legitimately computable even with zero golden answers. That line is worth its own sentence since it's the kind of distinction a deep interviewer is specifically listening for.

If the interviewer pushes further with 'how do you know the judge is right,' treat LLM-as-a-Judge as a calibrated proxy, not ground truth: measure its agreement against a small human-labelled set, use explicit per-claim rubrics rather than an opaque one-to-five score, and revalidate it periodically. In production, layer behavioural signals on top of all of this, abstention quality, citation usage, reformulation rate, escalation rate, and task completion, since those are available continuously and require no evaluation set at all. The overall shape to communicate is four levels of increasing maturity: reference-free metrics you can run on day one, a bootstrapped synthetic set you build in week one, a human-curated golden set you grow progressively, and production behavioural monitoring underneath all of it. You do not wait for a golden dataset to start evaluating; you use evaluation to build one.

Hint: This question recurs across formats, RAG, graph-RAG, and agent evaluation are all variants of 'how do you measure quality without a labelled answer,' and the decompose-rather-than-search-for-one-metric answer transfers directly across all three. See the boxed reference-based versus reference-free matrix in Appendix L for the compact version to have ready.

# 7. ML Fundamentals and Statistics

These questions appear at every level. Juniors are expected to know the basics; seniors are expected to connect them to practical system implications.

### Q1. Explain the bias-variance tradeoff.

Sample answer: Prediction error decomposes into bias (error from wrong assumptions: a linear model fitting a nonlinear relationship), variance (error from sensitivity to training data fluctuations: a model that memorises noise), and irreducible noise. High bias means underfitting: the model is too simple. High variance means overfitting: the model is too complex. The tradeoff is that reducing bias (adding model complexity) tends to increase variance, and reducing variance (regularisation, simpler model) tends to increase bias. In practice, you manage it through: cross-validation to detect overfitting, regularisation (L1/L2, dropout), ensemble methods (bagging reduces variance, boosting reduces bias), and data augmentation.

Hint: Be ready to give a concrete example: decision trees have low bias but high variance; deep trees overfit but shallow trees underfit. Random forests reduce variance by averaging many high-variance trees.

### Q2. What is p-value and what does it not mean?

Sample answer: A p-value is the probability of observing a test statistic as extreme as or more extreme than the one observed, assuming the null hypothesis is true. It does not tell you the probability that the null hypothesis is true, and it does not tell you the probability that your result is due to chance. A p-value under 0.05 does not mean the effect is large or practically significant: with enough data, even trivial effects become statistically significant. A p-value above 0.05 does not mean the null is true: it may mean insufficient power. What matters alongside statistical significance: effect size, confidence intervals, and whether the result replicates.

Hint: Know the difference between Type I error (false positive, rejecting a true null) and Type II error (false negative, failing to reject a false null). Alpha controls Type I; power (1 minus beta) controls Type II.

### Q3. How would you design an A/B test for a product change?

Sample answer: Define the primary metric and the minimum detectable effect you care about. Use a power calculation to determine sample size needed: typically power of 0.8, alpha of 0.05, and the minimum effect size gives you the required n per group. Ensure random assignment is at the right unit (user-level for most product changes, session-level only if users will not see both variants). Run for a predetermined duration, typically at least one full week to account for day-of-week effects, and do not stop early based on interim results (p-hacking). Analyse with a two-sample t-test for continuous metrics, chi-squared or z-test for proportions. Check for novelty effects and segment the results by user cohort.

Hint: Common A/B test pitfalls: peeking at results too early and stopping when significant (inflates Type I error), network effects (users in control group affected by users in treatment group), and survivorship bias in the analysis cohort.

## Q4. What is gradient descent and how does learning rate affect training?

Sample answer: Gradient descent is an optimisation algorithm that minimises a loss function by iteratively moving parameters in the direction opposite to the gradient. At each step, parameters are updated by subtracting the learning rate times the gradient. Stochastic gradient descent uses a single sample per step; mini-batch SGD uses a batch. Learning rate too high: the updates overshoot minima, training oscillates or diverges. Learning rate too low: training is slow and may converge to a poor local minimum. Modern practice uses adaptive optimisers (Adam, AdamW) that adjust the effective learning rate per parameter, plus learning rate scheduling (warmup followed by cosine decay or step decay).

Hint: Know vanishing and exploding gradients: in deep networks, gradients can become near-zero (vanish) or very large (explode) during backpropagation. Residual connections, layer normalisation, and gradient clipping are the main mitigations.

## Q5. When would you use precision vs recall vs F1 as your evaluation metric?

Precision: fraction of positive predictions that are actually positive. Use when false positives are costly: spam detection (flagging legitimate email as spam is bad), content moderation at low tolerance.

Recall: fraction of actual positives correctly identified. Use when false negatives are costly: disease screening (missing a case is worse than an unnecessary follow-up test), fraud detection (missing fraud is worse than blocking a legitimate transaction). F1: harmonic mean of precision and recall. Use when both false positives and false negatives matter and you want a single balanced metric. For imbalanced classes, prefer F1 over accuracy. For probabilistic outputs, use AUC-ROC (ranking ability) or AUC-PR (for high class imbalance where the positive class is rare).

Hint: The most important habit: always ask what the cost of each error type is before choosing a metric. The business context determines the right tradeoff.

## Q6. What is the core architectural difference between TensorFlow and PyTorch, and why does it matter?

Sample answer: The historical difference is static versus dynamic computation graphs. Original TensorFlow built a static graph ahead of time, enabling aggressive optimisation and easy deployment but awkward debugging. PyTorch uses eager execution by default, operations run immediately, so you can use standard Python debugging and dynamic control flow naturally, which made it dominant in research. TensorFlow 2.x adopted eager execution too, closing most of the gap, and both now offer a compilation step (torch.compile, tf.function) that traces eager code into an optimised graph for serving. By 2026 the meaningful difference is ecosystem: PyTorch dominates research and LLM serving; TensorFlow retains strength in mobile and edge deployment via TensorFlow Lite.

Hint: If asked which to use for a new project, the honest answer in 2026 is PyTorch by default unless you have a specific edge-deployment constraint, since the open-source model ecosystem is overwhelmingly PyTorch-first.

## Q7. What does autograd actually do, mechanically, in a framework like PyTorch?

Sample answer: Autograd builds a dynamic computation graph as the forward pass executes; each tensor requiring gradients carries a reference to the function that created it. Calling .backward() on a scalar loss traverses this graph in reverse, applying the chain rule at each node to compute the gradient of the loss with respect to every tensor requiring gradients, accumulating results into each tensor's .grad attribute. This is reverse-mode automatic differentiation, efficient because it computes gradients with respect to all inputs in a single backward pass regardless of how many inputs there are.

Hint: Know why the graph is freed after backward() by default (memory) and what retain_graph=True does if you need to call backward() more than once on the same graph.

## Q8. How does dropout actually work mechanically, and why does it reduce overfitting?

Sample answer: During training, dropout randomly zeroes activations in a layer at each forward pass with probability p, typically 0.2 to 0.5, and rescales remaining activations by 1/(1-p) so expected magnitude stays consistent (inverted dropout). At test time dropout is off and the full network is used. It reduces overfitting by preventing co-adaptation, since any neuron might be dropped on any pass, the network cannot rely on specific neuron combinations and learns features useful in combination with many random subsets of the rest of the network, approximating an implicit ensemble of thinned sub-networks.

Hint: Know the placement convention, dropout typically follows activations in fully-connected layers, is used more sparingly in convolutional layers (batch norm does more regularising there), and modern large transformers rely less on it since scale itself regularises.

## Q9. Beyond dropout and L1/L2, what other techniques fight overfitting, and when would you reach for each?

Sample answer: Early stopping halts training when validation loss stops improving, cheap and should be a default. Data augmentation increases effective training diversity without new labels. Batch normalisation has a regularising side effect from the noise in per-batch statistics. Label smoothing softens one-hot targets, preventing overconfidence and improving calibration. Ensembling reduces variance by averaging predictions across independently trained models, at multiplied training and serving cost. Reducing model capacity is the bluntest instrument, worth mentioning since not every overfitting problem needs a clever regulariser.

Hint: Connect the choice to the symptom, augmentation for too little data diversity, early stopping for a model that memorises given enough epochs, ensembling when compute allows, capacity reduction when nothing else works.

## Q10. How does a decision tree decide where to split, mechanically?

Sample answer: At each node, the tree considers every feature and split point and picks the split that most reduces impurity in the resulting children, Gini impurity or entropy for classification, variance reduction for regression. The algorithm is greedy, picking the locally best split without looking ahead, efficient but sometimes globally suboptimal. Growth continues recursively until a stopping condition, max depth, minimum samples per leaf, or no further improvement, and unconstrained trees split until every leaf is pure, which is why single trees have low bias but very high variance.

Hint: Be ready to state Gini impurity's formula intuitively, 1 minus the sum of squared class probabilities in a node, zero when pure, maximal when classes are evenly split.

## Q11. How does XGBoost differ from a random forest, and why does it typically perform better on tabular data?

Sample answer: A random forest bags many independent, deep, high-variance trees on bootstrapped samples and averages predictions, reducing variance. XGBoost boosts sequentially, each new tree fits the gradient of the loss with respect to the current ensemble's predictions, reducing bias progressively. XGBoost adds a regularisation term penalising tree complexity, a second-order Taylor approximation of the loss for more accurate split-finding, built-in missing-value handling, and efficient histogram-based parallel split-finding. On tabular data, boosted trees tend to beat both random forests and neural networks because tabular features are heterogeneous and non-smooth with complex interactions that axis-aligned splits capture naturally, whereas neural networks need far more data to learn the same interactions without that inductive bias.

Hint: If asked when not to use XGBoost, very high-dimensional sparse data (text, images) is usually better served by neural approaches, and tree ensembles do not extrapolate outside the training range, which matters for time-series forecasting.

**Q12. A bag has 3 blue balls and 20 black balls. What is the probability of drawing 2 blue balls in a row without replacement?**

Sample answer: 23 balls total. Probability the first is blue is 3/23. Given the first was blue, 2 blue remain out of 22, so the second is blue with probability 2/22, or 1/11. Multiply since these are sequential dependent draws: 3/23 times 1/11 equals 3/253, about 1.19 percent. The key mechanic is that draws are without replacement, so both the numerator (remaining blue balls) and denominator (total remaining) shrink together after the first draw.

Hint: A common follow-up is the probability of exactly one blue ball in two draws, remember to sum both orderings, blue-then-black and black-then-blue, which tests whether you understand combinations versus a single sequential path.

**Q13. What is the general approach for solving 'balls in a bag' or combinatorial probability questions under interview pressure?**

Sample answer: First decide whether order matters and whether draws are with or without replacement, which determines permutations, combinations, or sequential conditional probabilities. For an unordered outcome across several draws without replacement, combinations, favourable combinations over total combinations, is usually cleaner than multiplying sequential probabilities, though both give the same answer done correctly. For sequential reasoning, explicitly track how the numerator and denominator change after each draw, since forgetting that removing an item changes both is where most errors happen under time pressure.

Hint: Say your reasoning out loud as you go rather than jumping to a formula; interviewers weight the process, not just the final number, especially when the arithmetic itself is simple.

**Q14. What are the advantages and disadvantages of ReLU, sigmoid, and tanh as activation functions?**

Sample answer: Sigmoid squashes to (0, 1), interpretable as a probability, still standard for binary classification output layers, but suffers vanishing gradients, for large positive or negative inputs the curve flattens and gradients shrink toward zero, stalling learning in deep stacks; it is also not zero-centred, biasing downstream gradient updates. Tanh squashes to (-1, 1), is zero-centred and converges faster than sigmoid in hidden layers, but still saturates at its extremes. ReLU, max(0, x), became the default hidden-layer activation because it does not saturate for positive inputs, gradient exactly 1, so gradients propagate cleanly through many layers, and it is computationally trivial versus the exponentials in sigmoid and tanh. Its downside is the dying ReLU problem, a neuron whose input is always negative outputs zero with zero gradient everywhere in that regime and can get permanently stuck, which is why Leaky ReLU and GELU (used in most modern transformers) exist.

Hint: Connect this to where each is actually used today, sigmoid at output layers and inside LSTM gates, tanh inside LSTM and GRU cell states, ReLU or its variants (GELU, SwiGLU) dominating hidden layers in modern feedforward and transformer architectures, a fit-to-purpose decision, not a single winner.

### Q15. Why does ReLU not saturate, and what does 'saturate' actually mean in this context?

Sample answer: An activation saturates when its output goes nearly flat and insensitive to further input changes, so the local gradient approaches zero. Sigmoid and tanh saturate at both ends of their range. ReLU only saturates on the negative side, where output and gradient are both exactly zero, but on the positive side it is linear with slope 1 to infinity, never flattening. This asymmetry is why ReLU largely solved vanishing gradients for the positive-input regime while introducing the dying ReLU problem for the negative-input regime, trading one failure mode for a more localised one.

Hint: If asked about GELU specifically, it is smooth and non-monotonic near zero rather than having ReLU's sharp kink, which empirically improves optimisation in very deep transformer stacks, why GPT-style and BERT-style models use it in their feedforward sublayers.

## 12. Real Interview Logs: Questions Actually Asked in My Search

The questions below come from real interviews and internal technical discussions from my own search, grouped by the kind of engagement rather than by employer, in keeping with this book's practice elsewhere of describing what was asked without naming who asked it. Every question actually put to me is listed here, so the set is complete even where I have not repeated an answer. Where a question duplicates ground already covered earlier in this appendix, it is listed with a pointer rather than answered twice. Where it is genuinely distinctive, scenario-specific, or came up in an unusual form, it gets a full sample answer and hint, in the same format as the rest of this appendix.

## An Enterprise Architecture Review (CTO-Level Presentation)

This was less a conventional interview than a live walkthrough of a take-home system I had built, presented directly to technical leadership. All of the following came up:

– Explain your architecture end-to-end.
– How do you process millions of files?
– How do you extract metadata?
– How do you avoid duplicate metadata?
– How do you search efficiently?
– How would this scale?
– Why did you choose TF-IDF over an embedding-based approach?
– Why pickle instead of a database?
– How would you productionise it?
– How do you cache?
– What happens when new files arrive?
– How would you improve retrieval?

### Q1. Why did you choose a lightweight approach like TF-IDF and pickle files over a database and an embedding model, and when would that choice stop being defensible?

Sample answer: For a take-home or an early prototype, the right question is not 'what is the best possible architecture' but 'what proves the concept fastest with the least infrastructure risk.' TF-IDF needs no training, no GPU, no external API dependency, and is fast to implement and reason about; pickled objects avoid standing up a database for a demo that will run once. The tradeoff is honest: TF-IDF misses semantic similarity (synonyms, paraphrases) that embeddings capture, and pickle files do not scale past what fits comfortably in memory, have no concurrent-write safety, and are a deserialisation security risk if the file ever comes from an untrusted source. The choice stops being defensible the moment there is more than one writer, the corpus no longer fits in memory, or retrieval quality on paraphrased queries actually matters to the product, at which point the natural upgrade path is a real embedding model backed by a vector database, with TF-IDF or BM25 kept as a cheap first-stage filter in a hybrid retrieval setup rather than discarded entirely.

Hint: The interviewer is testing engineering judgement, not just architecture recall, so name the scaling ceiling explicitly rather than defending the simple choice as if it were correct at every scale.

## Q2. How do you avoid duplicate metadata when processing millions of files that may arrive from multiple sources or be re-uploaded?

Sample answer: Deduplicate at two levels. At the file level, hash the file content (not the filename, which can change) with something like SHA-256, and use that hash as the idempotency key, so re-processing an identical file is a no-op rather than a duplicate insert. At the metadata level, where two different files can describe the same underlying entity with slightly different text, normalise extracted fields (case-folding, whitespace, canonical date formats) before comparison, and use a similarity threshold, exact match on normalised key fields, or fuzzy matching for looser fields, to decide whether an incoming record should update an existing entry rather than create a new one. For new files arriving continuously, this dedup check needs to run as part of the ingestion pipeline itself, not as a periodic batch cleanup job, since letting duplicates accumulate and reconciling later is much more expensive than preventing them at write time.

Hint: Distinguish exact deduplication (file hashing, cheap and unambiguous) from semantic deduplication (near-duplicate metadata records), since interviewers sometimes want to see that you know these are different problems requiring different techniques.

## A Domain-Specific AI Role: Knowledge Graphs, RAG, and Fine-Tuning over Technical Standards

This role probed domain-specific application of standard AI techniques to a large body of technical standards and operational data. Questions clustered into three groups.

On knowledge graphs specifically:

- Can operational KPIs be represented as a knowledge graph?
- What would the nodes be?
- What would the edges be?
- How would you use graph reasoning over that structure?

### Q3. How would you model operational KPIs as a knowledge graph, what are the nodes and edges?

Sample answer: Nodes represent the entities the KPIs describe and the KPIs themselves: physical assets (equipment units, facility nodes, and their components), geographic or organisational groupings (sites, regions), time periods, and the KPI metrics as their own node type (call drop rate, throughput, latency), since treating a metric as a node rather than just an edge attribute lets you attach metadata to it, definitions, thresholds, units, and connect it to the specifications that define it. Edges represent relationships: an asset MEASURED_BY a KPI at a given time, a KPI DEFINED_IN a specific section of a technical standard, an asset PART_OF a larger site or region, and causal or correlational edges between KPIs learned from historical data, such as equipment temperature CORRELATES_WITH failure rate. Graph reasoning becomes useful once you have this structure: a multi-hop query like 'which specification defines the threshold for a KPI that is degrading at sites in this region' is a graph traversal, not a database join across a dozen normalised tables, and anomaly propagation, tracing how a fault at one asset could be affecting KPIs several hops away, is naturally a graph problem.

Hint: The interviewer is checking whether you default to treating a KPI as a flat table column, which is the natural instinct for anyone coming from a relational background, or whether you see the relational and definitional structure underneath it that makes a graph representation actually pay off.

On retrieval-augmented generation over technical specifications:

– Build a RAG system over a large corpus of technical standards documents.

– How would you retrieve the right specification sections?

– How would you reduce hallucinations?

– How would GraphRAG help compared to standard RAG here?

### Q4. Standard RAG questions on retrieval, chunking, and hallucination reduction are covered earlier in this appendix. How would GraphRAG specifically help over flat vector RAG for a large corpus of technical standards documents?

Sample answer: Technical specifications are heavily cross-referenced, a clause in one document defines a term used in another, a procedure references parameters defined elsewhere, and a KPI threshold in one section depends on a condition specified in a different section entirely. Flat vector RAG retrieves chunks based on surface similarity to the query and has no way to follow those cross-references, so a question that requires combining information from two linked but textually dissimilar sections often fails, the second chunk simply never gets retrieved because nothing in its wording matches the query. A knowledge graph built over the specification corpus, with edges capturing 'defines,' 'references,' and 'depends on' relationships extracted during ingestion, lets the retrieval step traverse from an initially retrieved chunk to the chunks it depends on, structurally rather than by similarity, which is exactly the failure mode multi-hop technical questions expose in a standard RAG pipeline.

Hint: Ground this in a concrete example if asked to go deeper, a KPI threshold that only makes sense once you know which operating condition it applies under, defined three sections away, is the kind of question that cleanly demonstrates the gap between flat retrieval and graph traversal.

On fine-tuning, the suggestion (rather than a direct question) was to fine-tune a small domain language model using QLoRA on a purpose-built vocabulary and compare it against the base model; the mechanics of that approach are covered under small language model training earlier in this appendix. Related dataset discussion referenced domain-specific QA benchmarks and specification corpora as training and evaluation sources, which is a useful reminder to know what public and internal datasets exist in your own domain before an interview, not a question with a single answer.

## Internal Enterprise AI Discussions (Not Formal Interviews)

Some of the most technically substantial questions I encountered were not interview questions at all, but proposals and design discussions inside a previous employer. They are worth including because they show the kind of open-ended, ambiguous framing that senior roles actually involve, closer to a design review than a quiz. Topics raised included:

- Predict ticket resolution time or likelihood from historical support data.
- Identify underperforming or inefficient network equipment from operational data.
- Build a natural-language-to-SQL chatbot over internal databases.
- Query and summarise results from a log search and analytics platform.
- Integrate a commercial AI coding assistant into an internal engineering workflow.
- Design an MCP-based architecture for connecting internal tools to an AI assistant.

### Q5. How would you build a model to predict how long a support ticket will take to resolve, or whether it will breach an SLA?

Sample answer: Frame it as a regression problem for time-to-resolution or a classification problem for SLA breach, and choose based on what the downstream action actually needs, a continuous estimate for capacity planning, or a binary flag for proactive escalation. Features fall into three groups: ticket content (category, priority, extracted entities from the free-text description, ideally via a lightweight NLP step rather than raw text into a tree model), historical patterns (this customer's or this issue type's average resolution time, current queue depth and agent workload at ticket creation time), and metadata (time of day, day of week, which team it was routed to). Gradient-boosted trees are a strong default here since ticket data is exactly the heterogeneous, tabular, interaction-heavy data that boosted trees handle well. The evaluation choice matters as much as the model: for SLA breach prediction specifically, this becomes an imbalanced classification problem similar to the rare-event prediction scenario covered under system design earlier in this appendix, precision-recall AUC and a business-cost-driven threshold, not accuracy.

Hint: Ask early whether the goal is prediction for its own sake or prediction to drive an intervention, escalating a ticket that is predicted to breach, since that changes whether false positives or false negatives are more costly and therefore which threshold and which metric actually matter.

### Q6. How would you architect MCP, the Model Context Protocol, into an internal tool so an AI assistant can access company systems securely?

Sample answer: MCP standardises how an AI assistant discovers and calls external tools and data sources, replacing bespoke, per-integration glue code with a common protocol. An MCP server exposes a defined set of tools, for instance query the ticket system, search internal documentation, read from a specific database view, each with a declared schema for inputs and outputs, and the AI client discovers and calls these tools through the protocol rather than through custom integration code written for each data source. The architecture question that actually matters is the security boundary: the MCP server should enforce the same authentication and authorisation as a human user would have, scoped to the minimum set of tools and data a given assistant deployment needs, with all calls logged and any tool that can mutate state, not just read, requiring an explicit and auditable permission separate from read-only tools. Treat it as you would any new API surface exposed to an automated caller, least privilege by default, not as a special case because the caller happens to be an LLM.

Hint: If asked what MCP actually solves versus a plain internal API, the honest answer is standardisation of the discovery and calling convention across many tools and many AI clients, not new capability that a bespoke integration could not already provide; its value is reducing the number of one-off integrations you have to build and maintain.

Natural-language-to-SQL and log-search-and-summarise assistants both reduce to the same underlying pattern, an LLM that translates a natural language question into a structured query against a specific schema, then formats the result back into natural language; the RAG and prompt engineering sections earlier in this appendix cover the relevant retrieval and grounding techniques, and the main addition specific to NL-to-SQL is validating the generated query against the actual schema and running it read-only before returning results, so a malformed or overly broad query is caught before it reaches the database rather than after.

## Coding Rounds

Across this search, coding assessments, not conceptual technical discussion, were consistently the elimination point, including at least two roles where the technical and system-design conversation went well and the process still ended at a Python or data-structures round. This is a data point worth taking seriously rather than a one-off: for a candidate whose strengths sit in architecture, research, and applied system design, coding fluency under timed pressure is a distinct skill that needs its own dedicated, repeated practice, not something that improves as a side effect of deep technical knowledge. The LeetCode pattern list and coding preparation guidance are covered under coding earlier in this appendix; the practical implication of this pattern is to weight practice time toward timed coding repetition specifically, ahead of further conceptual study, since conceptual gaps were not what closed doors in this search.

### General ML, Statistics, and SQL Screening Questions

These were largely standard screening questions, all already covered earlier in this appendix, listed here for completeness:

- Why would you use Random Forest over XGBoost, or the reverse? — covered under classical machine learning earlier in this appendix.
- Explain the bias-variance tradeoff. — covered under ML fundamentals and statistics earlier in this appendix.
- Explain regularisation and why a model overfits. — covered under ML fundamentals and statistics earlier in this appendix.
- How do you approach feature selection? — covered under feature engineering guidance elsewhere in this book.
- Precision versus recall, ROC versus PR curves. — covered under ML fundamentals and statistics earlier in this appendix.
- How does cross-validation work, and how do you handle class imbalance? — covered under ML fundamentals earlier in this appendix and under the rare-event prediction scenario under system design.
- Given a transactions table, find the top users by total spend. — this exact ranking-window-function pattern is answered under database and SQL earlier in this appendix.

### GenAI Screening Questions

GenAI questions were the fastest-growing category across this search and, by the more recent interviews, close to a default expectation rather than a specialisation. All of the following are answered under LLM concepts, RAG systems, or agentic AI earlier in this appendix:

- Explain RAG and how it works.

– Explain embeddings.
– Which vector database would you choose, and why?
– What chunking strategy would you use?
– What is metadata filtering and hybrid search?
– What is prompt engineering, and what techniques matter?
– What causes hallucinations, and how do you reduce them?
– What does temperature control?
– Explain function calling and tool use.
– What does agent architecture actually involve?

**Project Deep Dives**

Nearly every interview in this search, technical or not, spent significant time on a walkthrough of my own production work, more consistently than deep mathematics or even system design in the abstract. The recurring prompts were:

– Walk me through the architecture, end to end.
– Why this model, or this approach, and not an alternative?
– What metrics did you use, and why those?
– What was the biggest technical challenge?
– What was the biggest production issue, and how did you resolve it?
– What would you improve if you rebuilt it today?

There is no single sample answer for these, since the substance has to come from the specific project, but the pattern worth internalising is that this was the single most consistently weighted part of the process across every interview in this search, more reliable than deep mathematics, which came up rarely, and roughly as important as system design. Preparing a tight, honest, five-minute walkthrough of each major project, with the failure and the fix as vivid as the success, is worth more practice time than almost anything else on this list.

### Research Discussions

Where a candidate has publications or a public research portfolio, some interviewers used that as a springboard instead of, or in addition to, textbook questions, asking about the actual research areas represented in that portfolio rather than generic topics. The practical preparation for this is not a rehearsed answer but fluency: being able to state, in two or three plain sentences, what each of your own papers or projects actually claims, why it matters, and its most obvious limitation, since an interviewer probing your own work is really testing whether you can think critically about something you built yourself, not whether you can recite the abstract.

### Behavioural Questions

All standard, and all covered in the dedicated behavioural questions section earlier in this appendix: tell me about yourself, why are you leaving your current role, tell me about a difficult stakeholder, your biggest project, your biggest failure, and examples of leadership.

### A Consulting-Firm Senior GenAI Role: LLM Inference Systems Deep Dive

The conversation went almost entirely into the serving layer of LLMs, the engine that runs the model, rather than the application layer of RAG, agents, retrieval quality, and evaluation where most enterprise GenAI work actually happens.

All of the following came up:

– Why do you need vLLM at all? What problem does it solve?

– Is LLM inference memory bound or compute bound?

– Explain the KV cache. What is stored in it, and why does it dominate GPU memory under concurrent load?

– What hardware optimisations are needed to serve an open-source model efficiently?

## Q7. Is LLM inference memory bound or compute bound? Explain the prefill and decode phases.

Sample answer: It is both, but in different phases, and the distinction drives every serving optimisation. Every inference request has two operational phases. Prefill processes the entire input prompt in parallel to produce the first output token; because all prompt tokens go through the matrix multiplications at once, the GPU tensor cores are saturated and this phase is compute bound, limited by raw FLOPs. Decode then generates output autoregressively, one token at a time; the arithmetic per token is tiny, but for every single token the GPU must stream billions of model weights, plus the accumulated attention context, out of high-bandwidth memory into the processors. The compute units sit idle waiting for memory, so decode is memory-bandwidth bound. This is why time-to-first-token and tokens-per-second are optimised by different techniques: prefill benefits from faster attention kernels and prefix caching, while decode benefits from anything that shrinks or reuses memory traffic, quantisation, batching many concurrent requests so each weight fetch is amortised across users, and careful KV cache management.

Hint: If you remember one sentence, make it this one: prefill is compute bound, decode is memory-bandwidth bound. Interviewers use it as a gateway question; a candidate who has it can usually reason their way through everything that follows.

## Q8. What is the KV cache, why does it dominate GPU memory at scale, and what does vLLM actually do about it?

Sample answer: During attention, each generated token needs the key and value projections of every previous token. Without caching, those would be recomputed from scratch at every step, turning generation into a quadratic recomputation problem. The KV cache trades memory for speed: the key and value matrices of all processed tokens are kept in GPU memory and only the new token is computed each step. The catch is size. Under concurrent traffic with long contexts, the KV cache can consume more VRAM than the model weights themselves, and naive serving frameworks made it worse by pre-allocating one contiguous block per request sized for the maximum possible context, so a short request locked up memory it never used, causing out-of-memory failures at low actual utilisation. vLLM addresses this with PagedAttention, which manages the cache the way an operating system manages virtual memory: small non-contiguous pages allocated on demand, cutting memory waste from well over half to a few percent and fitting several times more concurrent users on the same GPU. On top of that, continuous batching inserts new requests into the running batch the moment any request finishes rather than waiting for a whole batch to complete, automatic prefix caching stores the KV cache of shared prefixes such as a common system prompt or shared RAG context so later requests skip that prefill work entirely, and KV cache quantisation to FP8 halves the cache footprint with negligible quality loss. Together these are the reason "just call the model in a loop" and "serve it with vLLM" can differ by a factor of two to four in the number of GPUs a deployment needs.

Hint: The business framing lands better than the systems framing in a consulting context: if a client deployment can carry the same traffic on 20 GPUs instead of 40, the saving over the life of the system is measured in crores. Being able to say why, in one paragraph, is the differentiator.

## Where This Layer of Knowledge Is Actually Used

It is worth being honest about how much of this an application-level GenAI career actually requires, because the answer shapes how much preparation time it deserves. There are broadly three kinds of GenAI engineer. Application engineers build RAG pipelines, agents, knowledge graphs, and evaluation harnesses; their question is how to improve answer quality. Platform engineers run models on Kubernetes with vLLM or Triton, autoscaling and GPU capacity planning; their question is how to serve hundreds of concurrent users. Systems engineers work on attention kernels, tensor parallelism, and CUDA; their question is how to squeeze out more tokens per second. At consulting firms and GCCs the large majority of GenAI work is the first kind, with a smaller platform slice and a very small systems slice concentrated in a central team.

The serving-layer slice is growing, though, for one structural reason: regulated clients. Banks, telecom operators, healthcare providers, and governments increasingly refuse to send confidential data to external model APIs, so they deploy open models such as Llama, Qwen, or Mistral inside their own infrastructure, and then someone has to answer whether the model fits on two GPUs or four, whether to quantise, and which inference engine to use. The consulting firms serving those clients advertise exactly this: LLMOps practices, GenAI platforms with LLM infrastructure optimisation, and cost rightsizing. So the interviewer asking about KV cache internals at a consulting firm is not necessarily showing off, even when the questions run well past what the median project there requires; the fairer reading is that they are testing whether a senior candidate could grow into the platform side, filtered through their own technical interests. Both things can be true at once, and neither changes what you should do about it.

What to do about it is not to spend months becoming a CUDA expert. The highest-return preparation, for the way these questions actually appear in interviews, is a bounded list: transformer internals including attention, the KV cache, positional embeddings, and FlashAttention at the level of what problem each solves; the major inference engines (vLLM, SGLang, TensorRT-LLM, Hugging Face TGI, Ollama) at the level of when you would pick each; GPU basics, meaning the memory-bandwidth versus compute distinction, quantisation, batching, and parallelism strategies; cloud deployment of models on the major platforms; and the recursion, tree, graph, and dynamic programming patterns that coding rounds keep drawing from. One encouraging note from this interview: an interviewer who skips straight to KV cache and memory bandwidth is assuming you already hold the standard LLM material. These questions are reserved for candidates being assessed at a senior level; the gap they probe is production systems familiarity, not foundational understanding.

For structured reading, Chip Huyen's AI Engineering (O'Reilly, 2025) is the single best match for this gap, covering inference optimisation, serving, and evaluation from an application engineer's side of the fence, with her earlier Designing Machine Learning Systems as the production-ML foundation underneath it.

Sebastian Raschka's Build a Large Language Model (From Scratch) is the fastest route to genuinely understanding attention and the KV cache rather than reciting them, because you implement both. Beyond books, the vLLM documentation and the PagedAttention paper (Kwon et al., 2023) are short, readable, and are the primary sources these interview questions are drawn from.

### The Pattern Across This Search

One thing held remarkably consistent across every interview logged here, across formal interviews and internal discussions alike: very few asked deep mathematics, most included system design or architecture, nearly all wanted a genuine deep dive into actual project work, and coding rounds were the single most common elimination point, even, and especially, when the technical conversation itself had gone well. If preparation time is limited, that ordering is the honest guide to where it should go: coding fluency first, project deep-dive narratives second, system design third, and conceptual theory last, not because theory does not matter, but because in this search it was consistently not what closed the door. One more pattern deserves calling out on its own: evaluation questions, specifically how do you know the system is actually good, recurred across formats that otherwise looked nothing alike, RAG rounds, graph-RAG and knowledge-graph rounds, and agent-design rounds all arrived at some version of the same question, and increasingly with the follow-up that no labelled dataset exists to check against. It was not a one-off; treat evaluation-without-ground-truth as core preparation rather than a specialist RAG topic, per the worked answer earlier in this appendix and the reference matrix in Appendix L.

## A Note on Using This Appendix

The questions here are representative, not exhaustive. The patterns are more important than any individual question: once you can explain attention from first principles, the specific question about scaled dot-product attention or flash attention is a minor variation.

Once you can design a fraud detection system, the recommendation system question is mostly the same framework applied to different constraints.

Practise out loud. Every question in this appendix should be answerable verbally, not just written. The interviewer cannot see your internal notes. What they can see is how clearly and confidently you think through a problem in real time.

Track which sections trip you up. A gap you identify here, before the interview, is a gap you can close. A gap that surfaces in the room is a gap that costs you the offer.

# Appendix H: Career Audit, Transition Plan, and Translation Guide

This appendix collects three short, practical tools for different moments in the search: assessing honestly where you are right now, planning the first ninety days once you have landed somewhere new, and translating an academic background into terms an industry hiring manager will recognise.

## Career Audit Worksheet

Use this worksheet once a year, or immediately after a job loss, a role change, or a period of feeling stuck. The goal is a specific diagnosis that tells you where to focus your effort in the next six months, not a comprehensive self-assessment.

Answer each prompt in writing, not in your head. The act of writing forces a precision that mental review does not.

### Section 1: Your Work Today

**What percentage of my typical week is execution work** (following defined processes, delivering against specifications, maintaining existing systems) versus judgment work (framing problems, making architectural decisions, evaluating trade-offs)?

Write your honest estimate: ____% execution, ____% judgment.

If execution is above 70 percent, your role is at structural risk from automation. This is not a crisis, but it is information.

**Could the execution portion of my work be done adequately by a well-prompted LLM or a junior professional with good tool literacy?**

Be specific about which tasks. List them.

**What is my domain depth?** Name the industry or domain where you have knowledge that goes beyond general ML competence. If you cannot name one, this is the gap to close first.

**What was the most consequential decision I made in the last six months?** If you cannot think of one, your role may not require the judgment that senior positions demand.

## Section 2: Your Market Position

**When did I last review 20-30 current job descriptions for roles I am realistically qualified for?** If longer than three months ago, do it before finishing this worksheet.

After reviewing JDs: what skills appear repeatedly that I do not currently have or cannot demonstrate? List them.

Current skills I have that appear frequently:

[write here]

Skills that appear frequently that I cannot demonstrate:

[write here]

Gap type (circle one): Positioning problem / Skills problem / Domain problem / Level problem

(See Chapter 11 for how to address each gap type.)

## Section 3: Your Public Footprint

**If a hiring manager searched my name right now, what would they find?** List every public artifact: GitHub repositories, published articles, conference talks, open-source contributions, LinkedIn posts with substantive content.

Public artifacts I have:

[list here]

**Of these, which ones demonstrate judgment and production thinking,** as opposed to tutorial reproduction or credential announcement?

Answer honestly. Tutorial reproductions: ____. Genuine judgment signals: ____.

**What would I work on publicly if I started today?** Name one specific project or article that would be genuinely useful to someone in my domain.

## Section 4: Financial and Optionality Position

**Financial runway:** If I lost my income today, how many months could I sustain my current expenses without distress? ______ months.

Target: 12 months minimum, 18 months for genuine career optionality. If below 6 months, financial runway is the most urgent priority before career strategy.

**Optionality:** What career moves are currently available to me that I am not taking? (Different companies, independent consulting, role changes, geographic moves.) Why am I not taking them?

**Learning rate:** Am I learning faster in this role than I would in the best alternative available to me? If no: why am I still here?

## Section 5: The Six-Month Plan

Based on the above, write three specific, concrete actions you will take in the next six months. Not aspirations. Specific actions with completion criteria.

Action 1: ______________________________________________

Completion criteria: ______________________________________

Action 2: ________________________________________

Completion criteria: ________________________________

Action 3: ________________________________________

Completion criteria: ________________________________

> *Review this worksheet in six months. The gap between what you wrote and what you did is as informative as the worksheet itself.*

## The 30-60-90 Day Plan for a New AI Role

Most career guides tell you how to get the job. Very few address what to do in the first three months once you have it. The first ninety days of a new role are disproportionately consequential: they establish your reputation, define the scope of work you are trusted with, and determine whether you are seen as a net contributor or a net consumer of the team's attention.

The framework below is structured around three distinct phases. Each phase has a different primary objective. Confusing the objectives, particularly trying to produce in the first thirty days before you have listened, is the most common mistake made by experienced professionals joining new organisations.

### Days 1-30: Understand Before You Propose

The objective of the first thirty days is to understand the systems, the people, the data, and the actual problems the team is trying to solve, before you form strong opinions about any of them. Producing comes later.

**Systems audit:** Document what ML systems currently exist in production. For each: what does it do, when was it last retrained, how is it monitored, who owns it, what are its known failure modes. If this documentation does not exist, creating it is a genuine contribution.

**Data audit:** Where does the training data come from, how is it labelled, what are the known quality issues, where are the joins or transformations that introduce risk. Do not assume the data is clean. Find out.

**Stakeholder mapping:** Who makes decisions about what gets built? Who is the primary consumer of model outputs? Who has tried to build something that failed? The last question is often the most informative.

**Listen in the first team meetings:** Resist the urge to offer solutions to problems you have just heard described. Ask clarifying questions. The person who identifies the actual problem is more valuable than the person who proposes a solution to the wrong one.

> *Success criterion for Day 30: you can describe the team's three most important technical problems in terms a non-technical stakeholder would recognise, and you know whose buy-in is required to address each one.*

## Days 31-60: One Small Win, Genuinely

The objective of the second thirty days is one concrete, visible contribution that the team actually notices. Not a large initiative. Not a proposal for a major new system. One thing that makes someone's work meaningfully easier or better.

Examples of good thirty-to-sixty-day wins: fixing a monitoring alert that was generating false positives and had been ignored for months. Adding a missing evaluation metric to an existing model that reveals a gap the team had not quantified. Documenting a data pipeline that only one person understood and that created single-point-of-failure risk. Writing a runbook for a production incident type that previously required tribal knowledge to resolve.

These are not glamorous. They are the contributions that experienced people notice and remember, because they reflect an understanding of what the team actually needs rather than what would look good on a future performance review.

**What to avoid:** proposing a complete system redesign, volunteering for the most visible project before you have demonstrated reliability on smaller things, or forming strong opinions about architectural decisions before you understand the constraints that produced them.

> *Success criterion for Day 60: one team member has told you, explicitly or implicitly, that something you did made their work easier.*

## Days 61-90: Propose Something Forward-Looking

By Day 90, you have enough context to propose something that goes beyond maintenance and incremental improvement. This is the moment to identify a genuine opportunity or gap and make a structured case for addressing it.

The proposal does not need to be large. It needs to be grounded: specific about the problem, clear about the approach, honest about the resource requirements, and connected to a business outcome the team cares about. A one-page brief is often more effective than a detailed technical design, particularly if the audience includes stakeholders who are not technical.

**Frame it as a question, not a conclusion:** 'I have noticed X pattern in the data, and I think it may be contributing to Y problem. I would like to spend two weeks investigating whether a Z approach could help. Here is what success would look like and how we would know if it is not working.' This is more persuasive than 'we should build Z' because it acknowledges uncertainty and proposes a bounded test rather than a commitment.

> *Success criterion for Day 90: you have a proposal on the table that reflects your understanding of the team's actual priorities, not just your technical interests, and at least one*

> *person with decision-making authority is interested in pursuing it.*

## India-Specific Notes

In GCC environments, the first ninety days often involve navigating a gap between what the India team is asked to deliver and what they have the authority to decide. Understanding the decision-making chain, particularly which decisions require headquarters sign-off and which can be made locally, is as important as understanding the technical systems. Frustration in the first three months at a GCC is almost always a navigation problem rather than a capability problem.

In early-stage startups, the first ninety days often involve discovering that the systems described in the interview are less complete than presented. Treat this as an opportunity rather than a disappointment. The person who builds foundational infrastructure when it is needed, rather than complaining about its absence, earns trust quickly in startup environments.

# Academic-to-Industry Translation

PhD graduates and postdoctoral researchers transitioning into industry AI roles are frequently filtered out by ATS systems not because their skills are insufficient but because they use academic vocabulary where production vocabulary is expected. The table below maps common academic achievements and descriptions to the language used in 2026 AI job descriptions.

This is not about misrepresentation. Every entry in the right column is an accurate description of the same work. It is about translation.

## Vocabulary Translation Table

### Research and Publication

**Academic:** Published 3 papers in peer-reviewed venues

**Industry:** Authored 3 research papers on [topic]; one accepted at [venue]; work cited [N] times

**Academic:** Presented at NeurIPS / ICML / ACL

**Industry:** Conference presenter at NeurIPS / ICML / ACL (top-tier ML/NLP venues)

**Academic:** Submitted preprint to arXiv

**Industry:** Published technical research on [specific topic] with [N] downloads / citations

## Technical Work

**Academic:** Implemented novel architecture for sequence modelling

**Industry:** Designed and implemented a custom transformer variant for [domain]; achieved [X]% improvement over SOTA baseline on [benchmark]

**Academic:** Ran experiments on SLURM cluster

**Industry:** Managed distributed training workloads across [N] GPUs using SLURM; reduced training time by [X]% through pipeline optimisation

**Academic:** Worked with large scale datasets

**Industry:** Processed and cleaned datasets of [N] million samples; built data pipelines handling [X] GB using [Python/Spark/etc.]

**Academic:** Supervised undergraduate research assistants

**Industry:** Mentored [N] junior researchers; managed task allocation and code review for a team of [N]

## Leadership and Collaboration

**Academic:** Collaborated with interdisciplinary research group

**Industry:** Worked cross-functionally with [domain] experts and software engineers to translate research into production-ready implementation

**Academic:** Secured research grant

**Industry:** Wrote and secured funding proposal worth [amount]; managed budget and deliverables across [duration]

**Academic:** Taught undergraduate course

**Industry:** Designed and delivered technical curriculum for [N] students; created hands-on lab components using [tools]

## The Cover Letter Framing

The most effective framing for a PhD transitioning to industry is not to apologise for the academic background but to make the transfer of value explicit. One paragraph that does this well:

> *My PhD in [field] at [institution] required me to define problems that had no known solution, design evaluation frameworks from scratch, implement and debug systems end-to-end, and communicate findings to audiences with different backgrounds. In industry terms: I have built and shipped ML systems, evaluated them rigorously, and explained technical decisions to non-technical stakeholders. What I am adding is deep domain expertise in [area] and the research instinct to question whether we are solving the right problem. I am looking for a role where that combination is useful.*

This paragraph works because it translates academic capabilities into industry expectations without minimising either. It does not say 'I have been in academia and want to try industry.' It says 'here is what I built and here is how it maps to what you need.'

# Appendix I: Portfolio and Resume Checklist

Two checklists that belong together because they get checked by the same people in the same sitting: whether your portfolio projects are genuinely production-grade, and whether your resume survives both an ATS filter and a human reading it five minutes later.

## The Production-Grade Portfolio Checklist

Use this checklist to evaluate each project in your portfolio before directing a hiring manager to it. A project that scores below 6 out of 10 is likely doing more harm than good: it signals tutorial consumption rather than production judgment.

Score each criterion from 0 (absent) to 1 (present and well-done). Half marks are acceptable for partial completion.

## The Ten-Point Checklist

### 1. Does the README explain the problem before the solution?

The first paragraph of the README should describe the real-world problem being addressed, not the technical approach. A recruiter who does not know your domain should understand why this matters within thirty seconds. Score: 0 / 0.5 / 1

### 2. Is there a clear statement of what the project does not do?

Production-grade thinking includes knowing the limitations of a system. A section on known limitations, edge cases, or design decisions that were deliberately excluded signals maturity. Score: 0 / 0.5 / 1

### 3. Is there a reproducible evaluation?

Not just a final accuracy number. A documented evaluation process: what dataset, what metrics, what baseline, how the metric was calculated. Someone else should be able to run your evaluation and get the same result. Score: 0 / 0.5 / 1

**4. Does the project handle at least one real failure mode?**

Does it include error handling for malformed inputs, empty retrieval results, API failures, or model timeouts? A project that only works on the happy path is not production-grade. Score: 0 / 0.5 / 1

**5. Is the code modular and readable?**

Functions do one thing. Variable names are descriptive. There are no notebook-style scripts with all logic in one cell. A reviewer should be able to understand the code structure without running it. Score: 0 / 0.5 / 1

**6. Is there a working demo, API endpoint, or deployed version?**

A live endpoint (even a free-tier deployment), a recorded demo, or a Colab notebook with pre-loaded state is significantly stronger than a repository that requires local setup to see anything. Score: 0 / 0.5 / 1

**7. Does the project reflect genuine domain judgment?**

A generic chatbot does not. A RAG pipeline over Indian High Court judgments that handles multilingual queries and accounts for jurisdictional variation does. The project should demonstrate that you understood a specific domain problem, not just a general ML pattern. Score: 0 / 0.5 / 1

**8. Are the design decisions explained?**

Why did you choose this chunking strategy over that one? Why this embedding model? Why this retrieval threshold? A section in the README or a companion article explaining design decisions is evidence of judgment, not just implementation. Score: 0 / 0.5 / 1

**9. Is there a cost or performance estimate?**

For LLM-based projects: approximate cost per 1,000 queries. For ML systems: inference latency on reference hardware. This signals that you think about production viability, not just proof-of-concept correctness. Score: 0 / 0.5 / 1

**10. Does the commit history tell a story?**

A project with one commit is a submission, not a project. A history of meaningful commits, showing iteration, debugging, and improvement, signals that this is real work rather than a polished one-shot exercise. Score: 0 / 0.5 / 1

## Scoring

**8-10:** Strong portfolio project. Direct hiring managers here confidently.

**6-7:** Acceptable. Consider strengthening 1-2 weak areas before using as primary evidence.

**4-5:** Borderline. Fix the most visible gaps or deprioritise this project in your portfolio.

**Below 4:** Tutorial-grade. Do not feature it prominently. Rebuild with a genuine problem.

# Resume and ATS Optimisation

Most AI professionals write resumes that describe what they did rather than what they achieved, and use internal project names rather than the language the market uses. Both errors reduce ATS match rates and reduce the speed with which a human reviewer grasps the relevance of the experience.

This appendix covers the ATS reality, the most common resume mistakes made by experienced AI professionals, and a before-and-after example for a senior ML engineer transitioning from a GCC role.

## How ATS Systems Work in Practice

Applicant Tracking Systems parse your resume for keywords and score the match against the job description. They do not read between the lines. If the JD says 'RAG pipeline' and your resume says 'retrieval-augmented generation system', you may not match. If the JD says 'LangGraph' and you list only 'agentic AI frameworks', you may not match.

The practical fix: read the job description carefully and mirror its specific terminology, not synonyms, not paraphrases. Call it translation, not dishonesty. If you built a retrieval-augmented generation pipeline, calling it a RAG pipeline in your resume is accurate and ATS-legible simultaneously.

Indian-market specific note: many GCC and IT services firms use platforms including Workday, SuccessFactors, Taleo, and iCIMS. Each has slightly different parsing behaviour. The safest approach: use a clean single-column format, avoid tables and text boxes (which many parsers cannot read), avoid headers and footers for key content, and save as .docx rather than PDF for initial applications unless PDF is specifically requested.

## The Most Common Mistakes

**Responsibilities without outcomes.** 'Developed machine learning models' tells the reviewer nothing. 'Developed a gradient boosting model for customer churn prediction that reduced churn rate by 12 percent in the first quarter of deployment' tells them everything relevant.

**Internal project names with no context.** 'Led Project Athena' is meaningless outside your former employer. Replace with what the project actually was: 'Led design and deployment of a RAG pipeline for internal knowledge retrieval serving 2,000 users across three business units.'

**Technology lists without application context.** A long list of tools (Python, TensorFlow, Spark, Kafka, Kubernetes) without context for where they were applied and at what scale is a weak signal. Integrate tools into achievement statements where possible.

**Underselling the engineering at execution-oriented roles.** Work done in GCC environments often involved production scale that product company work did not. State the scale explicitly: 'pipeline processing 50 million records daily', 'serving 300 concurrent users at under 200ms latency'.

## Before and After: Senior ML Engineer, GCC Background

### Before (common pattern)

Experience: Senior Data Scientist, [Company Name] GCC, 2021-2025

- Developed machine learning models for business use cases
- Worked with Python, SQL, and cloud platforms
- Collaborated with stakeholders across geographies
- Led Project Meridian data science initiative
- Participated in model deployment and monitoring activities

### After (ATS-legible, outcome-focused)

Experience: Senior Data Scientist, [Company Name] GCC, 2021-2025

- Designed and deployed a RAG pipeline over 40,000 internal policy documents, reducing average query resolution time from 18 minutes to under 90 seconds for 1,500 compliance staff. Stack: LangChain, Pinecone, GPT-4 (Azure), FastAPI.
- Built a customer churn prediction system using LightGBM on 3 years of transaction history (12M rows). Model achieved AUC 0.84 vs 0.71 baseline, contributing to a 9 percent reduction in voluntary churn in the first year.
- Established MLOps baseline for the team: Mlflow experiment tracking, Docker containerisation, weekly drift monitoring using Evidently AI. Reduced model retraining cycle from manual ad hoc to automated trigger-based.

Mentored 4 junior data scientists; 2 were promoted within 18 months.

> *The after version is not longer, just more specific. Every bullet answers: what was built, at what scale, with what outcome, using what tools. That is what a hiring manager and an ATS are both looking for.*

# Appendix J: Five Brief Treatments

The following sections address questions that did not fit neatly into the main chapters but that represent real career concerns. Each is brief. The goal is orientation rather than comprehensive treatment.

## 1. Why Nobody Cares About Your Titanic Project

Every year, thousands of data science portfolios contain the same four projects: a Titanic survival classifier, an Iris flower classifier, a movie recommendation system, and a generic text sentiment analyser. These are tutorial projects, useful for learning, useless as portfolio signals. Every hiring manager who reviews portfolios has seen hundreds of them. They do not demonstrate that you can solve a real problem. They demonstrate that you completed a course.

The projects that actually differentiate candidates are ones that: address a specific, real problem in a specific domain; involve non-trivial data collection or engineering; require judgment about problem framing rather than just model selection; and produce something that could plausibly be deployed or that someone would actually use.

In the Indian context, strong portfolio projects in 2026 look something like: a RAG pipeline over Indian court judgments that can answer questions about specific legal precedents; a transaction anomaly detector built on synthetic UPI-style data that accounts for the specific fraud patterns in Indian mobile payments; a multilingual NLP system that handles code-switching between English and a regional Indian language; a monitoring dashboard for a production ML model that detects drift and triggers retraining. These are not dramatically harder to build than a Titanic classifier. They are harder to define, which is why they signal more.

One project built on a problem you genuinely found interesting, documented honestly including what did not work, is worth more than ten tutorial reproductions. Choose the problem first, build the project second.

## 2. The Technical IC Track After 40: Staying Technical When the World Wants You to Manage

In the West, the distinction between the management track and the individual contributor track is institutionalised. Staff engineer, Principal engineer, Distinguished engineer, Fellow: these are well-defined career stages that recognise technical depth as genuinely senior, with compensation and organisational status to match. At Google, a Principal Engineer is peers with a VP. At Anthropic, a Staff Researcher has the autonomy and scope of a senior leader.

In the Indian technology sector, this track barely exists outside a handful of organisations. The implicit expectation, at GCCs, at IT services firms, and at many product companies, is that once you have enough experience, you manage people. Technical depth without management responsibility is read as a failure to progress. This expectation is wrong, and it is increasingly wrong, because the work that matters in 2026 requires depth, not headcount oversight. But the institutional expectation is real and must be navigated deliberately.

The practical path for a 40-year-old who wants to stay technical in the Indian market: target organisations where the IC track exists explicitly (global product companies, AI-first startups, research labs with India presence). Make the case for your role in terms of leverage rather than headcount: not how many people you manage, but how many projects and decisions benefit from your judgment. Build the public record that makes your technical authority legible outside any single organisation, because your employer's internal track limits do not apply to your external reputation. And be honest with yourself about what you actually want: managing people is a genuinely different job, not just a reward for doing the technical job well. Some people want it. Many more accept it because they cannot see another path.

## 3. What 2027 to 2030 Might Look Like

Predictions about AI timelines are reliably wrong in the specifics and sometimes right about the direction. With that caveat clearly stated, here is a grounded view of the forces likely to shape the field in the next three to four years, organised by what seems reasonably certain versus what remains genuinely uncertain.

What seems reasonably certain: agentic AI systems will move further into production, which will expose the evaluation and reliability problems that current hype elides. The companies that invested in evaluation infrastructure, testing frameworks, and monitoring pipelines before the agentic wave will have a significant advantage over those that rushed to deploy without it. The winners of the 2027-2029 period will be known for their evaluation rigour, not their agent architecture.

What is less certain but worth preparing for: multimodal capabilities (vision, audio, structured data, code in a single model) will become table stakes for production systems, which will create demand for people who understand how to evaluate and deploy multimodal pipelines at the boundary of current technical understanding. The sovereign AI question, whether nations build or mandate national AI infrastructure, will shape the Indian market significantly. India's approach to data localisation and model sovereignty will determine whether Indian AI professionals are primarily building on global infrastructure or building something distinctly local.

The skills that are likely to remain scarce regardless of which trajectory materialises: the ability to evaluate AI system outputs rigorously, the ability to translate between domain expertise and AI capability, the ability to design systems that degrade gracefully when AI components fail, and the human judgment required to know when a problem does not require AI at all. None of these are exotic. All of them require sustained engagement with real problems over time rather than tutorial consumption.

## 4. Pivoting into AI from a Non-AI Background

The book has been written primarily for people already working in data science, ML, or adjacent technical roles. But a significant fraction of readers will be approaching from adjacent or non-adjacent backgrounds: civil engineers, mechanical engineers, finance professionals, healthcare workers, legal practitioners, and others who see the shift happening and want to position themselves for it.

The honest message: the pathway exists, it is not fast, and the domain knowledge you already have is more valuable than you probably believe.

The domain knowledge point matters. A civil engineer who understands construction supply chains, material quality variance, and project scheduling constraints can build a more useful predictive maintenance model for a construction company than a fresh ML graduate who does not know the difference between compressive strength and tensile strength. A healthcare professional who understands clinical workflows, the specific ways diagnostic data is collected and recorded, and the regulatory requirements around patient data can build more trustworthy medical AI tools than a technically skilled person who has never interacted with a healthcare system. Domain expertise combined with ML skill is rare. Pure ML skill is not.

The mathematical foundation required is genuinely lower than most tutorials suggest. For the majority of applied AI roles, you need: linear algebra up to matrix multiplication and eigenvalues (Khan Academy is sufficient), probability up to Bayes' theorem and conditional probability, and statistics up to hypothesis testing and confidence intervals. You do not need a PhD in mathematics. You need these concepts well enough to reason about why a model is behaving the way it is.

Three portfolio projects that do not require a GPU and demonstrate real judgment: a RAG pipeline over documents from your domain (legal texts, medical literature, engineering standards) that can answer domain-specific questions; a structured prediction system using scikit-learn on real data from your field, documented with domain-informed feature engineering; and a deployment of a small open-source model using Ollama or llama.cpp that solves a specific task in your domain, with an evaluation framework you designed. These three projects, well-documented and honestly described, are more compelling to a hiring manager than any certification.

## 5. Who Owns Your Prompts: The Intellectual Property Question

Most AI professionals do not think carefully about intellectual property until they leave a company and want to use something they built. At that point, they discover that what they thought was their own knowledge and judgment may be legally entangled with their former employer in ways they did not anticipate.

The broad principle in Indian employment law, consistent with most jurisdictions: intellectual property created during employment, using company resources, in areas related to the company's business, belongs to the employer. This is expected and reasonable for core product work.

The ambiguity that matters more in 2026: system prompts, context schemas, RAG architectures, evaluation frameworks, and fine-tuning datasets that you developed as part of your professional work. If you spent eight months developing a domain-specific evaluation framework for LLM outputs at your employer, and it was built on company data and within company systems, the framework belongs to the company. The pattern of thinking that led to it, the intuition about what makes a good evaluation, the judgment you developed in the process, belongs to you. The specific artifact does not.

Practical steps that protect your transferable judgment without violating your obligations: document your thinking, not just your output. Write privately about why you made specific architectural choices, what failure modes you encountered, what you would do differently. This meta-level reasoning is not an employer artifact; it is your own developing expertise. Contribute to open-source projects in adjacent areas that are clearly outside your employment scope. Build public portfolio work on problems that are demonstrably not your employer's business. And before joining any company, read the IP assignment clause in your employment contract and ask, in writing, for clarity on what it covers. The companies that are unreasonable about this reveal something important about their culture early.

These five topics are not exhaustive. The field will produce new questions faster than any book can address them. The underlying orientation throughout this appendix, and throughout the book, is the same: understand the structures clearly, make decisions deliberately, and hold your specific skills loosely enough that the next wave does not catch you holding something that no longer moves.

# Appendix K: Mental Health Resources for Indian Tech Professionals

Chapter 6 describes the psychological texture of working in a fast-moving field, including chronic low-grade anxiety, imposter syndrome, and the specific pressures of the Indian professional context. This appendix provides concrete resources for when those pressures move beyond the manageable.

Seeking help is not a sign of weakness. In a field where the stakes are real and the pace is sustained, it is the decision that allows you to continue functioning at the level the work requires.

## Crisis and Immediate Support

**iCall (TISS):** 1800-599-0019 (toll-free). Psychosocial helpline run by the Tata Institute of Social Sciences. Available Monday to Saturday, 8am to 10pm. Trained counsellors. Free of charge.

**Vandrevala Foundation:** +91-1860-2662-345. 24/7 mental health helpline. Free. Available in multiple Indian languages.

**Snehi:** +91-44-24640050. Emotional support for adults. Chennai-based but serves pan-India.

**iSPOOL:** Online platform for peer support and professional counselling. Affordable sliding-scale pricing.

## Affordable Ongoing Therapy

**The Minds Foundation:** Low-cost therapy and group support, particularly for professionals. Online sessions available.

**Manastha:** Online platform connecting users with licensed therapists. Sliding-scale pricing starts at Rs 500 per session.

**YourDOST:** Online counselling platform widely used by Indian tech professionals. Many employers offer YourDOST access through Employee Assistance Programmes.

**InnerHour (now Amaha):** App-based mental health support with both self-guided tools and therapist access. Widely available on Android and iOS.

**Practo:** The Practo platform lists licensed psychiatrists and psychologists in most major Indian cities, including those offering online sessions.

## Employer-Based Resources

Many large Indian employers, particularly GCCs and MNCs, provide Employee Assistance Programmes that include free confidential counselling sessions, typically 6 to 12 per year. Check your HR portal or ask your HR business partner directly. EAP usage is confidential from your employer.

If your employer does not provide an EAP, this is worth raising with HR. The mental health and productivity literature is clear enough that most senior HR professionals recognise it as a legitimate request.

## For Burnout Specifically

Burnout is distinct from stress and from depression, though it can develop into either. It is characterised by three specific features: exhaustion that sleep does not resolve, cynicism about the work that was previously meaningful, and a reduced sense of professional efficacy despite maintaining output. If you recognise this pattern, the primary intervention is a structural change to the work, not time management.

The most useful first step is naming it to someone who can influence the conditions: a trusted manager, an HR partner, a mentor. Not performing resilience. The second step is talking to a mental health professional who has worked with occupational burnout specifically. The resources above can help find one.

# Appendix L: The AI Engineer Interview Primer

*A structured guide to the eight technical domains that determine whether you pass or fail senior AI interviews in 2026*

The AI Engineer interview in 2026 is testing something more specific than it appears to be. The surface question is whether you know LLMs. The underlying question is whether you understand the full stack those LLMs sit inside: the theory that explains why they behave as they do, the systems that make them usable at scale, the production infrastructure that makes them reliable, and the evaluation discipline that makes improvements trustworthy. Most candidates prepare for one layer of this. The ones who pass consistently prepare for all four.

The rough weighting across what companies actually evaluate: classical ML foundations and AI theory account for a relatively small share of most interviews, but candidates who lack them get exposed in follow-up questions. LLM internals and systems take up a larger share. The majority of interview time, especially at the senior level, focuses on whether you have built production applications and whether you understand what makes them fail. The distribution across these layers shifts depending on the role, the company, and how close to research versus engineering the position sits, but the pattern holds broadly.

What separates candidates who pass consistently from candidates who pass occasionally is the ability to reason across all four layers, rather than excelling in one and being thin in the others, more than raw technical knowledge. Prompt engineering fluency is assumed. What gets tested seriously at the senior level is the understanding of RAG architecture, agent orchestration and its failure modes, evaluation frameworks, fine-tuning trade-offs, and the production realities of running LLM systems at scale.

Work through each section out loud. The difference between knowing something and being able to explain it clearly under interview pressure is larger than most people expect. After each answer you practise, ask yourself: am I giving the Phase 1 answer (reciting a definition), the Phase 2 answer (describing an implementation), or the Phase 3 answer (reasoning about trade-offs and failure modes)? The phase of your answer often determines the phase of role you will be offered.

## 1. Classical Machine Learning

*Optional but a differentiator. Some companies, particularly research-heavy or older tech organisations, go deep here. Knowing it puts you ahead of most candidates.*

Supervised learning maps labelled inputs to outputs: classification, regression, prediction. Unsupervised learning finds structure in unlabelled data: clustering, dimensionality reduction, anomaly detection. The distinction matters because it shapes how you frame a problem before you touch a model.

Linear regression models a continuous output as a weighted sum of inputs. Logistic regression uses the sigmoid function to produce a probability for binary classification. SVMs find the maximum-margin hyperplane separating classes. Decision trees split on features recursively; random forests average many such trees to reduce overfitting. These are the algorithms that come up in phone screens and take-home diagnostics.

Gradient descent is the optimisation engine underneath almost everything else. The idea is to move model parameters in the direction that reduces error, guided by the gradient of the loss function. Learning rate controls step size. The key variants are batch gradient descent (all examples at once), stochastic (one example), and mini-batch (the standard in practice). Adam is the most widely used adaptive variant. If asked to explain it in an interview, imagine walking downhill in fog: the gradient tells you which direction is down, the learning rate tells you how large a step to take.

The concepts that transfer most directly from classical ML to LLM systems are: bias-variance trade-off (underfitting vs overfitting, which maps to model capacity choices), evaluation rigour (the discipline of held-out test sets, which maps to RAG evaluation and LLM-as-a-judge), and the understanding of why models fail, not just how they work when they succeed.

## 2. How LLMs Actually Work

*The most heavily tested section. You do not need to implement a transformer from scratch, but you need to explain one clearly.*

The training objective is simple: predict the next token given all previous tokens. Everything else, the reasoning, the knowledge, the apparent understanding, emerges from this objective applied at scale over enormous corpora. Keeping this in mind prevents overclaiming and helps diagnose failure modes.

### Tokenisation and embeddings

Models do not see words. They see tokens. Byte Pair Encoding (BPE) is the tokenisation method used by GPT-4, Claude, and LLaMA: frequently co-occurring character pairs are merged into single tokens iteratively, producing a vocabulary that handles both common words and rare subwords efficiently. This matters practically because tokenisation affects context window consumption, cost estimation, and the model's ability to process structured text like code, tables, or Indic scripts.

Tokens are converted to dense floating-point vectors called embeddings. Words with similar meaning cluster together in this high-dimensional space. The model also needs to know where each token sits in the sequence, since attention itself has no concept of order: positional encodings inject this information, either as fixed sinusoidal functions (the original transformer paper) or as learned embeddings or rotary embeddings (RoPE, used by modern LLMs).

### Self-attention and multi-head attention

Attention is the mechanism that allows every token to look at every other token when producing its output representation. Each token generates three learned projections: a query (what am I looking for?), a key (what information do I offer?), and a value (my actual content). Attention scores are computed as the dot product of queries and keys, scaled by the square root of the key dimension to prevent gradient saturation in the softmax, then multiplied by the values. The scaling factor matters: without it, large dot products cause the softmax to collapse to near-one-hot distributions, killing gradient flow.

Multi-head attention runs this mechanism in parallel across multiple smaller subspaces, then concatenates the results. Different heads learn to attend to different relationship types: one may capture syntactic structure, another semantic similarity, another long-range coreference. This is why the famous example works: in the sentence "The animal did not cross the street because it was tired," the model correctly resolves "it" to "animal" rather than "street."

### Encoder, decoder, encoder-decoder

Encoder models (BERT and its variants) read the full sequence bidirectionally and produce rich contextual representations. They are strong for classification, retrieval, and embedding tasks. Decoder-only models (GPT, Claude, LLaMA, Gemini) process tokens causally: each position can only attend to previous positions. They are trained to predict the next token, which makes them natural generators and the dominant architecture for chat and reasoning applications. Encoder-decoder models (T5, BART) use both: an encoder processes the input and a decoder generates the output, which is why they suit translation and summarisation. For most AI Engineer interview purposes, the decoder-only architecture is what matters most.

## 3. Building with LLM APIs

*The practical integration layer. Eighty percent of daily AI engineering work happens here.*

The three major API providers are OpenAI (GPT-4o and variants), Anthropic (Claude family), and Google (Gemini). Each exposes a chat completions interface: you send an array of messages with roles (system, user, assistant) and receive the model's next response. The system prompt sets persistent behaviour. The user and assistant turns represent the conversation history.

LLMs are stateless. Every API call is independent: the model has no memory of previous calls unless you explicitly include the conversation history in the request. This is a design property that requires deliberate memory management, not a limitation to work around. Common patterns include buffer memory (keep the last N turns), summary memory (compress older turns into a condensed representation), and vector memory (store past exchanges as embeddings and retrieve semantically relevant ones). When the accumulated history approaches the context window limit, you must truncate intelligently, summarise, or retrieve selectively rather than simply appending.

Context windows now range from 8k tokens for small models to over a million tokens for the largest. Knowing the window size of the model you are working with, and how to count tokens accurately, is table-stakes knowledge. The tiktoken library handles this for OpenAI models; Anthropic and Google provide their own token counting utilities.

## 4. Prompt Engineering and Context Engineering

*Not just being nice to the AI. This is engineering with measurable impact on output quality, cost, and latency.*

Zero-shot prompting provides no examples: just an instruction. One-shot provides one example; few-shot provides several. Few-shot is particularly effective for formatting, style, and extraction tasks where showing the model the desired output structure is more reliable than describing it. Chain-of-thought prompting asks the model to reason step by step before producing a final answer. It dramatically improves performance on multi-step reasoning tasks. Modern reasoning models generate internal chain-of-thought automatically, but explicitly requesting it in prompts is still effective for older models.

The KV cache is a critical performance mechanism. When generating tokens autoregressively, the model caches the key and value matrices computed for all previous tokens. Without caching, every new token would require recomputing attention across the entire sequence at quadratic cost. With caching, only the new token's attention needs to be computed. This is why generation speed increases after the first token: the prefill phase (processing the input) is expensive; the decode phase (generating output) is fast once the cache is populated.

Prompt caching is a distinct but related concept. Providers like Anthropic cache the full prompt across multiple API calls. If you send the same long system prompt or document context in every request, you pay only for the first call. Subsequent calls reuse the cached prefix at a fraction of the cost. For high-volume RAG applications, prompt caching combined with smaller models for routing can reduce inference costs substantially.

## 5. RAG and Vector Databases

*The most common production pattern. Appears in almost every AI Engineer interview.*

RAG (Retrieval-Augmented Generation) solves three problems that LLMs cannot solve alone: they hallucinate on facts not in their training data, their knowledge has a cutoff date, and they cannot access private or proprietary documents. RAG retrieves relevant content at inference time and provides it as context, grounding the model's response in real documents rather than parametric memory.

The pipeline: split documents into chunks, embed each chunk using an embedding model, store the vectors in a vector database, at query time embed the question, retrieve the top-k most similar chunks by cosine similarity, inject those chunks into the prompt, generate an answer. Poor chunking produces poor retrieval regardless of how good the model is. Common strategies include fixed-size chunking (simple but ignores content boundaries), semantic chunking (splits on sentence or paragraph structure), and hierarchical chunking (stores document-level and chunk-level embeddings for multi-step retrieval).

Vector databases you should be able to name and distinguish: Pinecone (managed, easy to start with, good for prototypes), Weaviate (open source, supports hybrid search combining vector and keyword matching), pgvector (a PostgreSQL extension that is underrated for most enterprise applications because it integrates with existing infrastructure and handles moderate scale without a separate service), Chroma (lightweight, good for local development and testing). The choice depends on scale, existing infrastructure, and whether you need hybrid search or pure vector search.

Advanced RAG patterns that come up in senior interviews: metadata-first retrieval (filter by structured attributes before doing vector search, dramatically improving precision for document collections with known structure), multi-vector retrieval (index both the document and a generated summary, retrieve from both), re-ranking (use a cross-encoder to re-score top-k results before passing to the LLM), and graph-augmented retrieval (use a knowledge graph to traverse entity relationships that flat vector search cannot capture).

LangChain and LlamaIndex are the two main frameworks. LangChain is broader: it covers agents, chains, and memory alongside retrieval, at the cost of significant abstraction overhead. LlamaIndex is more focused on indexing and retrieval and tends to be the better choice when RAG is the primary task. For senior roles, being able to implement RAG from scratch without relying on framework abstractions is a meaningful differentiator.

## 6. AI Agents

*The fastest-growing interview topic for senior roles. The questions that separate candidates who have read about agents from candidates who have built them.*

An agent is an LLM with access to tools and a planning loop. Instead of producing a single answer, it can search, calculate, call APIs, read databases, write files, and use the outputs of those actions to inform subsequent reasoning. The enabling mechanism is function calling: the model outputs structured JSON specifying which tool to invoke and with what parameters; the application executes the tool and returns the result; the model incorporates the result and continues.

The ReAct pattern (Reasoning and Acting) is the foundational agent loop: Thought, Action, Observation, repeat until a final answer is reached. It interleaves reasoning in natural language with structured tool calls, grounding the model's conclusions in real external data rather than purely parametric knowledge. Most production agent frameworks implement some variant of this pattern.

LangGraph implements stateful agent graphs and is the better choice for complex multi-step agents where you need fine-grained control over the execution flow. CrewAI uses a role-based multi-agent model (researcher, writer, critic) that maps naturally to workflows where different agents have distinct responsibilities and need to hand off between themselves. The Model Context Protocol (MCP) provides a standardised interface for connecting agents to external data sources and tools, applying least-privilege access control at the agent-tool boundary.

Where agents break: hallucinated tool calls (the model invokes a tool that does not exist, or passes parameters it fabricated); infinite loops (no termination condition, or the termination condition is itself poorly defined); context window exhaustion (in a long-running loop, the accumulated thought-action-observation history exceeds the model's context); cascading errors (a wrong tool result in step two corrupts all downstream reasoning); and goal drift (in multi-step tasks, the model loses sight of the original objective). The design response to each of these is worth knowing: schema validation before executing tool calls, hard iteration limits at the orchestrator level, context compression or summarisation mid-loop, checkpointing for retry without restart, and injecting the original objective into every prompt.

When not to use an agent: any task that is a deterministic single-step lookup, any task where latency or cost is the primary constraint, any task where the output must be fully auditable. Agents add unpredictability alongside capability. Being honest about this trade-off in interviews signals production awareness.

## 7. Linear Algebra for AI Engineers

*Only the bits that actually matter. Focus on what powers embeddings, attention, and retrieval.*

The dot product measures alignment between two vectors. Almost all LLM compute reduces to matrix multiplication: the transformer's attention scores, the feedforward layers, the projection matrices. If you understand that matrix multiplication is how the model transforms representations, you can reason about computational cost and the impact of model architecture choices.

Cosine similarity is how vector search works: it measures the cosine of the angle between two vectors, ranging from 1 (identical direction) to -1 (opposite). It is a normalised dot product, which means it ignores magnitude and focuses on direction. This is why two documents of very different lengths can still be retrieved as highly similar: the similarity is about meaning, not word count.

Matrix rank is the number of linearly independent dimensions. Low-rank matrices contain redundant information. This is why

LoRA works: the hypothesis underlying it is that the useful update to a weight matrix during fine-tuning lies in a low-dimensional subspace, which can be approximated by multiplying two much smaller matrices. Eigenvalues and eigenvectors appear in PCA and in the analysis of attention patterns, but surface-level understanding is sufficient for most interviews.

## 8. Fine-Tuning

*When prompting and RAG are not enough. A common interview question is knowing when each approach is the right tool.*

Fine-tuning updates model weights on domain-specific data, baking knowledge or behaviour into the parameters. Use it when the domain has distinct style, vocabulary, or format requirements, when you need reliable structured output that is hard to achieve through prompting, or when you need to serve a high volume of requests and want to use a smaller, cheaper model with domain-specific capability. Do not use fine-tuning to inject frequently changing factual knowledge: use RAG instead. A common mistake is fine-tuning when prompt engineering would have been sufficient and faster to iterate on.

PEFT (Parameter-Efficient Fine-Tuning) trains only a small subset of parameters rather than updating the full model. The dominant PEFT method is LoRA (Low-Rank Adaptation): instead of modifying the large weight matrix W directly, freeze W and add a low-rank update expressed as the product of two much smaller matrices A and B, where A is d by r and B is r by d, with r much smaller than d. Trainable parameters drop from d-squared to 2dr, typically a reduction of 90 percent or more. Optimizer state memory drops in proportion. QLoRA extends this by quantising the frozen base model weights to 4 bits, making it possible to fine-tune a 70-billion-parameter model on hardware that would not otherwise support it.

Instruction tuning trains the model to follow instructions reliably, typically on curated instruction-response pairs. This is what transforms a base language model into a useful assistant. Continued pre-training feeds the model additional raw text from a specific domain, extending its parametric knowledge but at much greater cost and with less predictable outcomes. Almost every practical fine-tuning task is instruction tuning or LoRA on a task-specific dataset, not continued pre-training.

## 9. The Last 10%: Production Systems

*What separates candidates who know from candidates who have shipped. These come from building real systems, not from studying.*

A framing correction before the content: for some senior GenAI interviews this material is no longer the last ten percent. The consulting-firm interview logged in Appendix G spent nearly its whole technical portion here, and the pattern it represents, application-level roles interviewed at platform depth, is becoming more common as regulated clients self-host models. Treat this section accordingly.

Start with the memory arithmetic, because an interviewer can and will do it in their head. Model weights occupy parameter count times bytes per parameter: four bytes at FP32, two at FP16 or BF16, one at INT8, half at INT4. To that add the KV cache, which grows with concurrent users, context length, and layer count and under production load can exceed the weights themselves, plus roughly ten to twenty percent for activations and overhead. Worked examples: a 7B model at FP16 is about 14 GB of weights; a 70B model at FP16 is about 140 GB, which means multiple GPUs or quantisation to 4-bit at roughly 35 GB; Mixtral 8x7B has about 47 billion total parameters, so FP16 needs roughly 94 GB and a single 80 GB A100 requires quantisation. If you claim a deployment, be able to walk this arithmetic aloud for it.

When one GPU is not enough, three parallelism strategies divide the work. Tensor parallelism splits individual weight matrices across GPUs, so every GPU participates in every layer; it needs fast interconnect and is the default for fitting a large model. Pipeline parallelism assigns whole layers to different GPUs and passes activations along the chain, cheaper on interconnect but prone to idle bubbles. Data parallelism replicates the full model and splits the requests, which scales throughput rather than model size. Production deployments combine them.

The engine landscape, at the level interviews test: vLLM is the open-source default, built around PagedAttention and continuous batching. Hugging Face TGI is the natural choice inside the HF ecosystem. TensorRT-LLM extracts peak performance from NVIDIA hardware at the cost of a heavier build and tuning process. SGLang targets structured outputs and agentic workloads with aggressive prefix cache reuse. Ollama is for local development and prototyping, not production concurrency. Knowing which one you would pick and why is worth more than internals knowledge of all five.

Latency has two phases: prefill (processing the input prompt, expensive and scales with prompt length) and decode (generating output tokens, faster once the KV cache is warm). Production latency optimisations include KV caching, batching multiple requests together to amortise the prefill cost, quantisation (reducing weight precision to 8-bit or 4-bit reduces memory bandwidth requirements and can accelerate inference), speculative decoding (use a small fast model to generate candidate tokens, verify with the full model in parallel), and continuous batching (process requests as a dynamic batch rather than waiting for a fixed batch to fill).

Cost attribution means tracking which users, features, or prompt components are consuming tokens and therefore money. Without this, it is impossible to optimise cost or understand the unit economics of an LLM application. Track input tokens and output tokens separately, since output token generation is more expensive. Use prompt caching to avoid paying for repeated static context.

Observability means being able to trace a single request through its full path: the prompt, the retrieval step, the model call, and the output. Tools like LangSmith, Phoenix, and Weights and Biases provide distributed tracing for LLM applications. Without structured logging of prompts, retrieved chunks, model outputs, and latency at each step, debugging a misbehaving RAG pipeline is guesswork.

Evaluation pipelines are what allow you to make changes confidently. For RAG systems, the RAGAS framework evaluates faithfulness (does the answer follow from the retrieved context?), answer relevance (does it actually answer the question?), and context recall (did retrieval surface the right documents?). LLM-as-a-Judge uses a strong model to evaluate the outputs of a weaker or task-specific model. Its limitations matter: judge models tend to prefer verbose outputs and outputs that match their own style, and they cannot reliably verify factual accuracy without external grounding. Golden datasets of human-annotated question-answer pairs remain the most reliable evaluation signal when they can be obtained.

### Evaluating RAG (and Graph-RAG) Without a Golden Dataset

This is one of the most frequently repeated interview questions across this search, and it recurs in RAG rounds, knowledge-graph rounds, and agent-evaluation rounds under slightly different wording each time: how do you know the system is good when there is no labelled answer set to check against? The wrong instinct is to say “I would use RAGAS” and stop. The right instinct is to decompose evaluation into layers that need different amounts of ground truth, some of them none at all, rather than searching for one metric that solves everything.

| Metric | Needs golden answer? | Needs retrieved context? |
|---|---|---|
| Faithfulness / groundedness | No | Yes |
| Answer relevance | No | No / optional |
| Context relevance | No | Yes |
| Citation correctness | No | Yes |
| Exact match / F1 vs. reference | Yes | No |
| Semantic similarity to reference | Yes | No |
| Retrieval Recall@K | Needs relevance–evidence labels | – |
| LLM-as-judge quality | Not necessarily | Depends on rubric |
| Task success / business outcome | No conventional gold answer | No |

Note that Recall@K, MRR, and NDCG@K all sit in the "needs relevance labels, not a golden answer" category, and that those labels are the bootstrappable part (via LLM judge or synthetic query generation), which is different from needing a reference answer at all.

Read the table as a decision aid, not a memorisation list: faithfulness, answer relevance, and context relevance are all reference-free and can run from day one, before any labelled data exists. Retrieval Recall@K needs relevance labels, but those can be bootstrapped synthetically, sample corpus chunks, generate questions each chunk answers, retain the source chunk as known evidence, and measure whether the retriever finds it, rather than hand-labelled from scratch. Only exact-match and semantic-similarity-to-reference metrics genuinely require a human-written golden answer, and those are the ones worth deferring rather than blocking on.

The maturity model to have ready verbally: Level 1 is reference-free evaluation you can run immediately (faithfulness, answer relevance, context utilisation, LLM-as-judge). Level 2 is a bootstrapped synthetic evaluation set built from the corpus itself (generated questions with known source chunks, giving Recall@K and MRR). Level 3 is a human-curated golden set grown progressively from real production queries and expert-validated answers. Level 4 is production behavioural monitoring that needs no evaluation set at all: task completion, user feedback, reformulation rate, escalation rate, cost, and latency. The single line worth ending on, because it is the thesis the question is actually testing for: no ground truth is not an excuse for no evaluation, it is an evaluation-design problem, and you use evaluation to progressively build the dataset rather than waiting for the dataset to start evaluating.

*See the full worked interview answer, including the graph-RAG extension (path correctness, entity-linking accuracy) and the LLM-as-judge calibration follow-up, in Appendix G, section 6, Q10.*

Reliability in production LLM systems means guardrails (input and output validation, content filtering, refusal handling), retries with exponential backoff for transient API failures, fallbacks to a cheaper or cached response when the primary model times out, and human-in-the-loop escalation for high-stakes or low-confidence outputs. None of these are glamorous. All of them are what make the difference between a demo and a system that runs for twelve months.

## The Final Checklist

Use this as a self-assessment before any interview. For each item, the test is not whether you can recite a definition but whether you can explain the concept clearly and reason about trade-offs under pressure.

Can you explain self-attention without referring to a paper?

Have you built a chat application with memory management?

Have you implemented a RAG pipeline without relying on framework abstractions?

Can you name three reasons to choose fine-tuning over RAG and three reasons to choose the reverse?

Can you explain cosine similarity in one sentence and tell me why it is used rather than Euclidean distance?

Can you describe LoRA including the matrix dimensions and why it saves memory?

Can you describe three agent failure modes and the design responses to each?

Can you name the metrics you would track for a production RAG application and explain what each tells you?

Can you explain the KV cache and prompt caching and why they are different?

For any model you claim to have deployed, can you walk through the memory arithmetic showing that it actually fit on the hardware you claim?

If you can answer all of these clearly and without notes, you are well ahead of most candidates in this market. The remainder of what distinguishes a strong hire from a very strong one comes from having built systems that ran in production and failed in ways that were not obvious in advance. That experience cannot be acquired by reading. It has to be accumulated by building, breaking, and fixing things until the failure modes become familiar enough to design against.

# About the Author

Joy Bose is a Senior Data Scientist and independent researcher based in Bengaluru, India. He holds a PhD in computational neuroscience from the University of Manchester, an MSc in Psychology and Neuroscience of Mental Health from King's College London, and an LLM from Golden Gate University School of Law (summa cum laude). He has spent over seventeen years working across machine learning, legal AI, neuromorphic computing, and contemplative technology, in product companies, research institutions, and independent practice across India and abroad. His published work includes arXiv papers on graph-constrained legal reasoning, spiking neural networks and transformer architecture, patent valuation via Shapley values, and multi-agent AI systems, as well as HuggingFace datasets for Indian matrimonial litigation and RTI decisions. His Google Scholar profile records over 700 citations, an h-index of 13, and 8 granted US and European patents. He writes at the intersection of AI, law, and contemplative practice, and maintains an active presence on arXiv, GitHub, Medium, and Substack under the handle joyboseroy.

www.ingramcontent.com/pod-product-compliance
Lightning Source LLC
LaVergne TN
LVHW052036200926
848481LV00005B/1690
* 9 7 9 8 9 0 5 4 0 0 3 0 8 *